Coleridge's Responses

Volume III: Coleridge on Nature and Vision

Coleridge's Responses

Selected Writings on Literary Criticism, the Bible and Nature

General Editor: John Beer, University of Cambridge

Volume I: *Coleridge on Writers and Writing*, edited by Seamus Perry
Volume II: *Coleridge on the Bible*, edited by Anthony John Harding
Volume III: *Coleridge on Nature and Vision*, edited by Samantha Harvey

The appearance of hitherto unpublished material during the last hundred years has brought out more fully the range and complexity of Coleridge's intelligence and knowledge. Complete publication of the *Notebooks* and *Collected Works*, together with that of the previously assembled *Collected Letters*, have made it increasingly evident that this was the most extraordinary English mind of the time. The specialist or more general student who wishes to know what Coleridge had to say on a particular subject may, however, find the sheer mass of materials bewildering, since in his less formal writings he passed quickly from one subject to another.

Coleridge's Responses, like its predecessor, *Coleridge's Writings* published by Palgrave, is a series addressed to such readers. In each volume a particular area of Coleridge's interest is explored, with an attempt to present his most significant statements and to show the development of his thought on the subject in question.

This major compilation not only arranges selections from Coleridge by themes but also, through notes and introductory material, elucidates and interprets the material. Covering Coleridge's wide-ranging criticism of other writers and statements on writing itself, his analysis and observation of nature and its powers and his enlightened view of the Bible achieved through constant study and annotation, this collection provides a comprehensive overview of his writings on these major areas of interest and knowledge.

Coleridge's Responses
Selected Writings on Literary Criticism, the Bible and Nature

Volume III:
Coleridge on Nature and Vision

Edited by SAMANTHA HARVEY

continuum

Continuum
The Tower Building
11 York Road
London SE1 7NX
www.continuumbooks.com

80 Maiden Lane, Suite 704
New York
NY 10038

British Library Cataloguing-in-Publication Data
A catalogue record for this book is available from the British Library.

Set ISBN: 978-08264-7576-3

Volume I: 978-0-8264-8372-0
Volume II: 978-0-8264-8374-4
Volume III: 978-0-8264-8373-7

Library of Congress Cataloging-in-Publication Data
Coleridge, Samuel Taylor, 1772–1834.
    Coleridge's responses : selected writings on literary criticism, the Bible, and nature / general editor, John Beer.
    p. cm.
    Includes bibliographical references.
    Contents: v. 1. Coleridge on writers and writing / edited by Seamus Perry -- v. 2. Coleridge on the Bible / edited by Anthony J. Harding -- v. 3. Coleridge on nature and vision / edited by Samantha Harvey.
    ISBN-13: 978-0-8264-7576-3 (set)
    ISBN-10: 0-8264-7576-0 (set)
    I. Beer, John B. II. Perry, Seamus. III. Harding, Anthony John. IV. Harvey, Samantha, 1972- V. Title.

    PR4472.B37 2007
    820.9--dc22

2006101744

Typeset by Fakenham Photosetting Limited, Fakenham, Norfolk
Printed and bound in Great Britain by Antony Rowe Ltd, Chippenham, Wiltshire

Contents

Acknowledgements

It has been an honour to work with John Beer, whose passion for Coleridge has seen this series through to its completion, and whose vast knowledge of Coleridge greatly aided the completion of this volume. I would also like to thank the editors of the *Coleridge's Writings* series, particularly David Vallins who wrote the companion volume on nature, *On the Sublime*. James Engell has been a guiding light in so many ways, and I am continually inspired by his luminous explications of the complexities of Coleridge's thought. Closer to home, special thanks are due to my research assistant Katya Cotey, for tirelessly checking quotations, the University of Colorado at Colorado Springs for making this assistance possible, and to the librarians for their patience and assistance with large numbers of fragile Coleridge materials. I am grateful to Princeton University Press for permission to reproduce passages from *The Notebooks of Samuel Taylor Coleridge*, ed. Kathleen Coburn (© Princeton University Press 1957–2002) and *Collected Works of Samuel Taylor Coleridge*, gen. ed. Kathleen Coburn (© Princeton University Press 1969–).

Finally, this book could not have been written without the dedicated support of my husband Silvino Lyra, who cared for our newborn daughter while this volume was being written. I hope that one day the three of us will see Coleridge's favourite inscription over the entrance at the temple of Delphi, 'Know Thyself.'

List of Abbreviations

AP	S.T. Coleridge, *Anima Poetæ: from the unpublished notebooks of Samuel Taylor Coleridge*. Ed. E.H. Coleridge. (London: William Heinemann, 1895).
AR (CC)	S.T. Coleridge, *Aids to Reflection*. Ed. John Beer. *Collected Works of Samuel Taylor Coleridge*. Vol. 9. (Princeton: Princeton U.P., 1993).
Ashe	S.T. Coleridge, *Lectures and Notes on Shakespeare and Other English Poets*. Ed. T. Ashe. (London: George Bell, 1884).
BL	British Library
BL (CC)	S.T. Coleridge, *Biographia Literaria*. Ed. James Engell and W. Jackson Bate. 2 vols. *Collected Works of Samuel Taylor Coleridge*. Vol. 7. (Princeton: Princeton U.P., 1983).
CC	S.T. Coleridge, *Collected Works of Samuel Taylor Coleridge*. General ed. Kathleen Coburn. Associate ed. Bart Winer. (Princeton: Princeton U.P., 1969–).
CCS	S.T. Coleridge, *On the Constitution of Church and State, according to the idea of each: with aids towards a right judgment on the late Catholic Bill*. (London: Hurst, Chance, 1830).
CH	Lucy E. Watson. *Coleridge at Highgate*. (London: Longmans, Green and Co., 1925).
CL	S.T. Coleridge, *Collected Letters of Samuel Taylor Coleridge*. Ed. E.L. Griggs. 6 vols. (Oxford: Clarendon Press, 1956–71).
CLE	S.T. Coleridge, *Letters*. Ed. E.H. Coleridge. 2 vols. (London: Heinemann, 1895).

CLU	S.T. Coleridge, *Unpublished Letters of Samuel Taylor Coleridge*. Ed. E.L. Griggs. 2 vols. (London: Constable, 1932).
CM (CC)	S.T. Coleridge, *Marginalia*. Ed. George Whalley *et al.* 6 vols. *Collected Works of Samuel Taylor Coleridge*. Vol. 12. (Princeton: Princeton U.P., 1980–2001).
CN	S.T. Coleridge, *The Notebooks of Samuel Taylor Coleridge*. Ed. Kathleen Coburn *et al.* 5 vols. (London: Routledge and Kegan Paul, 1957–).
CPW	S.T. Coleridge, *The Complete Poetical Works of Samuel Taylor Coleridge*. Ed. E.H. Coleridge. 2 vols. (Oxford: Clarendon Press, 1912).
ER	Joseph Cottle, *Early Recollections; chiefly relating to the late Samuel Taylor Coleridge, during his long residence in Bristol.* 2 vols. (London: Longman, Rees & Co. and Hamilton, Adams & Co., 1837).
F (CC)	S.T. Coleridge, *The Friend*. Ed. Barbara Rooke. 2 vols. *Collected Works of Samuel Taylor Coleridge*. Vol. 4. (Princeton: Princeton U.P., 1969).
IS	S.T. Coleridge, *Inquiring Spirit: A New Presentation of Coleridge from His Published and Unpublished Prose Writings*. Ed. Kathleen Coburn. (London: Routledge and Kegan Paul, 1950).
Lects 1808–19 (CC)	S.T. Coleridge, *Lectures 1808–1819 On Literature*. Ed. R.A. Foakes. 2 vols. *Collected Works of Samuel Taylor Coleridge*. Vol. 5. (Princeton: Princeton U.P., 1987).
Lects 1818–19 (CC)	S.T. Coleridge, *Lectures 1818–19 On the History of Philosophy*. Ed. R.J. de J. Jackson. 2 vols. *Collected Works of Samuel Taylor Coleridge*. Vol. 8. (Princeton: Princeton U.P., 2000).
LH	Robert Perceval Graves, *Life of Sir Rowan Hamilton, including selections from his poems,*

	correspondence, and miscellaneous writings. (Dublin: Hodges, Figgis, & Co., 1882–9).
LS (CC)	S.T. Coleridge, *Lay Sermons.* Ed. R.J. White. *Collected Works of Samuel Taylor Coleridge.* Vol. 6. (Princeton: Princeton U.P., 1972).
MC	S.T. Coleridge, *Coleridge's Miscellaneous Criticism.* Ed. T.M. Raysor. (Cambridge MA: Harvard University Press, 1936).
PL	S.T. Coleridge, *The Philosophical Lectures of Samuel Taylor Coleridge.* Ed. Kathleen Coburn. (London: Routledge and Kegan Paul, 1949).
PW (CC)	S.T. Coleridge, *Poetical Works.* Ed. J.C.C. Mays. 3 pts in 6 vols. *Collected Works of Samuel Taylor Coleridge.* Vol. 16. (Princeton: Princeton U.P., 2001).
Shedd	S.T. Coleridge, *The Complete Works of Samuel Taylor Coleridge.* Ed. W.G.T. Shedd. 7 vols. (New York: Harper, 1884).
STT	S.T. Coleridge, *Specimens of the Table Talk of Samuel Taylor Coleridge.* (London: John Murray, 1836).
SWF (CC)	S.T. Coleridge, *Shorter Works and Fragments.* Ed. H.J. Jackson and J.R. de J. Jackson. 2 vols. *Collected Works of Samuel Taylor Coleridge.* Vol. 11. (Princeton: Princeton U.P., 1995).
TL	S.T. Coleridge, *Hints Towards the Formation of a More Comprehensive Theory of Life.* Ed. Seth B. Watson. (London: John Churchill, 1848).
TT (CC)	S.T. Coleridge, *Table Talk.* Ed. Carl Woodring. 2 vols. *Collected Works of Samuel Taylor Coleridge.* Vol. 14. (Princeton: Princeton U.P., 1990).
~~Word~~	Coleridge's deletions of his text
< >	Coleridge's additions to his text

Conventions

In the *Shedd* edition, the editor chose to Americanize some of the spelling and some of Coleridge's italics were deleted. In order to honour Coleridge's intentions, the original italics and spelling have been restored.

Coleridge's spelling and usage errors have also been preserved as they appear in the text.

The first reference after each selection refers to the source of the printed text; the second reference, in brackets, refers to the page equivalent in *CC*, which is provided as a courtesy for the reader but is *not* a textual source unless otherwise cited.

Foreword

The appearance of hitherto unpublished material during the last hundred years has brought out more fully the range and complexity of Coleridge's intelligence and knowledge. Complete publication of the *Notebooks* and *Collected Works*, together with that of the previously assembled *Collected Letters*, has made it increasingly evident that this was the most extraordinary English mind of the time. The specialist or more general student who wishes to know what Coleridge had to say on a particular subject may, however, find the sheer mass of materials bewildering, since in his less formal writings he passed quickly from one subject to another. *Coleridge's Responses*, like its predecessor, *Coleridge's Writings*, is a series addressed to such readers. In each volume a particular area of Coleridge's interest is explored, with an attempt to present his most significant statements and to show the development of his thought on the subject in question.

Among the various interests attracting Coleridge during his career, poetry, and the appreciation and criticism of literature, remained constant presences and the achievement of the sublime a dominant aspiration. At the heart of his concerns, however, was a belief, or intuition, that if the recent growing interest in nature in his culture were to be developed further, his contemporaries would come to understand that it had only to be properly appreciated to reveal its underlying link with the divine. Whether or not that claim was valid has always of course been a matter for dispute; what cannot be contested, however, is the gift Coleridge displayed through his career for exploring and demonstrating its potentiality, and even its plausibility. Whether he was making minute observations of subtle countryside phenomena, or writing his most sensitive nature poetry, or indulging in metaphysical speculation, his concern to explore and demonstrate this relationship between nature and the divine was always at the heart of what he was doing. In that respect this volume will be seen to be central to the whole series.

Future progress of the work will throw more sidelights on such preoccupations. Collections devoted to the range of his criticism, to Shakespeare and to the Bible will all refer to them at times, but the present volume, by focusing on his capacity for analysis and minute observation in nature as well as his ability to range sweepingly over what she has to offer, and to insist on the centrality of mind as itself a crucial part of the nature it is seeking to explain, acts as a firm and central guide to ideas that permeate the whole of his work.

As always, the editorial work in the Princeton edition will be found invaluable by the reader who wishes to inquire further into particular matters.

JOHN BEER

Introduction

I. Visions of Nature, and the Nature of Vision

Throughout a lifetime of intellectual production, Coleridge produced thousands of pages of poems and prose, from highly polished lyric poems to spontaneous observations and speculations in the notebooks. His work spans an enormous range not only of genre, but also of quality, from stunning gems of insight to brambly disquisitions that seem to have no outlet. Despite the often miscellaneous feel of Coleridge's writing, upon closer examination it is apparent that there are many uniting strands of thought that run throughout his voluminous body of work. It is the purpose of this series to present some of these themes that continually reappear throughout Coleridge's lifetime as urgent intellectual and artistic questions.

Discovering these overarching themes requires a selective method of reading. Coleridge himself identified '4 Sorts of Readers. 1. Spunges that suck up every thing and, when pressed give it out in the same state, only perhaps somewhat dirtier'; Sand Glasses 'which in a brief hour assuredly let out what it has received' and Straining Bags 'who get rid of whatever is good & pure, and retain the Dregs'. The last type of readers, which 'are the only good, & I fear not the least numerous' were 'the Great-Moguls Diamond Sieves ... who assuredly retain the good, while the superfluous or impure passes away & leaves no trace'.[1] Coleridge's readers must attend to his writing in this way, by sifting the gems from the dross. The series *Coleridge's Responses* attempts to assist in this endeavour, by using various unifying themes as the sieve.

Working on Coleridge is like untangling the Gordian knot, in the sense that tugging on one seemingly independent strand turns out to affect every other part. Coleridge believed passionately in the interconnectedness of diverse systems of thought, from philosophy to science to poetry. Ineluctably there is some overlap in the *Coleridge's Writings* and *Coleridge's Responses* series, although each volume illuminates the others. *Nature and Vision* is intended to dovetail with David Vallins' volume *On the Sublime*, which also treats the subject of nature, particularly emotional responses to nature.

This volume will address the omnipresence of vision in Coleridge's work, both in visions of nature and his meditations on the nature of vision itself. That is, Coleridge was interested not only in *what* we perceive, but *how* we perceive. His concept of vision is multi-faceted: it is not simply a mechanical playing of light rays on the optic nerve, but a complex process involving the inner or spiritual eye as well as the physical eye. Vision is malleable and manifold, and subject to various influences, such as the voluntary powers of imagination and genius, involuntary responses such as emotion and dream-states, and cultivated capabilities such as reason and faith. Underlying and informing all vision, Coleridge cherished a deep-seated belief that God himself is intimately connected with all levels of human perception. Ultimately vision could span the spectrum from the humblest perceptions of nature to the most exalted spiritual truths.

Nature and Vision will explore three modes of vision that were important to Coleridge: the objective, the subjective, and the transcendental.[2] These modes commence with objective vision of the material forms of nature, ascend to creative or artistic vision, and finally culminate in the transcendental, in which the spiritual meaning of nature is perceived or at least intimated. These divisions correspond with an important theme in early nineteenth-century literature that I will refer to as the romantic triad, or the relationship between nature, humanity, and the divine.[3] Coleridge believed that through the perfection of human powers of vision, the relationship between the material and spiritual worlds could be apprehended. He claimed that 'our destiny & instinct is to unriddle the World, & he is the man of Genius who feels this instinct fresh and strong in his nature – who perceives the riddle & the mystery of all things even the commonest'.[4] The poet, if he mastered vision at its highest level, could potentially see into 'the mystery of all things' or the spiritual meaning of nature.

Far from being passive in this process, nature actually aids the human mind to see itself, the world, and even the divine. By providing 'Natural Symbols' or outer forms which contained inner spiritual meaning, nature instigated higher modes of seeing:

... all the merely bodily Feelings subservient to our reason, coming only at its call, and obeying its Behests with a gladness not without awe, like servants who work under the Eye of their Lord, we have solemnized the long marriage of our Souls by its outward sign & Natural Symbol. It is now registered in both worlds, the world of Spirit and the world of the Senses.[5]

Coleridge believed that God created nature as an 'outward sign' of spirit, through which human beings could descry the divine. In this sense, nature ministered to the human mind, as a kind of book or language that could be read for spiritual meaning. He stated, 'We understand Nature just as if at a distance, we looked at the Image of a Person in a Looking-glass, plainly and fervently discoursing – yet what he uttered, we could decypher only by the motion of the Lips, and the mien, and the expression of the muscles of the Countenance–'.[6] Although nature could be interpreted for spiritual meaning, this mode of vision required cultivation and development. Thus vision is both passive and active: the physical eye passively records impressions, yet the inner eye has to actively fathom the significance of natural forms.

This explains why vision became a lifelong obsession for Coleridge: cleansing, elevating and perfecting vision is in some sense redemptive: by rousing oneself continually to higher modes of perception, one engages in a continual spiritual process, with the highest goal being a transparent vision of nature, humanity and the divine. A unifying theme in Coleridge's thought is his interest in the freshness or vividness of perception, necessary not only for the poet, but also for the spiritual elevation of his readers. In *Aids to Reflection* he reflected, 'In philosophy equally as in poetry it is the highest and most useful prerogative of genius to produce the strongest impressions of novelty, while it rescues admitted truths from the neglect caused by the very circumstance of their universal admission.'[7] The role of the man of 'genius' is not only to see clearly, but to instigate the higher perceptive powers in his readers as well.

Refining the manifold powers of vision is a central motif that spans Coleridge's wide-ranging interests. His notebooks exhibit his desire to describe the natural world in all its myriad detail and splendour. His literary criticism heralded the importance of vivid and novel imagery for great poetry. His philosophical speculations urged the cultivation of the intellectual powers of reason and method. His religious beliefs called for mastering the art of reflection and faith as necessary to true spirituality. In all of these forms of vision, nature played an important role. Nature was a source of artistic inspiration, the key to philosophical and scientific discovery, and a book of spiritual meaning to be interpreted. Although he never formulated a final system that resolved the romantic triad of nature, humanity and the divine, all of his speculations necessitated the cultivation of vision as essential for a possible reconciliation of nature and spirit.

II. Unravelling 'the Riddle of the World'[8]

Coleridge believed that the perfection of vision, at its highest level, could potentially solve one of the great mysteries: the relationship between the spiritual and natural worlds. He wrote in *The Friend*, 'But to find no contradiction in the union of old and new, to contemplate the ANCIENT OF DAYS with feelings as fresh as if they then sprang forth at his own fiat, this characterizes the mind that feels the Riddle of the World, and may help to unravel it!'[9] The tissue of paradoxes involved in this 'Riddle' – the one and the many, the spiritual and the material, the temporal and the eternal – tantalized Coleridge throughout his intellectual career. This lifelong interest can be divided into three stages: a youthful intuition that nature and spirit were interrelated, which coincides with the early notebooks and poems; secondly, the search for an aesthetic, metaphysical and philosophical framework for nature and spirit, during the great prose works of his middle years; and finally, after failing to create such a system, an increasing reliance on religious modes of vision towards the end of his life. In this search Coleridge investigated countless intellectual sources, from literary theory, philosophy and science, and finally religious orthodoxy. A uniting strand in all these endeavours is his faith in the power of vision to reconcile and unify apparent opposites, including nature and spirit.

Coleridge's passion for nature and his conviction that it was linked with the spiritual world began in childhood. From an early age, he was convinced that the physical senses alone were not sufficient descriptors of reality. He recalled his childhood reading of the *Arabian Nights* as giving him an intuition of a spiritual world beyond the five senses:

For from my early reading of fairy tales and genii, etc., etc., my mind had been habituated *to the Vast*, and I never regarded *my* senses in any way as the criteria of my belief. I regulated all my creeds by my conceptions, not by my *sight*, even at that age. Should children be permitted to read romances, and relations of giants and magicians and genii? I know all that has been said against it; but I have formed my faith in the affirmative. I know no other way of giving the mind a love of the Great and the Whole.[10]

This intuitive 'love of the Great and the Whole' continued to develop hand in hand with a passion for the natural world throughout his early adulthood, the period of his greatest poetic production. In *Biographia Literaria*, he recounted how nature tutored and formed his literary and intellectual abilities: ' ... still there was a long and blessed interval, during which my natural faculties were allowed to expand, and my original tendencies to develop themselves: my fancy, and the love of nature, and the sense of beauty in forms and sounds'.[11] Nature was central in shaping all of his earliest intuitions, faculties and sensibilities, and yet never at the expense of faith in a spiritual world. However, Coleridge gradually became restless with a vague intuitive sense that nature and spirit were connected, more aware of its pantheistic implications, and increasingly preoccupied with finding an intellectual explanation for their relationship.

Coleridge's search for an intellectual framework to ground his ideas coincided with a turn away from poetry.[12] Thus began a long search for philosophical and metaphysical formulations to explain the relation between nature and spirit. An early enthusiasm for the materialist philosopher David Hartley, and his mechanical explanation for vision involving the 'hypothetical oscillating ether of the nerves'[13] seemed promising at first, but soon Coleridge rejected materialism as 'the philosophy of death':[14] it could not account for the dynamic powers of life, consciousness and change. The German idealist philosophers, especially Kant and Schelling, rescued Coleridge from the grip of materialism by positing the importance of the thinking and perceiving subject as the starting point for philosophy. However, Coleridge hoped for an even grander solution, by combining idealist philosophy with scientific discoveries of *Naturphilosophie*, an eclectic nineteenth-century scientific movement that sought a unified theory of philosophy, natural science and theology. Coleridge hoped to reveal such a system in a magnum opus to be named *Logosophia*. Like many of his projects it was never finished, nor was he ever able to fully systematize his wide-ranging thoughts. However, through these diverse endeavours runs a persistent commitment to cultivating various powers of vision.

In his later life, Coleridge focused more on harmonizing his Christian beliefs with his earlier intellectual intuitions. The religious doctrine of Trinitarianism proposed a unified, all-powerful God who also manifested himself in the multiplicity of nature. Various forms of spiritual vision are necessary for apprehending the 'three-in-one' identity of a Trinitarian God, who was both one and many, purely spiritual and yet also manifested in the material. Belief and faith continue where philosophical vision reaches its limits. While detailed descriptions of nature fade away in these later writings, Coleridge never abandoned nature: as ever, nature was still an essential part of his divine scheme.

III. Modes of Vision

As we have seen, Coleridge's interest in nature and vision was a lifelong preoccupation that evolved throughout his intellectual development. Each of the chapters in *Nature and Vision* will explore a different mode of seeing nature. Corresponding with his conception of an ascending series of perceptive powers, the chapters follow a similar arc from the lowest levels of objective vision to the highest and most exalted transcendental visions of nature. In each of these chapters, we see Coleridge's obsessive interest in perfecting vision as a necessary, and even redemptive, process that could potentially dissolve the boundaries between nature, humanity and the divine.

Chapter 1, 'Objective Vision', presents some of the observations of the natural world found in his early notebook entries. Inspired by Coleridge's rambles in the countryside, the notebooks include detailed descriptions of nature that exhibit both his passion for the beauty of nature and his commitment to portraying the natural world accurately. These entries are remarkable on several levels: they are notable for their objective powers of observation worthy of a naturalist, but also for fluid transitions from natural description to more abstract musings on the inward significance of these natural scenes. In these entries, the reader accompanies Coleridge on journeys through nature, in which both the inner and the outer vision are engaged in perceiving nature freshly:

> My walks therefore were almost daily on the top of Quantock, and among its sloping coombs. With my pencil and memorandum book in my hand, I was *making studies*, as the artists call them, and often moulding my thoughts into verse, with the objects and imagery immediately before my senses.[15]

Like the *plein-air* painters who first took their easels outdoors, Coleridge brought his notebooks with him on rambles to record nature as he experienced it in the moment. Striving for immediacy and vividness in his descriptions of nature, both visual and emotional, fulfilled his precept that a poet should combine 'the sense of novelty and freshness, with old and familiar objects'.[16] Coleridge's eye, far from being passive, was constantly shaping and 'moulding' what he saw.

The notebooks reveal Coleridge's remarkable eye for accurate description and naturalistic detail. Although no natural object was unworthy of his powers of description, he was drawn repeatedly to certain types of natural phenomena, especially the subtle changes and transformations in nature that seemed to manifest spiritual forces at work in the material world. As discussed at length in David Vallins' volume *Coleridge's Writings: On the Sublime*, Coleridge was drawn to landscape that was dramatic, extreme and awe-inspiring even to the point of terror, especially the mountains of the Lake District or the Alps. However, he also devoted notebook entries to more subtle scenery. He carefully documented natural ephemera, such as weather, cloudscapes, changing tints of light and shadow, and celestial phenomena like rainbows, glories and moon halos. The transformative effects of light, especially moonlight and shadow, on otherwise ordinary scenes also fascinated Coleridge. He studied forces that appeared to *animate* nature, such as wind, light or storms, observations which were attractive to his aesthetic and philosophical sensibility. He was also interested in optical illusions in which the gazing eye was misled in interpreting nature, because forces like imagination or emotion modified perception. These entries reinforce the idea that vision is a complex and multi-faceted process that defies a simple, mechanistic explanation.

In addition to their descriptive mastery, these notebook entries also record the emotional and spiritual resonances of Coleridge's experiences in nature. Natural forms are not only beautiful in themselves, they also awaken powers of vision and act as ciphers of spiritual meaning:

> O! Heaven! one thousandfold combinations of Images that pass hourly in this divine Vale, while I am dozing & muddling away my Thoughts and Eyes – O let me rouse myself – If I even begin mechanically, & only by aid of memory look round and call each thing by a name – describe it, as a trial of skill in words – it may bring back fragments of former Feeling – For we can live only by feeding abroad.[17]

In this passage inner and outer vision are invoked simultaneously – his 'Thoughts and Eyes' need to be rescued from dozing and dullness. Observing nature and calling 'each thing by a name', echoing Adam's naming of creation in Genesis, renews his emotional and spiritual connection to the world. This act of seeing, far from being a passive act, is active and rejuvenating, even redemptive: 'it may bring back fragments of former Feeling' or a sense of interconnection between the mind, nature and the divine.

Chapter 2, 'Visions of Nature in Lyric Poetry', seamlessly blends the beauty of objective visions of nature with the additional dimensions of artistic vision. Coleridge believed that poets are endowed with a special sensitivity to nature's outward forms. Additionally they are gifted with special inward powers of vision: namely being able to 'read' nature for spiritual meaning, and echo God's creation of nature in their own artistic productions. Thus the poet takes on a quasi-prophetic role as an interpreter (and creator) of the spiritual meanings of nature. The poems in this chapter illustrate three intersections of nature and vision: poems which take the form of visionary journeys, leading the reader's eye through nature; the role of the poet as an interpreter of nature; and finally, poems which celebrate an ecstatic vision of oneness between the natural and spiritual worlds.

In Coleridge's view, the poet needs manifold powers of vision to observe nature truly and communicate its meaning. For example, in the 'conversation poems' such as 'Frost at Midnight' and 'The Eolian Harp', various types of vision are invoked as the poems unfold. In the beginning, a loved one or a dear friend is addressed, making the poem a form of conversation requiring emotional connection and communication. Then the poems describe a natural scene in lush and evocative detail. Finally, the deeper spiritual meanings of these natural images are revealed. Three forms of vision are engaged: the outward and objective, the emotional and subjective, and the transcendental or spiritual perceptions. Thus in the creative world of these poems, the poet becomes a mediator between nature, the human world, and the divine.

Each group of poems in this chapter illustrates a different aspect of envisioning nature in poetry. In the first section, the poems take the form of visionary journeys, in which the reader's eye is guided through the natural world, while awakening manifold powers of vision. In his most famous poem of this type, 'This Lime-tree Bower my Prison', Coleridge concludes 'That Nature ne'er deserts the wise and pure' and 'may well employ/ Each faculty of sense, and keep the heart/ Awake to Love and Beauty',[18] emphasizing that nature stimulates all faculties of perception, from the physical to the emotional. Throughout the poem, these modes of vision are engaged simultaneously, making these poems inner as well as outer journeys.

In the next group of poems, the power of vision extends even further: nature is read as a book of spiritual meaning, or 'the language of God himself, as uttered by nature'.[19] Many of the early poems refer to nature's ministry, in which nature imparts spiritual lessons to the human mind. In *The Friend*, Coleridge writes 'Observe, how graciously Nature instructs her human children ... We not only see, but are enabled to discover by what means we see.'[20] Nature becomes a 'Great universal Teacher' whose outer forms guide and minister to the human mind. This idea is articulated in 'Frost at Midnight' in

> The lovely shapes and sounds intelligible
> Of that eternal language, which thy God
> Utters, who from eternity doth teach
> Himself in all, and all things in himself.
> Great universal Teacher! he shall mould
> Thy spirit, and by giving make it ask.[21]

Here nature is transformed into 'that eternal language' uttered by God himself, to teach 'Himself in all'. While the idea of nature as a book of God is not unique to Coleridge, the concept is boldly elevated in these early poems.

In the final section of poems, Coleridge presses poetic vision to its utmost extreme. Some of his early poems reveal moments of

ecstatic vision in which nature and spirit, creator and created, the
one and the many, dissolve into a transparent oneness:

> O dread and silent Mount! I gazed upon thee,
> Till thou, still present to the bodily sense,
> Didst vanish from my thought: entranced in prayer
> I worshipped the Invisible alone.[22]

Here we see two paradoxical modes of vision: a simultaneous
envisioning *and* disappearing of the outer form of a mountain. The
two forms of vision called for – material and spiritual, outward
and inward – blend in one ecstatic moment. At certain exalted
moments, Coleridge believed that it was possible to perceive the
spiritual powers working *in* and *through* nature. He used two Latin
terms to explain this distinction: *natura naturata*, referring to
physical or material nature, and *natura naturans*, referring to the
spiritual powers that inform and shape nature.[23] In Coleridge's
view the poet engages with both aspects of nature, revealing his
power to echo, to a lesser degree, God's creation.

Coleridge claimed 'Nature itself is to a religious Observer the
Art of God.'[24] Chapter 3 will more fully investigate this connection
between artistic creation and God's creation of nature. Coleridge
elaborated many theories about artistic vision, particularly the
definitions of symbol and imagination which bridged his literary,
philosophical and religious beliefs. He mused in a notebook entry
that 'In looking at the objects of Nature while I am thinking,
as at yonder moon dim-glimmering thro' the dewy window-
pane, I seem rather to be seeking, as it were *asking*, a symbolical
language for something within me that already and forever exists,
than observing anything new.'[25] This idea of nature acting as 'a
symbolical language' is vital to Coleridge's world view. Symbolism
is not a merely a picture-language or hieroglyphic to express
abstract qualities, but a representation 'consubstantial with the
truths, of which they are the *conductors*'.[26] In other words, natural
symbols are 'consubstantial' or sharing essence with the spiritual
truths they represent, indelibly linking the natural and spiritual
worlds. Creating symbols in art is an echo of God's creation of
nature: in both creative acts, spiritual truths embody themselves in
material form.

It is the role of the poet to look into nature to discover these
symbols. While creating symbols is natural to all humans, evident

in the creation of language itself, the poet is blessed with stronger and more vivid powers of vision:

> All minds must think by some *symbols* – the strongest minds possess the most vivid Symbols in the Imagination – yet this ingenerates a *want* ... for vividness of Symbol: which something that is *without*, that has the property of *Outness* (a word which Berkley preferred to 'Externality') can alone fully gratify/ even that indeed not fully – for the utmost is only an approximation to that absolute *Union*, which the soul sensible of its imperfection in itself, of its *Halfness*, yearns after, whenever it exists free from meaner passions ...[27]

In this passage, symbolism results from a religious yearning for 'absolute *Union*' of the inward and outward worlds. Heightened powers of vision, possessed by 'the strongest minds', are necessary for creating such symbols, marrying form and meaning. The second section of Chapter 3 presents some examples of such symbols created by Coleridge himself, such as the water-insect pulsing up a stream to the seed of the crocus. These metaphors are notable not only for their vividness, and their aptness in communicating certain abstract truths and principles, but also for the harmony between the organic and divine powers that Coleridge believed were at work in both symbol and the symbolized.

The poet's special powers of vision are defined by Coleridge as 'Genius'.[28] He devoted a good portion of *Biographia Literaria* to describing these rarified powers: 'The poet, described in *ideal* perfection, brings the whole soul of man into activity, with the subordination of its faculties to each other according to their relative worth and dignity.'[29] Thus the poet engaged many 'faculties' at once, becoming the master of the full range of perceptive powers:

> It is that pleasurable emotion, that peculiar state or degree of Excitement, which arises in the Poet himself, in the act of composition – & in order to understand this we must combine a more than ordinary Sympathy with the Objects, Emotions, or Incidents contemplated by the Poet in consequence of a more than common sensibility, with a more than ordinary Activity of the Mind as far as respects the Fancy & Imagination – Hence a more vivid reflection of the Truths of Nature & the Human Heart united with that constant exertion of Activity which modifies &

corrects these truths by that sort of pleasurable Emotion, which the exertion of all our faculties give in a certain degree ...[30]

The poet must have a 'more than common' sympathy with nature, artistic sensibility, a well-developed imagination – each of these are rarefied modes of vision that must be mastered in order to reflect the 'Truths of Nature & the Human Heart'.

The final sections of this chapter investigate the highest mode of poetic vision: the imagination. Coleridge's definition is one of his most important intellectual contributions, and one that impacted on later literary thought. He conceived of the imagination as a mode of vision that not only passively perceived the outer world, but actively created art as an echo of God's creation, or 'repetition in the finite mind of the eternal act of creation in the infinite I AM'.[31] The imagination transcends the merely literary: in Coleridge's view, poets were akin to prophets in their ability to perceive *and* communicate spiritual truths through symbols. However, these high levels of vision are difficult to achieve and sustain: the final set of quotations reveals Coleridge's anxiety when the imagination falters, or in his own words, when the 'genial spirits fail'.[32]

Chapter 4, 'The Natural and the Supernatural', explores the imagination as a mode of vision from a different angle. The imagination is not only an artistic, voluntary power used to create art, but also an involuntary power that could radically alter perception. Coleridge was interested in the supernatural, or phenomena that resist explanation by natural laws, because such phenomena illustrated the transformative effects of imagination on everyday experience. In particular, he was fascinated by the forces that modify, distort or amplify vision, such as moonlight, intense emotions, volition, drugs, fevers, dreams. These altered states of vision suggest that perception is not a straightforward mechanical process, but an interplay between the objective and subjective worlds, in which nature and mind collaborate:

> In Youth and early Manhood the Mind and Nature are, as it were, two rival Artists, both potent magicians, and engaged, like the king's Daughter and the rebel Genie in the Arabian Nights' Enternts., in sharp conflict of Conjuration – each having for it's object to turn the other into Canvas to paint on, Clay to mould, or Cabinet to contain. For a while the Mind seems to have the better in the contest, and makes of Nature what it likes ... But

alas! Alas! That Nature is a wary wily long-breathed old Witch ...
She is sure to get the better of Lady MIND in the long run.[33]

Mind and nature are 'two rival Artists, both potent magicians' that
conjure and shape reality. The mind can project meaning onto
nature, but nature also forms and shapes the mind. Instances of
the supernatural raise questions about the nature of perception,
as they inevitably call into question which power is predominant:
mind or nature.

This interest in altered states of vision, particularly the psychological explanations for distortions of perception, was ahead of its
time. Long before Freud discussed the role of the subconscious,
Coleridge posited that in certain states of consciousness, deep
desires modified perception. And yet, these states are not entirely
dismissed as fantasy or illusion either. Coleridge's thoughts on
mysticism also straddle this divide. Although he derided many
mystical writers for confusing their peculiar individual visions with
universal truths, he was still fascinated by the nature of mysticism
and read deeply into the works of Swedenborg and Böhme.
However cautious he was about mysticism, he refers repeatedly to
exalted states of vision in which the impossible becomes possible:
extremes meet, polarities collapse, boundaries dissolve, and a
vision of the supernatural – or that which lies beyond the natural
world – is possible. The first set of selections present examples
of such quasi-mystical visions which gave 'the mind a love of the
Great and the Whole'.[34]

Accounting for supernatural phenomena also raised myriad
questions about the nature of perception itself. The second set of
quotations in Chapter 4 involve accounts of ghosts, apparitions
and other unusual phenomena. Coleridge was sceptical about the
existence of ghosts, not because he didn't believe wholly in the
spiritual manifesting in the material world, but because he thought
that it was more likely that these phenomena were created by the
imagination affecting vision through various influences. He regarded
these supernatural accounts as 'affording some valuable materials
for a theory of perception and its dependence on the memory and
imagination'.[35] He hoped that study of the forces which modified
perception could yield insight into the nature of vision itself.

While Coleridge questioned the objective reality of supernatural
phenomena, he was less equivocal about the power of supernatural

imagery in literature. A central aim of his poetic sensibility was to reinvigorate language by creating imagery that was vivid and fresh; the strangeness of the supernatural served this function by captivating the reader's imagination. He praised his childhood reading of the *Arabian Nights* because in these tales 'there is the same activity of mind as in dreaming, that is – an exertion of the fancy in the combination and recombination of familiar objects so as to produce novel and wonderful imagery'.[36] This use of the supernatural to present the familiar in an unfamiliar light provided a central premise in Coleridge's collaboration with Wordsworth in *Lyrical Ballads*. The goal of that poetic volume was to illustrate 'the two cardinal points of poetry, the power of exciting the sympathy of the reader by a faithful adherence to the truth of nature, and the power of giving the interest of novelty by the modifying colours of imagination'.[37] While Wordsworth would evoke 'the truth of nature' in his poems for *Lyrical Ballads*, Coleridge would present a purely imaginative world, one lit by moonlight and haunted by supernatural elements. The effect of 'persons and characters super-natural' would be to 'transfer from our inward nature a human interest and a semblance of truth sufficient to procure for these shadows of imagination that willing suspension of disbelief for the moment, which constitutes poetic faith'.[38] In this 'suspension of disbelief' Coleridge could usher his reader to a visionary world of pure imagination, in which normal logical expectations were temporarily suspended in a special act of seeing.

Thus the use of the supernatural in literature ventures beyond mere novelty, to a deeper programme whereby the reader is trans-ported, however briefly, into an imaginative world. The final part of this chapter contains selections from Coleridge's two great super-natural poems, 'The Rime of the Ancient Mariner' and 'Christabel', to illustrate the power and strangeness of supernatural imagery. However, such elements were not limited to poetry, as selections from several of Coleridge's 'allegoric visions' reveal; in these prose selections the reader also embarks on weird visionary journeys, in which elaborate supernatural imagery illustrates theoretical points. Also included in this chapter are two poems influenced by opium, a drug which powerfully altered perception and provided a doorway into supernatural reveries, both ecstatic and demonic. All of these selections invoke altered states of vision, which engage the reader's imagination and refresh their perceptive powers.

The supernatural illuminates an interesting intersection between modes of vision: on one hand, objective views of nature and on the other, the subjective forces that modify visions of nature. As we have seen in the progression of chapters thus far, in Coleridge's view the human mind is capable of many kinds of perception, from the sensory perception of the physical eye, to the artistic interpretations of genius and imagination, to the altered states of vision invoked in perceiving the supernatural. Each of these modes of vision requires different faculties through which the outer world is perceived and shaped. The remainder of *Nature and Vision* will investigate more abstract modes of vision, particularly the philosophical and religious, which increasingly preoccupied Coleridge in his middle and later years.

Chapter 5 investigates a central philosophical conundrum involving nature and vision: namely 'the Riddle of the World'[39] or the question of how exactly the material world and spiritual world are interrelated. Coleridge always had a strong inner intuition that nature and spirit were reconcilable, but the exact nature of this relationship puzzled and frustrated him for his entire life. He found existing philosophical positions on this question unsatisfactory, although pantheism, mysticism, materialism and Platonic and German idealism all intrigued him at various points in his intellectual career. Instead of accepting one philosophical theory, he attempted to harmonize many different philosophical systems, a project for which he has been much derided – with charges both of misinterpretation and of imputed plagiarism. However, if we set aside judgement of Coleridge as a philosopher, we see an important continuation of his interest in nature and vision.

From his earliest writings, Coleridge intuited that in high levels of seeing, nature and spirit could potentially be seen transparently, revealing the immaterial within the material, or unity in multiplicity. He was firmly committed to finding a philosophical explanation for this vision. An early notebook entry reveals the urgency of this preoccupation:

I would make a pilgrimage to the Deserts of Arabia to find the man who could make understand how the *one can be many!* Eternal universal mystery! It seems as if it were impossible; yet it *is* – & it is every where! – It is indeed a contradiction *in Terms*: and only in Terms! – It is the co presence of Feeling & Life, limitless by their very essence, with Form, by its very essence limited – determinate – definite. –[40]

Seeing how 'the one can be many' is at once a paradox and contradiction, and yet 'it is every where!' Coleridge strove diligently to find a philosophical solution to this 'Eternal universal mystery' that harmonized his intuitions of unity with his Christian beliefs, since early attempts to describe such a unity bordered on pantheism. Although this question had been broached in many philosophical traditions, he was not satisfied with existing formulations, which he felt gravitated towards one of two extremes:

> But in fact it is demonstrably impossible, that the Riddle of the World should be solved by a Philosophy, which commences by drawing a circle, that can never open, around it; and which therefore must for ever stagger to and fro between two intolerable Positions – first, an absolute Identity, that monopolizing all *very* Being leaves only a Universe of mere Relations without focuses, to which they refer – i.e. when the Looking-glasses are themselves only Reflections. 2. A real Nature, in which Potential Being is a the bona fide Antecedent to all actual Being, and every higher Power is the Creature and Product of the lower – all therefore of the lowest.[41]

Coleridge struggled between the two philosophical extremes of idealism and materialism. On one hand, materialism made 'every higher Power' the 'Product of the lower', which did not respect a hierarchical superiority of the divine. Idealism mandated 'an absolute Identity' that entailed a 'Universe of mere relations', in which nature subsequently faded away. Neither position was satisfactory for Coleridge, who sought instead for a higher fusion of these philosophical extremes. He sought a hierarchical model in which God is the highest power, informing nature yet not merging indiscriminately with it; yet he also refused to abandon nature as irrelevant or separate from God either. This entailed an intermediary position:

> Observe: we must not worship God, as if *his* Ways were as *our* Ways. We must not apply to him, neither, as tho' God were the same with Sensible Nature, or the sum total of the Objects of our bodily Senses. And to speak aloud to God and by the sound and meaning of our words to suppose ourselves influencing him

as we in this way influence our fellow-men, this is a *delirious* Superstition. O in that, which comprizing both transcends both, what precious Mysteries lie hid.[42]

Coleridge never succeeded in forging this philosophical fusion systematically, but equally he never discarded the conviction that such a fusion was possible. To find a middle ground between materialism and idealism, a position which 'comprizing both transcends both', he focused on the human faculties of vision to explain the relation of nature and spirit. Rather than God or nature being inherently divided or limited, it is our *vision* of God and nature that is limited.

Once reaching this conclusion that our perception is the limiting factor in seeing the world truly, Coleridge exhorted his readers to elevate their philosophical vision. He was indebted to Kant's distinction between the reason and understanding as a critical first step in delineating the higher and lower philosophical powers of the mind. He was also influenced by the intellectual movement of *Naturphilosophie*, which sought for a unified theory combining natural science, philosophy and theology. As Coleridge gradually left poetry and literary theory behind, he focused instead on formulating an ascending arc of powers, commencing from the lowest sensory perceptions to the highest transcendental intuition. While seeing nature and responding to it emotionally is an instinctive and natural mode of vision, higher forms of vision require active refinement. Chapter 5 presents various methods through which philosophical vision could be cultivated: by identifying different faculties of perception; by creating proper terminology and definitions; by training the mind according to a philosophic 'method' and, finally, looking toward advances in science to fill in the missing links between the material and spiritual worlds.

Ultimately Coleridge sought for a philosophy that addressed all areas of human endeavour, anticipating the time when 'we shall have Philosophy, that will unite in itself the warmth of the mystics, the definiteness of the Dialectician, and the sunny clearness of the Naturalist, the productivity of the Experimenter and the Evidence of the Mathematician'.[43] Unlike his literary theories, which he enacted in his own poetry and literary criticism, much of his philosophical musing remained speculative. His hope for a unified philosophical system was never achieved; yet by examining his philosophical musings, we can appreciate the depth and breadth of his passion to unite the natural and spiritual worlds.

Chapter 6 concludes *Nature and Vision* with the keystone of Coleridge's intellectual thought: religious vision. All of his endeavours were in some way related to his religious belief that God not only stands at the apex of all creation, but intimately informs all of its workings, including the human mind and the natural world. Perhaps he stood on firmer ground when he put aside philosophical speculation, and grounded his intellectual framework on religious foundations instead. Although his thinking becomes more abstract in his later thought, he does not abandon nature in favour of the ineffable divine; rather, we see him continually striving to incorporate nature into his religious plan.

Once again, the power of vision is emphasized as necessary to perceiving the interrelation of nature and spirit. Coleridge devoted one of his best-known prose works, *Aids to Reflection*, to the art of reflection, described as 'an intention to form the human mind anew after the DIVINE IMAGE'.[44] Thus vision is turned inward and upward, rather than being directed to the outside world. Yet nature is not forgotten: this form of reflective vision is simply a higher, more refined faculty of seeing:

> For all things are but parts and forms of its progressive manifestation, and every new knowledge but a new organ of sense and insight into this one all-inclusive verity, which, still filling the vessel of the understanding, still dilates it to a capacity of yet other and yet greater truths, and thus makes the soul feel its poverty by the very amplitude of its present, and the immensity of its reversionary wealth.[45]

Earlier chapters of *Nature and Vision* traced each different 'organ of sense', from the physical eye, to the artistic imagination, to philosophical perception. However, the highest of all perceptive powers is religious vision, which as it 'dilates to a capacity of yet another and yet greater Truths' could reach the highest levels of human seeing. Coleridge believed that by cultivating this kind of spiritual seeing, we could potentially return to our original state of oneness with God and nature:

> It seems as if the soul said to herself: from this state hast *thou* fallen! Such shouldst thou still become, thyself all permeable to

a holier power! thyself at once hidden and glorified by its own transparency, as the accidental and dividuous in this quiet and harmonious object is subjected to the life and light of nature; to that life and light of nature, I say, which shines in every plant and flower, even as the transmitted power, love and wisdom of God over all fills, and shines through, nature![46]

In Coleridge's thought, all roads lead to Rome, as it were: the power of vision, if pursued to its highest level, could potentially unify nature and spirit. This state of oneness and transparency is at the heart of all his intellectual and artistic endeavours. Nature, rather than being superfluous in this highest form of seeing, actually aids in the cultivation of vision, since 'The wonderful Works of God in the sensible World are a perpetual Discourse, reminding me of his Existence, and Shadowing out to me his perfections.'[47] The material world is a shadow of the divine, created in order to direct human vision upwards towards its perfect source.

Chapter 6 investigates various modes of religious vision. The first section examines Coleridge's commitment to the art of 'reflection', or turning the mind inward upon itself. Such meditations not only entail high levels of perception, but also hint at their limits. Although the power of reason is celebrated as a high form of seeing, it is superseded by a religious power, that of faith: 'Religion passes out of the ken of Reason only where the eye of Reason has reached its own horizon; and that Faith is then but its continuation.'[48] Here Coleridge becomes more of a mystic than a philosopher, claiming that faith not only subsumes reason, but is an intuition and an apprehending: 'faith must be a light, a form of knowing, a beholding of truth'.[49] Thus at the apex of human capabilities of vision, the objective powers, the imaginative powers, and the rational powers are crowned by a religious and intuitive mode of vision.

However, Coleridge still yearned for a system to ground his beliefs: resorting to the quasi-mystical power of faith was not enough to solve the 'Riddle of the World'. In his later life, he turned to the notion of Trinitarianism as a possible way to harmonize the natural and spiritual worlds. The notion of a tripartite God as the Father, the Son and the Holy Ghost approximated to Coleridge's complex conception of the divine as undivided, all-powerful, and yet creative. The idea of the 'Logos' or the *word* of God as a manifestation of divine creativity, evident in the creation of the natural world and of the human mind, was an attractive formulation for Coleridge. The penultimate section details some of these Trinitarian musings; however, his penchant for coinages and terminology sometimes obscures his attempts to find a lucid formula inclusive of nature and spirit.

Finally, we end where we begin, like the Coleridgean symbol of the serpent whose tail is in its mouth: the exploration of nature and vision has come full circle. From his earliest fascination with material observations of nature, to the highest conceptions of the divine shining through nature, Coleridge reveals that a transparent vision of nature, the divine and humanity is a millennial hope that fuelled all of his thought:

> In this and no other, that the objects of the Christian Redemption will be perfected on this earth; – that the kingdom of God and his Word, the latter as the Son of Man, in which the divine will shall *be done on earth as it is in heaven,* will *come*; – and that the whole march of nature and history, from the first impregnation of Chaos by the Spirit converges toward this kingdom as the final cause of the world. Life begins in detachment from Nature, and ends in union with God.[50]

Coleridge yearned for a 'Christian Redemption' when nature, spirit, and humanity would be seen transparently, and all divisions and limitations of vision would be transcended; but these wishes are always stated in the future tense, which suggests that Coleridge is not a mystic but a millennial thinker who believes in the *possibility*, but not the *actuality*, of the highest levels of vision. However, we see that throughout a lifetime of intellectual production, Coleridge never relinquished his commitment to seeing nature and spirit as one. When he muses, 'Life begins in detachment from Nature, and ends in union with God', he idealizes the full scope of human vision, from seeing nature's humblest forms to the highest mystic visions of oneness with spirit.

Notes

1 *CN* III 3242 25.5
2 These terms, taken from German idealism, which Coleridge so admired, were interpreted and adapted by him in his own ways. In

particular, Coleridge's use of the term 'transcendental' is complex and varies significantly from Kant's definitive philosophical use of the term; however, Coleridge's interpretation (or misinterpretation) was essential to his intellectual framework, and additionally it was significant for the development of romanticism both in England and abroad. See footnotes 4 and 5 in Chapter 5 for more on Coleridge and German idealism.

3 The romantic triad is inspired in part by M.H. Abrams' discussion of the centrality of these themes in romanticism. See M.H. Abrams, *Natural Supernaturalism: Tradition and Revolution in Romantic Literature* (London: Oxford University Press, 1971).

4 *CM (CC)* I 747

5 *CN* II 2600 17.211

6 *CN* III 3659 24.45

7 *AR (CC)* 11

8 *F (CC)* II 73–4

9 *F (CC)* II 73–4

10 *CLE* I 16–17 [*CL* I 354]

11 *BL (CC)* I 17

12 Coleridge considers 'Well were it for me perhaps, had I never relapsed into the same mental disease; if I had continued to pluck the flower and reap the harvest from the cultivated surface, instead of delving in the unwholesome quicksilver mines of metaphysic depths' (*BL (CC)* I 17). While metaphysics were a vital intellectual endeavour for Coleridge, it was an obsession that indubitably marked the end of his greatest poetic production.

13 *BL (CC)* I 106. David Hartley was the founder of the materialist philosophy of associationism and one of Coleridge's early influences, after whom Coleridge's first son was named.

14 *LS (CC)* 89

15 *BL (CC)* I 196

16 *BL (CC)* II 17

17 *CN* III 3420 13.14

18 *CPW* I 178–81 [*PW (CC)* I 351]

19 *SWF (CC)* I 485

20 *F (CC)* I 47

21 *CPW* I 240 [*PW (CC)* I 452]

22 *CPW* I 376 [*PW (CC)* II 717]

23 For more on *natura naturata* and *natura naturans* see *AR (CC)* 252n, *AR (CC)* 558–9 and *Lects 1818–19 (CC)* II 556–7.

24 *CN* III 4397 22.73

25 *CN* II 2546 17.104

26 *LS (CC)* 29

27 *CN* III 3325 21 1/2.19

28 In Coleridge's view, Shakespeare represented this ideal of genius most perfectly, as will be discussed in *Coleridge's Respones: on Writers and Writing.*

29 *BL (CC)* II 15
30 *CN* III 4111 M.12
31 *BL (CC)* I 304
32 *CPW* I 362–8 [*PW (CC)* II 697]
33 *CLE* II 742 [*CL* V 496–7]
34 *CLE* I 16–17 [*CL* I 354]
35 *Shedd* II 134–6 [*F (CC)* I 145]
36 *MC* 193 [*Lects 1808–19* II 191]
37 *BL (CC)* II 5
38 *BL (CC)* II 5
39 *CM (CC)* II 1018
40 *CN* I 1561 21.281
41 *CM(CC)* II 1018
42 *IS* 379
43 *IS* 126
44 *AR (CC)* 25
45 *Shedd* VI 188–9 [*LS (CC)* 179]
46 *Shedd* I 461 [*LS (CC)* 69]
47 *CN* III 4005 M.7
48 *Shedd* III 594 [*BL (CC)* II 247]
49 *Shedd* V 565 [*SWF (CC)* II 844]
50 *Shedd* V 513 [*CM (CC)* III 417]

O! Heaven! one thousandfold combinations of Images that pass hourly in this divine Vale, while I am dozing & muddling away my Thoughts and Eyes – O let me rouse myself – If I even begin mechanically, & only by aid of memory look round and call each thing by a name – describe it, as a trial of skill in words – it may bring back fragments of former Feeling – For we can live only by feeding abroad.

CN III 3420 13.14

Chapter One

Objective Vision: 'we can live only by feeding abroad'

Our exploration of nature and vision begins with Coleridge's objective descriptions of the natural world. In his early years, he was fond of walking in the countryside and observing nature, often with notebook in hand to jot down his impressions. These entries provided a sourcebook of vivid imagery and ideas that were often incorporated into later poetry and prose, and they also illustrate a lifelong commitment to honing and refining his objective powers of vision.

The notebook entries describing natural scenes are remarkable for their accuracy, vibrancy and range of natural description. On the grandest scale, Coleridge often describes panoramas in a kind of visionary journey, guiding the reader's eye through a scene in its vastness and complexity. His accounts are replete with accurate geographical description, to such a degree that it is possible, for example, to take a walk in Coleridge's very footsteps in the Lake District that is based on his notebook entries. In addition to the precise descriptions of the permanent features of the landscape, he was also gifted with a painterly capacity to relate subtle atmospheric effects, elevating these descriptions to a poetic recreation of the experience in nature itself. Yet Coleridge's powers of observation are not limited to the grand and sublime: he also attended to the smallest scale, with a naturalist's eye for scientific detail. His descriptions of a lizard's 'forepaw throbbing with a visible pulse'[1] or a spider spinning his web and 'heaving in the air, as if the air beneath was a pavement elastic to his Strokes'[2] reveal his capacity for relating exquisite observations of minutiae, as well as the grand panorama.

The selections below also illustrate Coleridge's interest in natural ephemera, such as changing light, weather, wind and other forces that appeared to animate nature with living and spiritual energies. Descriptions of skyscapes, seascapes and dramatic weather such as storms reflected Coleridge's intuition that nature was not dead and static, but dynamic and evolving. He was especially fascinated with celestial phenomena, with countless descriptions of the moon and moonlight, rainbows, glories and other effects of light and atmosphere that seemed to suggest a spiritual presence in the natural world.

Although Coleridge was committed to relating the physical world accurately and objectively, the notebook entries also document the transforming and sometimes distorting power of the imagination. The final selections in this chapter describe optical illusions that Coleridge observed in nature, which he attributed to the human powers of 'Queen Imagination'[3] and 'Logic the Friend of Perception'[4] that altered the mechanics of perception. Even in these objective descriptions of nature, envisioning nature transcends the physical eye.

I. Visionary journeys

Some of Coleridge's notebook entries resemble visionary journeys, in which the reader's eye is led through the totality of grand panoramas, balancing geographical description with the subtleties of light and atmosphere playing upon a scene. In these journeys, outer visions of nature often flow into more inward meditations inspired by these landscapes.

From his Lakeland notebook, October 1803

– A grey Day, windy – the vale, like a place in Faery, with the autumnal Colours, the orange, the red-brown, the crimson, the light yellow, the yet lingering Green, Beeches all & Birches, as they were blossoming Fire & Gold! – & the Sun in slanting pillars, or illuminated small parcels of mist, or single spots of softest greyish

Light, now racing, now slowly gliding, now stationary/ – the
mountains cloudy – the Lake has been a mirror so very clear,
that the water became almost invisible – & now it rolls in white
Breakers, like a Sea; & the wind snatches up the water, & drifts
it like Snow/ – and now the Rain Storm pelts against my Study
Window! ... why have I not an unencumbered Heart! these beloved
Books still before me, this noble Room, the very centre to which a
whole world of beauty converges, the deep reservoir into which all
these streams & currents of lovely Forms flow – my own mind so
populous, so active, so full of noble schemes, so capable of realizing
them/ this heart so loving, so filled with noble affections – O ...
wherefore am I not happy?

CN I 1577 21.297

From his Lakeland notebook, November 1799

Sunday Morning left our bad Inn, & went down the lake by the
opposite shore – the hoar-frost on the ground, the lake calm &
would have been mirrorlike but that it had been *breathed* on by
the mist – & that shapely white Cloud, the Day-moon, hung over
the snowy mountain opposite to us – . / We passed the first *Great*
Promontory, & What a scene! Where I stand, on the shore is a trian-
gular Bay, taking in the whole of the water view – on the other shore
is a straight deep wall of Mist/ & one third of the bare mountains
stands out from behind it – the top of the wall only in the sun – the
rest black – & now it is all one deep wall of white vapour, save that
black streaks shaped like strange creatures, seem to move in it &
down it, in opposite direction to the motion of the great Body! – &
over the forke of the Cliff behind, in shape so like a cloud, the Sun
sent cutting it his thousand silky Hairs of amber & green Light – I
step two paces, and have lost the Glory, but the edge has exactly
the soft richness of the silver edge of a cloud behind which the Sun
is travelling! – The fog has now closed over the Lake, & we wander
in darkness, save that the mist is here & there prettily color'd by the
wither'd fern, over which it hovers –

CN I 551 5.123

From his Lakeland notebook, August 1800

... – the evening now lating, I had resolved to pass it by; but Nature
twitched me at my heart strings – I ascended it – thanks to her!

Thanks to her – What a scene! nothing behind me! – as if it would be an affront to that which fronts me! ...

travelling along the ridge I came to the other side of those precipices and down below me on my left – no – no! no words can convey any idea of this prodigious wildness/ that precipice fine on this side was but its ridge, sharp as a <jagged> knife, level so long, and then ascending so boldly – what a frightful bulgy precipice I stand on and to my right how the Crag which corresponds to the other, how it plunges down, like a waterfall, reaches a level steepness, and again plunges! –

The Moon is above Fairfield almost at the full! – now descended over a perilous peat-moss then down a Hill of stones all dark, and darkling, I climbed stone after stone down a half dry Torrent and came out at the Raise Gap/ And O! my God! How *did* that opposite precipice look – in the moonshine – its name Stile Crags. –

CN I 798 5 1/2.42

From his notebook in Scotland, August 1803

About 2 miles from the Ferry, the views of the Foot of the Loch begin to be highly interesting & the Lake itself always highly so from the multitude & fine Shape of its Bays – But here as I leaned against an ash Tree, I saw such a visionary Scene! – One promontory from the Right ran down into ~~along~~ the Lake like a stretched out Arm bent downwards with a *bend* as if to support something, then a long Island midway the Lake/ then from the ~~right~~ left another promontory much resembling the former, but varying in the Steepness of its Segments/ Again from the Right a high Headland falling down steep & high as far as the Tower/ & in the far distance & exact Center of the View a small Sugar Loaf Hill – all these in exquisite Harmony, every ridge branch out, every intervening Distance softened by the rainy Air/

CN I 1471 7.24

From his Lakeland notebook, October 1803

Oct. 21ˢᵗ, 1803. Friday Morning. – A drisling rain. Heavy masses of shapeless Vapour upon the mountains (O the perpetual Forms of Borrodale!) yet it is no unbroken Tale of dull Sadness – slanting Pillars travel across the Lake, at long intervals – the vaporous mass whitens, in large Stains of Light – on the <Lakeward> ridge of that huge arm-chair, of Lowdore, fell a gleam of softest Light, that brought out the rich hues of the late Autumn. – The woody Castle Crag between me & Lowdore is a rich Flower-Garden of Colours, the brightest yellows with the deepest Crimsons, and the infinite Shades of Brown & Green, the *infinite* diversity of which blends the whole – so that the brighter colours seem as *colors* upon a ground, not colored Things.

Little wool-packs of white bright vapour rest on different summits & declivities – the vale is narrowed by the mist & cloud – yet thro' the wall of mist you can see into a bason of sunny Light in Borrodale – the Birds are singing in the tender Rain, as if it were the Rain of April, & the decaying Foliage were Flowers and Blossoms. The pillar of Smoke from the Chimney rises up in the Mist, & is just distinguishable from it; and the Mountain Forms in the Gorge of Borrodale consubstantiate with the mist & cloud even as the pillared Smoke / a shade deeper, & a determinate Form. – <Cleared up. the last thin Fleeces on the bathed Fells.>

CN I 1603 21.363

From his notebook in Italy, January–March 1806

To conceive an idea of Olevano you must first imagine a round bason formed by a circle of mountains, the diameter of the Valley about 15 or 16 miles/ These mountains all connected and one; but of very various heights, and the lines in which they sink and rise of various Sweep and Form, sometimes so high as to have no visible superior behind, sometimes letting in upon the Plain one Step ~~behind~~ above them from behind, sometimes two, and three; and in one place behind the third a bald bright Skull of a mountain (for the Snow that wholly covered it lay so smooth & shone so bright in the Sun, that the whole suggested the idea of a polished Skull, and the Snow seeming rather a property or attribute than an accident or adjunct rendered the baldness more intense rather than diminished it.

The other higher mountains that looked in from behind on the bason with more or less command were lit up with snow-relicts, scarcely distinguishable from Sunshine on bare and moist rock opposed to deep Shade, save when (as often happened) both the one and the other were seen at the same time, when they formed one of the gentlest diversities possible, and yet the distinction

evident and almost obvious – How exquisitely *picturesque* this effect
is (in the strictest sense of the word) Mr. Alston has proved in his
Swiss Landskip, of which it is not too much to say – quam qui non
amat, illum omnes et Musæ et Veneres odere. – The vale itself is
diversified with a multitude of Rises, from Hillocks to Hills, and the
~~northern~~ Eastern Side of the <circular> mountain Boundary ~~runs~~
vaults down into the vale in Leaps, forming Steps. – <The first>
Hills ~~that~~ sink to rise into <a> higher Hill that sinks to rise into a
yet higher and the mountain boundary itself is the fifth Step. – On
the third Step, which is broad and heaves in many Hillocks, some
bare & like Cairns, some green, stands Olevano, its old ruinous
Castle with church-like Tower cresting the height of this third Step/
the town runs – down the Ridge in one narrow Line almost like
a Torrent of Houses; and where the last House ends, more than
half of the whole ridge, a narrow back of bare jagged grey rock
commences, looking like the ruins of a Town/ a green field finishes
the ridge, which passes into the vale by a Copse of young Oaks/ one
different heights on other Steps ~~and do~~ or other Hills the towns of
Civitella, Pagliano, Avita, Santo Spirito ~~all~~ stick like Eagle-nests, or
seem as if the rock had chrystallized into those forms/ but how shall
I describe the beauty of the ~~rounds~~ roads, winding up the different
Hills, now lost & now re-appearing in different arcs & segments of
Circles – how call up before you those different masses of Smoke
over the vale – I count 10 from this one point of view <for they
are burning weeds> in different distances, now faint now vivid,
now in shade & now their exquisite blue glittering in Sunshine/~~but~~
Our House stands by itself, about a quarter of a mile from the
Town and its steep Ridge, on a level Ridge a little lower than it.
– This description I have written, standing or sitting on the ~~step~~
breast of the fourth Step, or that height ~~into~~ which <immediately
commands> Olevano. – But from our House we look down into
the Vale of Valleys – for so it may well be called, for the whole Vale
heaves and swells like a plate of cut and knobbly Glass, or a Spread
of wood knotty and at the same time blistered/ for the higher &
larger Ranges of Hills include as in a plain a multitude of smaller
elevations, swells, and ridges, which from a great Height appear as
one expanse – even as a stormy Sea might appear from a Balloon;
but lower down you see the Land-billows – & when in the Vale you
are in a Labyrinth of sweet Walks, glens, green Lanes, with Hillsides
for Hedges – some of the Hills & Hillocks wooded, some bare &

pastured, several with white Cottages on their sides or summits, & one & sometimes two or three pines by the Cottage Garden Gate.

CN II 2796 16.341

The selections below blend description of natural images with more abstract meditations on the 'organ of vision' and the complexity of perception. Viewing nature is the first step; the second is to 'subjugate [natural images] to our Intellect'. Nature and mind are inextricably linked, since vision is a faculty not only of the physical eye, but the inner eye as well:

From his notebook in Scotland, September 1803

Between the Lake & the Peep of the Lake a mountain of very various, but all superficial & gentle segments, runs down in between almost as gently as a man would ~~rest~~ lie on a bed, so imperceptibly declining from an Horizontal Line into a Slope/ – Those who hold it undignified to illustrate Nature by Art – how little would the truly dignified say so – how else can we bring the forms of Nature within our voluntary memory! – The first Business is to subjugate them to our Intellect & voluntary memory – then comes their Dignity by Sensation of Magnitude, Forms & Passions connected therewith.

CN I 1489 7.39

From his notebook in Malta, January 1805

This Evening was the most perfect & the brightest Halo ~~around~~ circling the roundest and brightest moon I ever beheld – so bright was the Halo, so compact, so entire a circle, that it gave the whole of its area, the moon itself included, the appearance of a solid opake body – an enormous Planet/ & as if <this Planet had> ~~there were~~ a <circular belt-like> Trough ~~over~~ of some light-reflecting Fluid for its rim, (that is the Halo) and its centre, i.e. the Moon, a small circular bason of some fluid that still more copiously reflected, or that even emitted light; <and as if> the interspatial area ~~being~~ were somewhat equally substantial, but sullen/ – thence I have found occasion to meditate on the nature of the sense of magnitude; its absolute dependence on the idea of *Substance*; the consequent difference between *magnitude* and *Spaciousness*; the dependence of the idea of substance on double-touch/& thence to evolve all our feelings & ideas of magnitude, magnitudinal sublimity, &c from a scale of our own bodies – so why if *form* constituted the sense, i.e. if it were pure vision, as a perceptive sense abstracted from *feeling* in the organ of vision, why do I seek for mountains when in the flattest countries the Clouds present so many so much more romantic & *spacious* forms, & the coal-fire so many so much more varied & lovely forms? – And whence arises the pleasure from musing on the latter/ do I not more or less consciously fancy myself a Lilliputian, to whom these would be mountains – & so by this factitious scale make them mountains, my pleasure being consequently playful, a voluntary poem in *hieroglyphics* or picture-writing – '*phantoms* of Sublimity' which I continue to know to be *phantoms?* – And form itself, is not its main agency exerted in individualizing the Thing, making it *this*, & *that*, & thereby facilitating this shadowy measurement of it by the scale of my own body?

Yon long not unvaried ridge of Hills that runs out of sight each way, it is *spacious*, & the pleasure derivable from it is from its *running*, its *motion*, its assimilation to action/ & here the scale is taken from my *Life*, & *Soul* – not from my body. Space <is one of> the Hebrew names for God/ & it is the most perfect image of *Soul, pure Soul* – being indeed to us nothing but unresisted action. – Wherever action is resisted, limitation begins – & limitation is the first constituent of body – the more omnipresent it is in a given space, the more that is *body* or matter// but thus all body necessarily presupposes soul, inasmuch as all resistance presupposes action/ Magnitude therefore is the intimate *union* blending, the most perfect union, thro' its whole sphere, in every minutest part of it, of action and resistance to action/ it is spaciousness in which Space is *filled up*; & feelingly stopped <as we well say – i.e. transmitted by incorporate accession, not destroyed.> and In all limited things, that is, in all *forms*, it is at least fantastically *stopped*/ and thus from the positive *grasp* to the mountain, from the mountain to the Cloud, from the Cloud to the blue depth of Sky, that which, as one on the top of Etna in a serene atmosphere, seems to go *behind* the Sun, all is *gradation*, that precludes division indeed, but not distinction/

CN II 2402 21.567 (b)

II. Naturalist detail

In addition to his gift for relating grand panoramas, Coleridge also observed the minutiae in nature with equal reverence and subtlety. The following quotations consist of vivid descriptions of ordinary natural objects such as trees, rocks, blossoms and animals, which are extraordinary observations – worthy of a naturalist.

From his notebook, journeying through England, October 1810

The ruin of the Oak 40 feet in circumference – The Daws mixing with the Rooks & flying from the Belfry Octagon, 70 feet high up to the summit of the two Ashes, at least 40 feet higher –

The park surmounting the woody hill-sides with its new 100 tints, the witch-elm fringed as clouds when the moon mounts up from behind them, the wild Crab, or wilder vine so old – the Birch all bright Painter's sunshine, the crimson Dogwood, &c &c &c – these surmounted by the strange Park with its brown-red fern, & Oak Trees, whose Fathers might have furnished Time's Cradle, & they its Coffin – scattered as Heroes routed after deadly battle, now out of the reach of pursuit, & standing at distances in their war-ranks, as if waiting for their comrades to fill up the spaces – but they had fallen!

The Mountain Ash splitting the Holly – one with its roots in the air midway where the Trunk splits into branches, but this Trunk the Tap root of this Ash, which now, shot down thro' the Holly – but the Holly has now utterly disappeared – it is only a Mountain Ash, with its own roots rotting in mid air at the top of its own trunk/

The church itself in the ruins compared to the young Tree growing in the Hollow of the old Hollow Tree/

The waterfall = an overshot wheel, the first 1/5 perpendicular & falling in the segment of the circle, created by the jutting rock which is hidden even from suspicion by the mass & foam of the water/

At night my mistaking the river looked at upward between the woods & with its dark background for a stupendous Cataract, the distant stream being lifted up to the eye, like as a wet road appears a jasper colum half upreared/

The looking down a dell filled up with wood rising up from unequal ground, & forming such a sweet play of Surfaces. What is the source of this peculiar pleasure? – A surface that is yet not a surface? or rather a substratum counterfeited by the deep Drapery of the true Substratum?

CN III 3990 14.73

From his notebook in Scotland, August 1803

The Rocks, by which we passed, under the brow of one of which I sate, beside an old blasted Tree, seemed the very link by which Nature connected Wood & Stone/ The Rock Substance was not distinguishable in grain, cracks, & colors from old scathed Trees, Age- or Lightning-burnt/ Right opposite to me the willowy Mountains with the broken wild craggy summits, & half way up one very large blasted Tree, white & leafless/– Here too I heard with a deep feeling the swelling unequal noise of mountain Water from the streams in the Ravines/

CN I 1469 7.22

From his notebook, September 1824

Now the Breeze thro' the <stiff &> brittle-becoming Foliage of the Trees counterfeits the sound of a rushing stream, or Water-flood <suddenly sweeping by>. The sigh, the modulated continuousness of the murmur is exchanged for the confusion of *overtaking* sounds, the self-evolutions of the *One* for the clash or stroke of even commencing Contact of the *Multitudinous* – without interspace by confusion/– the short Gusts rustle, and the ear feels the unlithsome dryness before the eye detects the coarser duller ~~green~~ tho' deeper Green/deadninged and not awakened into the hues of decay, Spring's echoes from the sepulchral Vault of Winter – Nature's Palinode – the memory of the aged year, conversant with the forms of its Youth, and forgetting all the interval – feebly reproducing

CN IV 5165 16.396

From his notebook, April 1826

Spring Flowers, I have observed, look best in the Day, and by Sunshine: but Summer or Autumnal Flower-pots by Lamp or Candlelight. April 18, 1826 – I have now before me a Flower-pot of Cherry-blossoms, Polyanthuses, double Violets, Periwinkle, Wall-flowers &c – but how dim & dusky they look! – The Scarlet Anemone is an exception & 3 or 4 of these with all the rest of the Flower-Glass Sprays of white Blossoms, and one or two Periwinkles for the sake of the dark green Leaves, green stems, and flexible elegant forms – make a lovely Group, both by Sun & by Candlelight.–

CN IV 5356 23.60

From his notebook in Malta, April 1805

Having had showers (23 April) I smelt the orange blossoms long before I reached St Antonio/ when I entered, it was overpowering/ the Trees were indeed oversnowed with Blossoms, and the ground snowed with the fallen leaves/ the Bees in on them, & the <golden ripe> fruit on the inner branches glowing thro/ Note/ my reflection on the multitude of orange flowers.

CN II 2565 15.148

From his Lakeland notebook, October–November 1802

The first sight of green fields with the numberless nodding gold cups, & the winding River with alders on its bank affected me, coming out of a city confinement, with the sweetness & power of a sudden Strain of Music.

CN I 1256 21.220

In the selections below, Coleridge turns his powers of observation to small creatures. He reverently enters their world, without diminishing their dignity or individuality. These selections evidence the scope of his objective powers of vision, capable of invoking both the grandest panoramas as well as the jewel-like detail.

From his Lakeland notebook, October 1803

On St Herbert's Island, I saw a large Spider with most beautiful legs floating in the air on his Back by a single Thread which he was spinning out, and still as he spun, heaving in the air, as if the air beneath was a pavement elastic to his Strokes/– from the Top of a very high tree he had spun his Line, at length reached the Bottom, tied his Thread round a piece of Grass, & re-ascended, to spin another/ a net to hang as a fisherman's Sea net hangs in the Sun & Wind, to dry.

CN I 1598 21.358

From his notebook in Malta, July 1804

Lizard half-erect stands still as I stop – I stop a long while/ he turns his head & looks sidelong at me/ – Crawls two or three paces by stealth – stops again/ I walk off briskly, turning my head tho' & looking at him/ he is too cunning – & has not moved – at length I really move away – and off – he is gone! –

Glide across the sunny walk like shooting Stars, green, grey, speckled/ exquisite grace of motion/ all the delicacy of the Serpent and a certain dignity ~~from the~~ from even just the ~~semi~~ increasing erectness of it to ~~the two low~~ its ~~forefeet~~ hind paws – /Dragon flies. 1. purple. 2 & most common, a deep crimson – not so long in the *Sheath* as our finest ones in England/ Butterflies/glorious ones, but their flight unwieldy – I could catch them with ease. – The Lizard's motion, & the Dragon-fly's – both darting and angular, yet how different/ the Dr.'s always & naturally angular/ the Lizard's only by choice/ – This is Friday, July 13th/ at St Antonio's – Yesterday and to day I seem to *live*/ O Sara! – yes, I could be happy here with *you!* – Let me write to her to day. – Lizard green with bright gold spots all over – firmness of its *stand-like* feet, where the *Life* of the *threddy* Toes makes them both seem & be so firm, so solid – yet so very, very supple/ one pretty fellow, whom I had fascinated by stopping & gazing at him as he lay in a <thick> network of Sun & Shade, after having turned his head from me so as but for the greater length of its Tail to form a crescent with the outline of its body – then turned his Head to me, depressed it, & looked up half-watching; half-imploring, at length taking advantage of a brisk breeze that made all the Network dance & Toss, & darted off as if an Angel of Nature had spoken in the Breeze – Off! I'll take care, he shall not hurt you/ – I should like if I could know what they eat, or if they eat bread, to tame one/

Lizard driven headlong before a gust into the Harbour/ turns his head & innocent eye sidelong toward me, his side above his forepaw throbbing with a visible pulse – a minute & then a slow timid creep off for an inch or so – then stops/

CN II 2144 K.35, 37

From his notebook in London, May 1808

O that sweet Bird! Where is it? – it is encaged somewhere out of Sight – but from my bedroom at the Courier office, from the windows of which I look out on the walls of the Lyceum, I hear it, early Dawn – often alas! then lulling me to late Sleep – again when I awake – & all day long. – It is in Prison – all its Instincts ungratified – yet it feels the Influence of Spring – & calls with unceasing Melody to the Loves, that dwell in Fields & Greenwood bowers –; unconscious perhaps that it calls in vain. – O are they the Songs of a happy enduring Day-dream? has the Bird Hope? Or does it abandon itself to the Joy of its Frame – a living Harp of Eolus? – O that I could do so! –

CN III 3314 20.5

From his notebook, 1819–20

The Humming Moth with its glimmer-mist of rapid unceasing Motion before, the Humble Bee within the flowery Bells and Cups, and the Eagle *even* <level> with the clouds, himself a cloudy speck, surveys the Vale from Mount to Mount. From the Cataract flung on down in the Gale the broadest Fleeces of the Snowy Foam Light on the Bank. Flowers or the Water-lilies in the stiller Bay, below –

CN IV 4631 21 1/2.96

III. Natural ephemera

Coleridge was fascinated with the ever-changing forces in nature. Descriptions of celestial bodies like the moon and stars, dynamic changes of weather and the transformative effects of light suggest that nature is animate: it changes, grows and decays, and even casts different moods depending on effects of light and darkness. Of course many of these impressions are created and magnified by the human imagination, but Coleridge's attraction to ephemera fulfilled his intuition that the natural and spiritual worlds are both driven by the same dynamic forces.

a. Celestial bodies

The moon, stars and sun are favourite images for Coleridge. Endlessly varied and yet directed by changeless rhythms, celestial bodies are apt symbols for the paradoxes that intrigued him: the natural and the spiritual, the one and the many, the poles of light and dark, positive and negative. The bewitching effects of the moon elicited especially powerful emotional responses, as seen below:

From his notebook in Malta, February 1805

Friday– Saturday 12–1 °clock/ What a sky, the not yet orbed moon,
the spotted oval, blue at one edge from the deep utter Blue of
the Sky, a *mass* of *pearl*-white Cloud below, distant, and travelling
to the Horizon, but all the upper part of the Ascent, and all the
Height, such *profound* Blue, *deep* as a deep river, and deep in color,
& those two <depths> so entirely *one*, as to give the meaning and
explanation of the two different significations of the epithet (here
so far from divided they were scarcely *distinct*) scattered over with
thin pearl-white Cloudlets, hands, & fingers, the largest not larger
than a flowing Veil/ Unconsciously I stretched forth my arms as
to embrace the Sky, and in a trance I had worshipped God in the
Moon/ the Spirit not the Form/ I felt in how innocent a feeling
Sabeism might have begun/ O not only the Moon, but the depths
of the Sky! – the Moon was the *Idea*; but deep Sky is of all visual
impressions the nearest akin to a Feeling/ it is more a Feeling than
a Sight/ or rather it is the melting away and entire union of Feeling
& Sight/

CN II 2453 17.27

From his Lakeland notebook, September 1801

Sept. 15. Observed the great half moon setting behind the mountain
Ridge, & watched the shapes its various segments presented as it
slowly sunk – first, the foot of a Boot, all but the heel – then, a
little pyramid Δ – then a star of the first magnitude – indeed it was
distinguishable from the evening Star at its largest – then rapidly
a smaller, a small, a very small star – and as it diminished in size,
so it grew paler in tint – and now where is it? Unseen; but a little
fleecy cloud hangs above the mountain Ridge, & is rich – with an
amber Light.

CN I 983 21.35

b. Skyscapes

*Coleridge's notebooks contain many descriptions of changing weather
and the transformative effect it had upon the landscape. Dramatic
weather appeared to animate nature, echoing Biblical accounts of natural
phenomena revealing God's will, either in destructive ways such as*

storms or in providential ways, such as the rainbow. Coleridge especially liked to describe skyscapes, whose constant changes seemed to mimic the flux of human thought and emotion itself.

From his notebook in Malta, December 1804

O that Sky, that soft blue mighty Arch, resting on the mountains or solid Sea-like plain/ what an awful adorable omneity in unity. I know no other perfect union of the sublime with the beautiful, that is, so that they should both be felt at the same moment tho' by different faculties yet each faculty predisposed by itself to receive the specific modification from the other. To the eye it is as an inverted Goblet, the inside of a ~~gold~~ sapphire Bason; = perfect beauty <in shape and color>; to the mind <it is> immensity, but even the eye <feels as if it were to> look thro' with dim sense of the non ~~differ~~resistance/ it is not exactly the feeling ~~from~~ a given to the organ by solid & limited things/ the eye itself feels that the limitation is in its own power not in the Object, but pursue this in the manner of the Old Hamburgh Poet –

CN II 2345 21.530

From his Lakeland notebook, September–October 1802

The stedfast rainbow in the fast-moving, hurrying, hail-mist! What a congregation of Images & Feelings, of fantastic Permanence amidst the rapid Change of Tempest – quietness the Daughter of Storm.

CN I 1246 21.263

From his Lakeland notebook, December 1800

The thin scattered ~~clouds~~ rain-clouds were scudding along the Sky, above them with a visible interspace the crescent Moon hung, and partook not of the motion – her own hazy Light ~~light~~ fill'd up the concave, as if it had been painted & the colors had run. – Dec. 19. 1800.

CN I 875 21.85

From his notebook in Malta, December 1804

The most common appearance in wintry weather is that of the sun – under a sharp defined level line of <stormy> cloud that stretches one-third or half round the circle of the horizon, of thrice the height that intervenes between it & the horizon, which last is about a sun & a half – the sun comes out a mass of brassy light, himself lost & diffused in his stormy splendor. Compare this with the beautiful summer set of color without cloud.

CN II 2301 21.485

From his notebook, spring 1808

A Storm seen by a Flash of Lightning – storm clouds enclosing as in a quasi-circle the stormy Light – the quasi-circle ~~by~~ *run-up-into*, to the left hand at the lower end by a falling-Mountain-like cloud with a table-slope rising into two heads – then two wild lower clouds; making as it were the rocks at the entrance of a Harbour put by these a storm-driven Hulk – the sea in deep troughs – The Castle wall four round points – a *stub* in the water, and then a much higher fragment of a wall; but far lower than the Ruin – like a huge upright Tombstone/ Trees sheltered, & seeming timidly ~~fearful~~ grateful for their shelter behind the Castle – Out in the Foreground two great rock-stones a *cub* by the left hand one, and 5 lesser *Cubs* by the right – the wild root nearer the sea, between the two rocks, but only a little way from the left rock – that root how hieroglyphic of human Life – of a man cast on shore, and raising himself up by both arms from his *prostration*.

CN III 3258 14.94

From his notebook at sea, April 1804

Half past 7 almost a calm/ to the Left the arc of Heaven which I have before me shipless, cloudless/ I turn round, and lo! the arc which was behind me, & now to my right hand before, the whole Convoy the Leviathan in the seeming centre & outside of them (for our Ship is the foremost & the outermost by half a mile) exactly comprised under one magnificent twi-cleft white mountain of Cloud/ beginning with & ending with the Ships/ – / or the other black clouds with stripes & streaks of darkening Gold/ and mid way between our Top mast & the Right Horizon the crescent Moon with the old Moon in her Lap, and below it 20 times its own Diam. a bright Planet –

CN II 2009 9.115

From his Lakeland notebook, October 1801

Thursday Evening, 1/2 past 6. Oct. 22, 1801. All the mountains black & tremendously obscure, except Swinside – which looks great a light green wood growing on the other mountains – At this time I saw one after the other, nearly in the same place, two perfect Moon Rainbows – the one foot in the field below my garden, the other in the field nearest but two to the Church – It was grey-moonlight-mist-color. <Friday morning, Mary Hutchinson arrived.>

CN I 999 21.151

From his Lakeland notebook, December 1803

Tuesday 1/2 past 3. beautiful Sun set – the Sun setting behind Newlands across the foot of the Lake. The Sky cloudless, save that there is a cloud on Skiddaw, one on the highest Mountain in Borrodale, some on Helvellin, and that the Sun sets in a glorious Cloud/ these Clouds are of various shapes, various Colours – & belong to their mountains, & have nothing to do with the Sky. – N.B. Something metallic, silver playfully & imperfectly gilt, & highly polished; or rather something mother of pearlish, in the Sun gleams upon Ice, thin Ice.

CN I 1701 21.415

From his notebook in Malta, December 1804

15 Dec. 1804. Saw the limb of a rainbow footing itself on the Sea at a small apparent distance from the Shore, a thing of itself, no substrate cloud or even mist visible, but the distance glimmered thro' it as thro' a thin semitransparent hoop –

CN II 2340 21.524

From his Lakeland notebook, November 1803

Wednesday Morning, 20 minutes past 2°clock. November 2ⁿᵈ. 1803. The Voice of the Greta, and the Cock-crowing: the Voice seems to grow, like a Flower on or about the water beyond the Bridge, while the Cock crowing is nowhere particular, it is at any place I imagine & do not distinctly see. A most remarkable Sky! The Moon, now waned to a perfect Ostrich's Egg, hangs over our House almost – only so much beyond it, garden-ward, that I can see it, holding my Head out of the smaller Study window. The Sky is covered with whitish, & with dingy *Cloudage*, thin dingiest Scud close under the moon & one side of it moving, all else moveless; but there are two great Breaks of Blue Sky – the one stretching over our House, & away toward Castlerigg, & this is speckled & blotched with white Cloud – the other hangs over the road, in the line of the Road in the shape of an ellipse or shuttle, I do not know what to call it – this is unspeckled, all blue – 3 Stars in it/ more in the former Break – all unmoving. The water leaden white, even as the grey gleam of Water is in latest Twilight. – Now while I have been writing this & gazing between whiles (it is 40 M. past Two) the Break over the road is swallowed up, & the Stars gone, the Break over the House is narrowed into a rude Circle, & on the edge of its circumference one very bright Star – see! already the white mass thinning at its edge *fights* with its Brilliance – see! it has bedimmed it – & now it is gone – & the Moon is gone. The Cock-crowing too has ceased. The Greta sounds on, for ever. But I hear only the Ticking of my Watch, in the Pen-place of my Writing Desk, & the far lower note of the noise of the Fire – perpetual, yet seeming uncertain/ it is the low voice of quiet change, of Destruction doing its work by little & little.

CN I 1635 21.383

c. Seascapes

The ocean is another powerful natural image for Coleridge that inspired meditations on the one and the many: myriad waves within the sea evoke the paradox of 'the million millions of forms, and yet the individual unity in which they subsisted'. As in earlier selections, outward observations of natural forms often turn to inward reflections.

From his notebook at Malta, November 1804

Those crinkled every varying circles, which the moonlight makes on the not calm, yet not wavy, sea. –
　　Quarantine, Malta. Nov. 10. Saturday 1804.

CN II 2266 21.337

From his notebook at Malta, December 1804

O said I as I looked at the blue, yellow, green & purple green Sea, with all its hollows & swells, & cut-glass surfaces – O what an

Ocean of lovely forms! – and I was vexed, teased, that the sentence sounded like a play of Words. But it was not, the mind within me was struggling to express the marvelous distinctness & uncon-founded personality of each of the million millions of forms, & yet their undivided Unity in which they subsisted.

CN II 2344 21.528

From his notebook at Malta, December 1804

A brisk Gale, and the spots of foam that peopled the *alive* Sea most interestingly combined with the numbers of white Sea Gulls; so that repeatedly it seemed, as if the foam-spots had taken Life and Wing & flown up/ the white precisely same color Birds rose up so close by the ever perishing white wave head, that the eye was unable to detect the illusion which the mind delighted indulging –

CN II 2345 21.529

From his notebook in Scotland, August 1803

See the shapes below me, in 3 yards of water/smooth water in a vault, smooth water close to the smooth rock – a hollow, unquiet, & changeful between the waters/water with glassy wrinkles, water with a thousand wrinkles all lengthways, water all puckered & all over dimples, over smooth rock rough with tiny roughnesses, the boiling foam below this fall.

CN I 1450 7.3

IV. Optical illusions

Coleridge was fascinated by optical illusions and their philosophical implications for perception. Occasions of mistaken vision, for example mistaking a leaf for a bird, or a shadow for a solid body, suggest that certain human powers such as imagination, logic or emotional expec-tation could dramatically alter perceptions of nature. In this section, Coleridge's careful objective descriptions of nature blend with a more abstract grappling with the powers that modify, amplify or embellish vision, which is a salient theme in the next two chapters.

From his notebook in Italy, November–December 1805

<Logic Friend of Perception!>

Vesuvius covered with smoke – cloud from the weight of the atmos-phere/ I saw on its sides two narrow streams or slips of Fire, rapidly undulating its flame-color in a fast-flowing Torrent of melted Gold or Copper/ – but why begin there? why end there? I see no reason! I meditated & in that act cast my eye somewhat down/ & again looking up, with an altered angle, perceived that it was two Pennants waving on this side the Bay, Logic the Friend of Perception.

CN II 2720 16.311

From his notebook on the way to Scotland, August 1803

Seat of limestone, in the limestone Bank of the Dell Brook, coming out from the rock, like a thick Slate, or London Flag Stone/ – above it some 4 or 5 feet a low ruined Garden wall, overgrown with gooseberry Trees, which formed a thick busy *Shed* over the seat – & above these a double-blossomed Cherry Tree in its barren Pomp, stretching out beyond the Shed, & dropping its [? flashing/glinting] Blossoms into the River/ ... Out of the little parlour window looking across the market place & over the market House, a group of Ashes, of which the hithermost hath its topmost Twig exactly like a Rook or Magpie perching on the topmost Twig. N.B. The manifest magnitude which this Twig attained by its assimilation to a familiar Form, the size of which had been exempted by its old acquaintance, Queen Imagination, from all chances of perspective.

CN I 1426 16.7

From his notebook at Malta, April 1805

Thought and Reality two distinct corresponding Sounds, of which no man can say positively which is the ~~Sound~~ Voice and which the Echo.

O the beautiful Fountain or natural Well at Upper Stowey! The images of the weeds which hung down from its sides, appeared as plants growing up, straight and upright, among the water weeds that really grow from the Bottom of the well/ & so vivid was the Image, that for some moments & not till after I had disturbed the water, did I perceive that ~~they~~ their roots were not neighbours, & they side-by-side companions. So – even then I said – so are the happy man's *Thoughts* and *Things* – (in the language of the modern Philosophers, Ideas and Impressions.)

CN II 2557 17.115

From his notebook at Malta, July–August 1804

Motion at a great distance/ its visibility increased by all that increases the distinct visibility of the moving object – This Saturday, August 3rd, 1804, in the Room immediately under the Tower in St Antonio's, as I was musing on the difference, whether ultimate or only of degree, between 'auffassen' and 'anerkennen' (an idea received, and an idea *agnized*) I saw on the Top of the distant Hill a Shadow <on the sunny ground> moving very fast & wavelike, yet always in the same place; which I should have immediately attributed to the Windmill close by; but the Windmill (which I saw distinctly too) appeared at rest. On steady gazing however (& most plainly with my spy-glass) I found that it was not at rest, but that this *was* its Shadow – The Windmill itself was ~~sunny~~ white in the sunshine & sunny white clouds at its Back; the Shadow black on the white ground. –

CN II 2153 21.454

In the final selections, Coleridge describes how he gradually disentangles the optical illusion from the objective reality, revealing the complex factors that modify human perception.

From his notebook, February 1807

In the forest the spots of moonlight of the wildest outlines, not unfrequently approaching so near to the shape of man, & the domestic animals most attached to him, as to be easily conjured into them by ~~a~~ fancy~~ful~~, and mistaken by terror, moved & started as the wind stirred the Branches; that it almost seemed, like a flight of ~~Faery~~ lucent spirits, of ~~Moonlight~~, Sylphs and Sylphids dancing & ~~capable of~~ capering in a world of Shadows/ once where our path was ~~overshadowed~~canopied by the meeting Boughs for a stone-throw, as I hallo'd to those behind me, a sudden flash of Light darted down as it were, upon the path close before me, with such rapid & indescribable effect, that my life seemed snatched away from me – not by terror, but by the whole attention being suddenly, & unexpectedly, seized hold of – if one could conceive a violent Blow given by an unseen hand, yet without pain, or local sense of injury – of the weight falling here, or there – it might ~~not ill~~ assist in conceiving the feeling. – This I found was occasioned by some very large Bird, who, scared by my noise, had suddenly flown upward, and by the spring of his feet or body had driven down the branch on which he was a-perch.

CN II 2988 11.57

From his Lakeland notebook, January 1804

Images of Calmness on ~~Grasmere~~ Rydale Lake, Jan. 14/ ~~new~~ fresh Delves in the Slate Quarry I *mistook* for smoke in the reflection/ An islet Stone, at the bottom of the Lake, the reflection so bright as to be heaved up out of the water/ the Stone & its reflection looked so compleatly one, that Wordsworth remained for more than 5 minutes trying to explain why that Stone had no Reflection/ & at last found it out by me/ the shore, & green field, ~~with~~ a Hill bank below that Stone, & with Trees & Rock forming one brilliant picture without was such, that look at the Reflection & you annihilated the water/ it is all one piece of bright Land/ just half wink your Eyes & look at the Land, it is then *all* under water, or with that glossy Unreality which a Prospect has, when seen thro' Smoke.

CN II 1844 16.227

From his Lakeland notebook, November 1803

a pretty optical fact occurred this morning. As I was returning from Fletcher's, up the back lane, & just in sight of the River, I saw floating high in the air, somewhere over the ~~Mr~~ Banks's, a noble *Kite* – I continued gazing at it for some time; when turning suddenly round I saw at an equidistance on my right, i.e. over the middle of our field, a pair of Kites – floating about – I looked at them for some seconds when it occurred to me that I had never before seen two Kites together – instantly the vision disappeared – it was neither more nor less than two pair of Leaves, each pair on a separate Stalk, on a <young> Fruit tree that grew on the other side of the wall, not two yards from my eye. The leaves being alternate did, when I looked at them as leaves, strikingly resemble wings – & they were the only leaves on the Tree. – The magnitude was given by the imagined Distance; that Distance by the former adjustment of the Eye, which *remained* in consequence of the deep impression, the length of time, I had been looking at the Kite, the pleasure, &c – & a new Object impressed itself on the eye/ &c &c.

CN I 1668 21.403

From his notebook at Bath, September 1814

The ear-deceiving Imitation of a steady soaking Rain, while the Sky is in full uncurtainment of sprinkled Stars and milky Stream and dark blue Interspaces – the Rain had held up for two Hours or more – but so deep was the silence of the Night, that the *Drip* from the Leaves of the Garden Trees *copied* a steady Shower –

20 Sept^r, 1814. – Ashley, Box, Bath.

CN III 4220 20.20

Notes

1 *CN* II 2144 K.35, 37
2 *CN* I 1598 21.358
3 *CN* I 1426 16.7
4 *CN* II 2720 16.311

Chapter Two

Visions of Nature in Lyric Poetry: 'My eye shall dart thro' infinite expanse'

Envisioning the beauty of nature, its emotional resonance and the spiritual meaning of natural forms were central themes in Coleridge's poetical work. His nature poems are remarkable for their seamless transitions between different modes of vision, including outward descriptions of nature that turn to inward meditations, seeing nature as a 'book' to be read for divine meaning, and ecstatic visions of oneness or transparency between the natural and spiritual worlds. The lyric poems in this chapter envision nature on many levels simultaneously, blending the exquisite natural description of the notebooks with theories of art that will be further discussed in the next chapter.

The first selections continue the theme of visionary journeys. As in many of the notebook entries, the reader's eye is guided through the beauty of a natural scene and the poet's meditations, making these poems inner as well as outer journeys. The next set of poems relates the poet's prophetic ability to read nature as a book of divine meaning.[1] Coleridge believed that the poet is endowed with special powers of vision: he is gifted not only with a sensitivity to the beauty of nature, but he is also capable of interpreting its spiritual meaning, and communicating these truths to others. In *The Friend* Coleridge writes 'Observe, how graciously Nature instructs her human children … We not only see, but are enabled to discover by what means we see.'[2] Nature is the language of God, in which spiritual truths are manifested in material form; the poet's special powers of vision allow him to be the interpreter of 'nature's ministry'. In the final set of poems, Coleridge raises poetic vision to an almost mystical extreme, in which the poet not only reads meaning into nature, but sees nature and spirit as unified. In his later life, he regretted the pantheistic implications of these poems.[3] However, they reveal his insistent conviction that the natural and spiritual world might be one, if only vision could be elevated to a high enough perspective.

Coleridge's poetry invokes many levels of vision: objective views of natural beauty, subjective and emotional resonances, and, finally, transcendental views in which natural form itself disappears, revealing its spiritual essence. The ability to blend these widely divergent modes of vision harmoniously in poetic form marks the zenith of Coleridge's creative genius.

I. Lyric journeys

Ironically, or perhaps appropriately, the finest poem relating a visionary journey describes a ramble Coleridge was unable to take: because of an injured foot, he could not accompany his companions, and instead imagined their walk while sitting in his neighbour Tom Poole's garden, under a lime tree. It is particularly interesting to note the ebb and flow of inward and outward modes of vision in this poem, as the reader's eye is guided through the landscape.

'This Lime-tree Bower my Prison' (1798)

Well, they are gone, and here must I remain,
This lime-tree bower my prison! I have lost
Beauties and feelings, such as would have been
Most sweet to my remembrance even when age
Had dimmed mine eyes to blindness! They, meanwhile,
Friends, whom I never more may meet again,
On springy heath, along the hill-top edge,
Wander in gladness, and wind down, perchance,
To that still roaring dell, of which I told;
The roaring dell, o'erwooded, narrow, deep,
And only speckled by the mid-day sun;
Where its slim trunk the ash from rock to rock
Flings arching like a bridge; – that branchless ash,
Unsunn'd and damp, whose few poor yellow leaves
Ne'er tremble in the gale, yet tremble still,
Fann'd by the water-fall! and there my friends
Behold the dark green file of long lank weeds,
That all at once (a most fantastic sight!)
Still nod and drip beneath the dripping edge
Of the blue clay-stone.

                    Now, my friends emerge
Beneath the wide wide Heaven – and view again
The many-steepled tract magnificent
Of hilly fields and meadows, and the sea,
With some fair bark, perhaps, whose sails light up
The slip of smooth clear blue betwixt two Isles
Of purple shadow! Yes! they wander on
In gladness all; but thou, methinks, most glad,
My gentle-hearted Charles! for thou hast pined
And hunger'd after Nature, many a year,
In the great City pent, winning thy way
With sad yet patient soul, through evil and pain
And strange calamity! Ah! slowly sink
Behind the western ridge, thou glorious Sun!
Shine in the slant beams of the sinking orb,
Ye purple heath-flowers! richlier burn, ye clouds!
Live in the yellow light, ye distant groves!
And kindle, thou blue Ocean! So my friend
Struck with deep joy may stand, as I have stood,
Silent with swimming sense; yea, gazing round
On the wide landscape, gaze till all doth seem
Less gross than bodily; and of such hues
As veil the Almighty Spirit, when he makes
Spirits perceive his presence.

                    A delight
Comes sudden on my heart, and I am glad
As I myself were there! Nor in this bower,
This little lime-tree bower, have I not mark'd
Much that has sooth'd me. Pale beneath the blaze
Hung the transparent foliage; and I watch'd
Some broad and sunny leaf, and lov'd to see
The shadow of the leaf and stem above
Dappling its sunshine! And that walnut-tree
Was richly ting'd, and a deep radiance lay
Full on the ancient ivy, which usurps
Those fronting elms, and now, with blackest mass
Makes their dark branches gleam a lighter hue
Through the late twilight: and though now the bat
Wheels silent by, and not a swallow twitters,

Yet still the solitary humble-bee
Sings in the bean-flower! Henceforth I shall know
That Nature ne'er deserts the wise and pure;
No plot so narrow, be but Nature there,
No waste so vacant, but may well employ
Each faculty of sense, and keep the heart
Awake to Love and Beauty! and sometimes
'Tis well to be bereft of promis'd good,
That we may lift the soul, and contemplate
With lively joy the joys we cannot share.
My gentle-hearted Charles! when the last rook
Beat its straight path along the dusky air
Homewards, I blest it! deeming its black wing
(Now a dim speck, now vanishing in light)
Had cross'd the mighty Orb's dilated glory,
While thou stood'st gazing; or, when all was still,
Flew creeking o'er thy head, and had a charm
For thee, my gentle-hearted Charles, to whom
No sound is dissonant which tells of Life.

CPW I 178–81 [*PW (CC)* I 351–4]

*In another poem recounting an imagined journey, Coleridge guides his
friend Charles Lloyd through the Somerset landscape near Adscombe,
where he planned to rent a cottage and hoped to persuade Lloyd to join
him. The luminous natural imagery blends with emotional evocations
of an idealized harmony between friends and family, echoes of a larger
harmony between nature and humanity.*

'To a Young Friend, on his proposing to domesticate with the Author'
(1796)

A mount, not wearisome and bare and steep,
    But a green mountain variously up-piled,
Where o'er the jutting rocks soft mosses creep,
Or colour'd lichens with slow oozing weep;
    Where cypress and the darker yew start wild;
And, 'mid the summer torrent's gentle dash
Dance brighten'd the red clusters of the ash;
    Beneath whose boughs, by those still sounds beguil'd,
Calm Pensiveness might muse herself to sleep;
    Till haply startled by some fleecy dam,

That rustling on the bushy cliff above
With melancholy bleat of anxious love,
   Made meek enquiry for her wandering lamb:
Such a green mountain 'twere most sweet to climb,
E'en while the bosom ach'd with loneliness –
How more than sweet, if some dear friend should bless
   The adventurous toil, and up the path sublime
Now lead, now follow: the glad landscape round,
Wide and more wide, increasing without bound!

   O then 'twere loveliest sympathy, to mark
The berries of the half-uprooted ash
Dripping and bright; and list the torrent's dash –
   Beneath the cypress, or the yew more dark,
Seated at ease, on some smooth mossy rock;
In social silence now, and now to unlock
The treasur'd heart; arm link'd in friendly arm,
Save if the one, his muse's witching charm
Muttering brow-bent, at unwatch'd distance lag;
   Till high o'er head his beckoning friend appears,
And from the forehead of the topmost crag
   Shouts eagerly: for haply *there* uprears
That shadowing Pine its old romantic limbs,
   Which latest shall detain the enamour'd sight
Seen from below, when eve the valley dims,
   Tinged yellow with the rich departing light;
   And haply, bason'd in some unsunn'd cleft,
A beauteous spring, the rock's collected tears,
Sleeps shelter'd there, scarce wrinkled by the gale!
   Together thus, the world's vain turmoil left,
Stretch'd on the crag, and shadow'd by the pine,
   And bending o'er the clear delicious fount,
Ah! dearest youth! it were a lot divine
To cheat our noons in moralising mood,
While west-winds fann'd our temples toil-bedew'd:
   Then downwards slope, oft pausing, from the mount,
To some low mansion, in some woody dale,
Where smiling with blue eye, Domestic Bliss
Gives *this* the Husband's, *that* the Brother's kiss!

Thus rudely vers'd in allegoric lore,
The Hill of Knowledge I essayed to trace;
That verdurous hill with many a resting-place,
And many a stream, whose warbling waters pour
 To glad, and fertilise the subject plains;
That hill with secret springs, and nooks untrod,
And many a fancy-blest and holy sod
 Where Inspiration, his diviner strains
Low-murmuring, lay; and starting from the rock's
Stiff evergreens, (whose spreading foliage mocks
Want's barren soil, and the bleak frosts of age,
And Bigotry's mad fire-invoking rage!)
O meek retiring spirit! we will climb,
Cheering and cheered, this lovely hill sublime;
 And from the stirring world up-lifted high
(Whose noises, faintly wafted on the wind,
To quiet musing shall attune the mind,
 And oft the melancholy *theme* supply),
 There, while the prospect through the gazing eye
 Pours all its healthful greenness on the soul,
We'll smile at wealth, and learn to smile at fame,
Our hopes, our knowledge, and our joys the same,
 As neighbouring fountains image each the whole:
Then when the mind hath drunk its fill of truth,
 We'll discipline the heart to pure delight,
Rekindling sober joy's domestic flame.
They whom I love shall love thee, honour'd youth!
 Now may Heaven realise this vision bright!

CPW I 155–8 [*PW (CC)* I: 276–9]

One of Coleridge's most elaborate visionary journeys follows, a poem replete with both panoramic description and superb naturalistic detail. Although it lacks the structural cohesion of the two earlier conversation poems, it captures instead the rhythms of an actual ramble through the woods, particularly the mingling flow of physical sensations with abstract musings inspired by visions of a loved one.

Selections from 'The Picture, or the Lover's Resolution' (1802)

Through weeds and thorns, and matted underwood
I force my way; now climb, and now descend

O'er rocks, or bare or mossy, with wild foot
Crushing the purple whorts; while oft unseen,
Hurrying along the drifted forest-leaves,
The scared snake rustles. Onward still I toil,
I know not, ask not whither! A new joy,
Lovely as light, sudden as summer gust,
And gladsome as the first-born of the spring,
Beckons me on, or follows from behind,
Playmate, or guide! The master-passion quelled,
I feel that I am free. With dun-red bark
The fir-trees, and the unfrequent slender oak,
Forth from this tangle wild of bush and brake
Soar up, and form a melancholy vault
High o'er me, murmuring like a distant sea.

Here Wisdom might resort, and here Remorse;
Here too the love-lorn man who, sick in soul,
And of this busy human heart aweary,
Worships the spirit of unconscious life
In tree or wild-flower. – Gentle lunatic!
If so he might not wholly cease to be,
He would far rather not be that he is;
But would something that he knows not of,
In winds or waters, or among the rocks!

    But hence, fond wretch! breathe not contagion here!
No myrtle-walks are these: these are no groves
Where Love dare loiter! If in sullen mood
He should stray hither, the low stumps shall gore
His dainty feet, the briar and the thorn
Make his plumes haggard. Like a wounded bird
Easily caught, ensnare him, O ye Nymphs,
Ye Oreads chaste, ye dusky Dryades!
And you, ye Earth-winds! you that make at morn
The dew-drops quiver on the spiders' webs!
You, O ye wingless Airs! that creep between
The rigid stems of heath and bitten furze,
Within whose scanty shade, at summer-noon,
The mother-sheep hath worn a hollow bed –
Ye, that now cool her fleece with dropless damp,
Now pant and murmur with her feeding lamb.

Chase, chase him, all ye Fays, and elfin Gnomes!
With prickles sharper than his darts bemock
His little Godship, making him perforce
Creep through a thorn-bush on yon hedgehog's back.

 This is my hour of triumph! I can now
With my own fancies play the merry fool,
And laugh away worse folly, being free.
Here will I seat myself, beside this old,
Hollow, and weedy oak, which ivy-twine
Clothes as with net-work: here I will couch my limbs,
Close by this river, in this silent shade,
As safe and sacred from the step of man
As an invisible world – unheard, unseen,
And listening only to the pebbly brook
That murmurs with a dead, yet tinkling sound;
Or to the bees, that in the neighbouring trunk
Make honey-hoards. The breeze, that visits me,
Was never Love's accomplice, never raised
The tendril ringlets from the maiden's brow,
And the blue, delicate veins above her cheek;
Ne'er played the wanton – never half disclosed
The maiden's snowy bosom, scattering thence
Eye-poisons for some love-distempered youth,
Who ne'er henceforth may see an aspen-grove
Shiver in sunshine, but his feeble heart
Shall flow away like a dissolving thing.

Sweet breeze! thou only, if I guess aright,
Liftest the feathers of the robin's breast,
That swells its little breast, so full of song,
Singing above me, on the mountain-ash.
And thou too, desert stream! no pool of thine,
Though clear as lake in latest summer-eve,
Did e'er reflect the stately virgin's robe,
The face, the form divine, the downcast look
Contemplative! Behold! her open palm
Presses her cheek and brow! her elbow rests
On the bare branch of half-uprooted tree,
That leans towards its mirror! Who erewhile
Had from her countenance turned, or looked by stealth,

(For Fear is true-love's cruel nurse), he now
With steadfast gaze and unoffending eye,
Worships the watery idol, dreaming hopes
Delicious to the soul, but fleeting, vain,
E'en as that phantom-world on which he gazed,
But not unheeded gazed: for see, ah! see,
The sportive tyrant with her left hand plucks
The heads of tall flowers that behind her grow,
Lychnis, and willow-herb, and fox-glove bells:
And suddenly, as one that toys with time,
Scatters them on the pool! Then all the charm
Is broken – all that phantom-world so fair
Vanishes, and a thousand circlets spread,
And each mis-shape the other. Stay awhile,
Poor youth, who scarcely dar'st lift up thine eyes!
The stream will soon renew its smoothness, soon
The visions will return! And lo! he stays:
And soon the fragments dim of lovely forms
Come trembling back, unite, and now once more
The pool becomes a mirror; and behold
Each wildflower on the marge inverted there,
And there the half-uprooted tree – but where,
O where the virgin's snowy arm, that leaned
On its bare branch? He turns, and she is gone!
Homeward she steals through many a woodland maze
Which he shall seek in vain. Ill-fated youth!
Go, day by day, and waste thy manly prime
In mad love-yearning by the vacant brook,
Till sickly thoughts bewitch thine eyes, and thou
Behold'st her shadow still abiding there,
The Naiad of the mirror!

            Not to thee,
O wild and desert stream! belongs this tale:
Gloomy and dark art thou – the crowded firs
Spire from thy shores, and stretch across thy bed,
Making thee doleful as a cavern-well:
Save when the shy king-fishers build their nest
On thy steep banks, no loves hast thou, wild stream!

    This be my chosen haunt – emancipate
From Passion's dreams, a freeman, and alone,
I rise and trace its devious course. O lead,
Lead me to deeper shades and lonelier glooms.
Lo! stealing through the canopy of firs,
How fair the sunshine spots that mossy rock,
Isle of the river, whose disparted waves
Dart off asunder with an angry sound,
How soon to re-unite! And see! they meet,
Each in the other lost and found: and see
Placeless, as spirits, one soft water-sun
Throbbing within them, heart at once and eye!
With its soft neighbourhood of filmy clouds,
The stains and shadings of forgotten tears,
Dimness o'erswum with lustre! Such the hour
Of deep enjoyment, following love's brief feuds;
And hark, the noise of a near waterfall!
I pass forth into light – I find myself
Beneath a weeping birch (most beautiful
Of forest trees, the Lady of the Woods),
Hard by the brink of a tall weedy rock
That overbrows the cataract. How bursts
The landscape on my sight! Two crescent hills
Fold in behind each other, and so make
A circular vale, and land-locked, as might seem,
With brook and bridge, and grey stone cottages,
Half hid by rocks and fruit-trees. At my feet,
The whortle-berries are bedewed with spray,
Dashed upwards by the furious waterfall.
How solemnly the pendent ivy mass
Swings in its winnow: All the air is calm ....

CPW I 369–74 [*PW (CC)* II 712–16]

At the start of his career Coleridge explores the idea that journeys into nature are actually inner journeys, and asks that 'New Scenes of Wisdom may each step display,/ And knowledge open, as my days advance!' References to vision pepper this short poem, referring both to inner and outer sight.

'Life'[24] (perhaps 1789, 1791)

As late I journey'd o'er the extensive plain
  Where native Otter sports his scanty stream,
Musing in torpid woe a Sister's pain,
  The glorious prospect woke me from the dream.

At every step it widen'd to my sight –
  Wood, Meadow, verdant Hill, and dreary Steep,
Following in quick succession of delight, –
  Till all – at once – did my eye ravish'd sweep!

May this (I cried) my course thro' Life portray!
New scenes of Wisdom may each step display,
  And Knowledge open as my days advance!
Till what time Death shall pour the undarken'd ray,
  My eye shall dart thro' infinite expanse,
And thought suspended lie in Rapture's blissful trance!

CPW I 11–12 [*PW (CC)* I 15]

II. Reading nature

a. The poet-prophet

Many of Coleridge's poems feature a lone figure wandering through nature, interpreting its forms. Two such figures appear in the poems below: the first, the Minstrel 'wont to rove' and in the second, the 'humble man' who proves an even more prophetic reader of nature: 'Sweet influences trembled o'er his frame;/ And he, with many feelings, many thoughts,/ Made up a meditative joy, and found/ Religious meanings in the forms of nature!'

Selections from 'Monody on the Death of Chatterton'

... O Spirit blest!
Whether the Eternal's throne around,
Amidst the blaze of Seraphim,
Thou pourest forth the grateful hymn;
Or soaring thro' the blest domain
Enrapturest Angels with thy strain, –
Grant me, like thee, the lyre to sound,
Like thee with fire divine to glow; –
But ah! when rage the waves of woe,
Grant me with firmer breast to meet their hate,
And soar beyond the storm with upright eye elate! ...

Ye woods! That wave o'er Avon's rocky steep,
To Fancy's ear sweet is your murmuring deep!
For here she loves the cypress wreath to weave,
Watching, with wistful eye, the saddening tints of eve.
Here, far from men, amid this pathless grove,
In solemn thought the Minstrel wont to rove,
Like star-beam on the slow sequestered tide
Lone-glittering, through the high tree branching wide.
And here, in Inspiration's eager hour,
When most the big soul feels the madning power
    These wilds, these caverns roaming o'er,
    Round which the screaming sea-gulls soar,
With wild unequal steps he passed along,
Oft pouring on the winds a broken song:
Anon, upon some rough rock's fearful brow
Would pause abrupt – and gaze upon the waves below.

Shedd VII 22–3 [*PW (CC)* I 142–3]

Selections from 'Fears in Solitude' (1798)

A green and silent spot, amid the hills,
A small and silent dell! O'er stiller place
No singing sky-lark ever poised himself.
The hills are heathy, save that swelling slope,
Which hath a gay and gorgeous covering on,
All golden with the never-bloomless furze,
Which now blooms most profusely; but the dell,
Bathed by the mist, is fresh and delicate
As vernal corn-field, or the unripe flax,
When, through its half-transparent stalks, at eve,
The level sunshine glimmers with green light.
Oh! 'tis a quiet spirit-healing nook!
Which all, methinks, would love; but chiefly he,
The humble man, who, in his youthful years,
Knew just so much of folly, as had made
His early manhood more securely wise!
Here he might lie on fern or withered heath,
While from the singing lark (that sings unseen
The minstrelsy that solitude loves best),
And from the sun, and from the breezy air,

Sweet influences trembled o'er his frame;
And he, with many feelings, many thoughts,
Made up a meditative joy, and found
Religious meanings in the forms of Nature!
And so, his senses gradually wrapt
In a half sleep, he dreams of better worlds,
And dreaming hears thee still, O singing lark,
That singest like an angel in the clouds!

CPW I 256 [*PW (CC)* I 470]

b. Nature's ministry

The poet-prophet is gifted with a sensitivity to the 'ministry of nature', such as the 'Lessons of love and earnest piety' taught by nature in the poem below (a composition of uncertain date). Coleridge believed that God created nature as a manifestation of his spirit, and that by knowing nature, one could discover nature's divine source. These poems begin with descriptions of the outer forms of nature, only to reveal their deeper spiritual import towards the end of the poems. Interestingly, the last two poems, written during the period of his greatest inspiration, address Coleridge's children and his hope that, as they grow, they will be tutored by nature's ministry.

'To Nature' (1820?)

It may indeed be phantasy, when I
    Essay to draw from all created things
    Deep, heartfelt, inward joy that closely clings;
And trace in leaves and flowers that round me lie
Lessons of love and earnest piety.
    So let it be; and if the wide world rings
    In mock of this belief, it brings
Nor fear, nor grief, nor vain perplexity.
So will I build my altar in the fields,
    And the blue sky my fretted dome shall be,
And the sweet fragrance that the wild flower yields
    Shall be in incense I will yield to Thee,
Thee only God! and thou shalt not despise
Even me, the priest of this poor sacrifice.

CPW I 429 [*PW (CC)* II 992–3]

'Frost at Midnight' (1798)

The Frost performs its secret ministry,
Unhelped by any wind. The owlet's cry
Came loud – and hark, again! loud as before.
The inmates of my cottage, all at rest,
Have left me to that solitude, which suits
Abstruser musings: save that at my side
My cradled infant slumbers peacefully.
'Tis calm indeed! so calm, that it disturbs
And vexes meditation with its strange
And extreme silentness. Sea, hill, and wood,
This populous village! Sea, and hill, and wood,
With all the numberless goings-on of life,
Inaudible as dreams! the thin blue flame
Lies on my low burnt fire, and quivers not;
Only that film, which fluttered on the grate,
Still flutters there, the sole unquiet thing.
Methinks, its motion in this hush of nature
Gives it dim sympathies with me who live,
Making it a companionable form,
Whose puny flaps and freaks the idling Spirit
By its own moods interprets, every where
Echo or mirror seeking of itself,
And makes a toy of Thought.

      But O! how oft,
How oft, at school, with most believing mind,
Presageful, have I gazed upon the bars,
To watch that fluttering *stranger*! and as oft
With unclosed lids, already had I dreamt
Of my sweet birth-place, and the old church-tower,
Whose bells, the poor man's only music, rang
From morn to evening, all the hot Fair-day,
So sweetly, that they stirred and haunted me
With a wild pleasure, falling on mine ear
Most like articulate sounds of things to come!
So gazed I, till the soothing things, I dreamt,
Lulled me to sleep, and sleep prolonged my dreams!
And so I brooded all the following morn,
Awed by the stern preceptor's face, mine eye

Fixed with mock study on my swimming book:
Save if the door half opened, and I snatched
A hasty glance, and still my heart leaped up,
For still I hoped to see the *stranger's* face,
Townsman, or aunt, or sister more beloved,
My play-mate when we both were clothed alike!

Dear Babe, that sleepest cradled by my side,
Whose gentle breathings, heard in this deep calm,
Fill up the interspersèd vacancies
And momentary pauses of the thought!
My babe so beautiful! it thrills my heart
With tender gladness, thus to look at thee,
And think that thou shalt learn far other lore,
And in far other scenes! For I was reared
In the great city, pent 'mid cloisters dim,
And saw nought lovely but the sky and stars.
But *thou*, my babe! shalt wander like a breeze
By lakes and sandy shores, beneath the crags
Of ancient mountain, and beneath the clouds,
Which image in their bulk both lakes and shores
And mountain crags: so shalt thou see and hear
The lovely shapes and sounds intelligible
Of that eternal language, which thy God
Utters, who from eternity doth teach
Himself in all, and all things in himself.
Great universal Teacher! he shall mould
Thy spirit, and by giving make it ask.

Therefore all seasons shall be sweet to thee,
Whether the summer clothe the general earth
With greenness, or the redbreast sit and sing
Betwixt the tufts of snow on the bare branch
Of mossy apple-tree, while the nigh thatch
Smokes in the sun-thaw; whether the eave-drops fall
Heard only in the trances of the blast,
Or if the secret ministry of frost
Shall hang them up in silent icicles,
Quietly shining to the quiet Moon.

CPW I 240 [*PW (CC)* I 452–6]

'*The Nightingale: A Conversation Poem*' (1798)

No cloud, no relique of the sunken day
Distinguishes the West, no long thin slip
Of sullen light, no obscure trembling hues.
Come, we will rest on this old mossy bridge!
You see the glimmer of the stream beneath,
But hear no murmuring: it flows silently,
O'er its soft bed of verdure. All is still,
A balmy night! and though the stars be dim,
Yet let us think upon the vernal showers
That gladden the green earth, and we shall find
A pleasure in the dimness of the stars.
And hark! the Nightingale begins its song,
'Most musical, most melancholy' bird!
A melancholy bird? Oh! idle thought!
In Nature there is nothing melancholy.
But some night-wandering man, whose heart was pierced
With the remembrance of a grievous wrong,
Or slow distemper, or neglected love,
(And so, poor wretch! filled all things with himself,
And made all gentle sounds tell back the tale
Of his own sorrow) he, and such as he,
First named these notes a melancholy strain.
And many a poet echoes the conceit;
Poet who hath been building up the rhyme
When he had better far have stretched his limbs
Beside a brook in mossy forest-dell,
By Sun or Moon-light, to the influxes
Of shapes and sounds and shifting elements
Surrendering his whole spirit, of his song
And of his fame forgetful! So his fame
Should share in Nature's immortality,
A venerable thing! and so his song
Should make all Nature lovelier, and itself
Be loved like Nature! But 'twill not be so;
And youths and maidens most poetical,
Who lose the deepening twilights of the spring
In ball-rooms and hot theatres, they still
Full of meek sympathy must heave their sighs
O'er Philomela's pity-pleading strains.

My Friend, and thou, our Sister! we have learnt
A different lore: we may not thus profane
Nature's sweet voices, always full of love
And joyance! 'Tis the merry Nightingale
That crowds, and hurries, and precipitates
With fast thick warble his delicious notes,
As he were fearful that an April night
Would be too short for him to utter forth
His love-chant, and disburthen his full soul
Of all its music!

                    And I know a grove
Of large extent, hard by a castle huge,
Which the great lord inhabits not; and so
This grove is wild with tangling underwood,
And the trim walks are broken up, and grass,
Thin grass and king-cups grow within the paths.
But never elsewhere in one place I knew
So many nightingales; and far and near,
In wood and thicket, over the wide grove,
They answer and provide each other's song,
With skirmish and capricious passagings,
And murmurs musical and swift jug jug,
And one low piping sound more sweet than all –
Stirring the air with such an harmony,
That should you close your eyes, you might almost
Forget it was not day! On moonlight bushes,
Whose dewy leaflets are but half-disclosed,
You may perchance behold them on the twigs,
Their bright, bright eyes, their eyes both bright and full,
Glistening, while many a glow-worm in the shade
Lights up her love-torch.

                         A most gentle Maid,
Who dwelleth in her hospitable home
Hard by the castle, and at latest eve
(Even like a Lady vowed and dedicate
To something more than Nature in the grove)
Glides through the pathways; she knows all their notes,
That gentle Maid! And oft, a moment's space,
What time the moon was lost behind a cloud,

Hath heard a pause of silence; till the moon
Emerging, hath awakened earth and sky
With one sensation, and these wakeful Birds
Have all burst forth in choral minstrelsy,
As if some sudden gale had swept at once
An hundred airy harps! And she hath watched
Many a nightingale perch giddily
On blossomy twig still swinging from the breeze,
And to that motion tune his wanton song
Like tipsy Joy that reels with tossing head.

Farewell, O Warbler! till to-morrow eve,
And you, my friends! farewell, a short farewell!
We have been loitering long and pleasantly,
And now for our dear homes. – That strain again!
Full fain it would delay me! My dear babe,
Who, capable of no articulate sound,
Mars all things with his imitative lisp,
How he would place his hand beside his ear,
His little hand, the small forefinger up,
And bid us listen! And I deem it wise
To make him Nature's play-mate. He knows well
The evening-star; and once, when he awoke
In most distressful mood (some inward pain
Had made up that strange thing, an infant's dream –)
I hurried with him to our orchard-plot,
And he beheld the moon, and, hushed at once,
Suspends his sobs, and laughs most silently,
While his fair eyes, that swam with undropped tears,
Did glitter in the yellow moon-beam! Well! –
It is a father's tale: But if that Heaven
Should give me life, his childhood shall grow up
Familiar with these songs, that with the night
He may associate joy. – Once more, farewell,
Sweet Nightingale! once more, my friends! farewell.

CPW I 264 [*PW (CC)* I 516–20]

c. The book of nature

*If the book of nature is 'the language of God himself, as uttered by
nature',*[5] *it also articulates 'that eternal language, which thy God utters
…'*[6] *References to reading meaning into natural forms, and the requisite
powers of vision needed to do so, abound in his poetry from an early
stage. In the first poem below, the moon is read as a symbol of hope, 'as
changeful and as fair!'*

'Sonnet: To the Autumnal Moon' (1788)

> Mild Splendour of the various-vested Night!
> 　Mother of wildly-working visions! hail!
> I watch thy gliding, while with watery light
> 　Thy weak eye glimmers thro' a fleecy veil;
> And when thou lovest thy pale orb to shroud
> 　Behind the gather'd blackness lost on high;
> And when thou dartest from the wind-rent cloud
> 　Thy placid lightning o'er the awaken'd sky.
> Ah such is Hope! as changeful and as fair!
> 　Now dimly peering on the wistful sight;
> Now hid behind the dragon-wing'd Despair:
> 　But soon emerging in her radiant might
> She o'er the sorrow-clouded breast of Care
> 　Sails, like a meteor kindling in its flight.

CPW I 5 [*PW (CC)* I 103]

*In the following poem, describing the cottage at Clevedon where he and
his wife spent the early period of their marriage, Coleridge shifts from
describing the beauty of a natural scene to reading its spiritual import,
making the expansive claim that 'God, methought,/ Had built him there
a Temple: the whole World/ Seem'd imag'd in its vast circumference'.*

*Selections from 'Reflections on having left a Place of Retirement'
(1795)*

> Low was our pretty Cot: our tallest Rose
> Peep'd at the chamber-window. We could hear
> At silent noon, and eve, and early morn,
> The Sea's faint murmur. In the open air
> Our Myrtles blossom'd; and across the porch
> Thick Jasmins twined: the little landscape round

Was green and woody, and refresh'd the eye.
It was a spot which you might aptly call
The Valley of Seclusion! ...

   But the time, when first
From that low Dell, steep up the stony Mount
I climb'd with perilous toil and reach'd the top,
O! what a goodly scene! *Here* the bleak mount,
The bare bleak mountain speckled thin with sheep;
Grey clouds, that shadowing sport the sunny fields;
And river, now with bushy rocks o'er-brow'd,
Now winding bright and full, with naked banks;
And seats, and lawns, the Abbey and the wood,
And cots, and hamlets, and faint city-spire;
The Channel *there*, the Islands and white sails,
Dim coasts, and cloud-like hills, and shoreless Ocean –
It seem'd like Omnipresence! God, methought,
Had built him there a Temple: the whole World
Seem'd *imag'd* in its vast circumference:
No *wish* profan'd my overwhelméd heart.
Blest hour! It was a luxury, – to be! ...

                    CPW I 106 [*PW (CC)* I 261–3]

A poem written in Germany in May 1799 also begins with an objective description of nature's beauty, then shifts inward to a musing note: 'for I had found/ That outward forms, the loftiest, still receive/ Their finer influence from the Life within' – again reading nature for spiritual meaning.

'Lines written in the Album at Elbingerode in the Harz Forest' (1799)

I stood on Brocken's sovran height, and saw
Woods crowding upon woods, hills over hills,
A surging scene, and only limited
By the blue distance. Heavily my way
Downward I dragged through fir groves evermore,
Where bright green moss heaves in sepulchral forms
Speckled with sunshine; and, but seldom heard,
The sweet bird's song became a hollow sound;
And the breeze, murmuring indivisibly,
Preserved its solemn murmur most distinct

From many a note of many a waterfall,
And the brook's chatter; 'mid whose islet-stones
The dingy kidling with its tinkling bell
Leapt frolicsome, or old romantic goat
Sat, his white beard slow waving. I moved on
In low and languid mood: for I had found
That outward forms, the loftiest, still receive
Their finer influence from the Life within;–
Fair cyphers else: fair, but of import vague
Or unconcerning, where the heart not finds
History or prophecy of friend, or child,
Or gentle maid, our first and early love,
Or father, or the venerable name
Of our adoréd country! O thou Queen,
Thou delegated Deity of Earth,
O dear, dear England! how my longing eye
Turned westward, shaping in the steady clouds
Thy sands and high white cliffs!

　　　　　　　　　　　　My native Land!
Filled with the thought of thee this heart was proud,
Yea, mine eye swam with tears: that all the view
From sovran Brocken, woods and woody hills,
Floated away, like a departing dream,
Feeble and dim! Stranger, these impulses
Blame thou not lightly; nor will I profane,
With hasty judgment or injurious doubt,
That man's sublimer spirit, who can feel
That God is every where! the God who framed
Mankind to be one mighty family,
Himself our Father, and the World our Home.

　　　　　　　　　　　　CPW I 315 [*PW (CC)* I 574–9]

Fragment[7] *(1803)*

Bright clouds of reverence, sufferably bright,
That intercept the dazzle, not the Light;
That veil the finite form, the boundless power reveal,
Itself an earthly sun of pure intensest white.

　　　　　　　　　　　　CPW II 998 [*PW (CC)* I 802–3]

III. Transparency of nature and spirit

In this final section of poems, the power of vision is pressed to its utmost and transcendent extreme: nature and spirit are seen as one. Although he intuitively believed such union was possible, Coleridge wrestled with its pantheistic implications. Later in his life he relied more on vision – both its potential and its limits – to explain why it is so difficult to see the spiritual in nature. However, in these early poems, Coleridge is less cautious and writes of a mystical and ecstatic union of the inner and outer worlds. Paradoxically, these poems reverence the beauty of nature and yet the outer forms of nature temporarily disappear in the moment that the spiritual is apprehended. Despite all of its myriad complexity, ultimately nature is subsumed into a higher spiritual identity, and the poet worships 'the Invisible alone'.

'Hymn before Sun-rise, in the Vale of Chamouni' (1802)

Hast thou a charm to stay the morning-star
In his steep course? So long he seems to pause
On thy bald awful head, O sovran Blanc,
The Arve and Arveiron at thy base
Rave ceaselessly; but thou, most awful Form!
Risest from forth thy silent sea of pines,
How silently! Around thee and above
Deep is the air and dark, substantial, black,
An ebon mass: methinks thou piercest it,
As with a wedge! But when I look again,
It is thine own calm home, thy crystal shrine,
Thy habitation from eternity!
O dread and silent Mount! I gazed upon thee,
Till thou, still present to the bodily sense,
Didst vanish from my thought: entranced in prayer
I worshipped the Invisible alone.

　　Yet, like some sweet beguiling melody,
So sweet, we know not we are listening to it,
Thou, the meanwhile, wast blending with my Thought,
Yea, with my Life and Life's own secret joy:
Till the dilating Soul, enrapt, transfused,
Into the mighty vision passing – there
As in her natural form, swelled vast to Heaven!

Awake, my soul! not only passive praise
Thou owest! not alone these swelling tears,
Mute thanks and secret ecstasy! Awake,
Voice of sweet song! Awake, my heart, awake!
Green vales and icy cliffs, all join my Hymn.

Thou first and chief, sole sovereign of the Vale!
O struggling with the darkness all the night,
And visited all night by troops of stars,
Or when they climb the sky or when they sink:
Companion of the morning-star at dawn,
Thyself Earth's rosy star, and of the dawn
Co-herald: wake, O wake, and utter praise!
Who sank thy sunless pillars deep in Earth?
Who filled thy countenance with rosy light?
Who made thee parent of perpetual streams?

And you, ye five wild torrents fiercely glad!
Who called you forth from night and utter death,
From dark and icy caverns called you forth,
Down those precipitous, black, jaggéd rocks,
For ever shattered and the same for ever?
Who gave you your invulnerable life,
Your strength, your speed, your fury, and your joy,
Unceasing thunder and eternal foam?
And who commanded (and the silence came),
Here let the billows stiffen, and have rest?

Ye Ice-falls! ye that from the mountains' brow
Adown enormous ravines slope amain –
Torrents, methinks, that heard a mighty voice,
And stopped at once amid their maddest plunge!
Motionless torrents! silent cataracts!
Who made you glorious as the Gates of Heaven
Beneath the keen full moon? Who bade the sun
Clothe you with rainbows? Who, with living flowers
Of loveliest blue, spread garlands at your feet? –
God! let the torrents, like a shout of nations,
Answer! and yet the ice-plains echo, God!
God! sing ye meadow-streams with gladsome voice!
Ye pine-groves, with your soft and soul-like sounds!

And they too have a voice, yon piles of snow,
And in their perilous fall shall thunder, God!

Ye living flowers that skirt the eternal frost!
Ye wild goats sporting round the eagle's nest!
Ye eagles, play-mates of the mountain-storm!
Ye lightnings, the dread arrows of the clouds!
Ye signs and wonders of the element!
Utter forth God, and fill the hills with praise!

Thou too, hoar Mount! with thy sky-pointing peaks,
Oft from whose feet the avalanche, unheard,
Shoots downward, glittering through the pure serene
Into the depth of clouds that veil thy breast –
Thou too again, stupendous Mountain! thou
That as I raise my head, awhile bowed low
In adoration, upward from thy base
Slow travelling with dim eyes suffused with tears,
Solemnly seemest, like a vapoury cloud,
To rise before me – Rise, O ever rise,
Thou kingly Spirit throned among the hills,
Thou dread ambassador from Earth to Heaven,
Great Hierarch! tell thou the silent sky,
And tell the stars, and tell yon rising sun,
Earth, with her thousand voices, praises God.

CPW I 376 [*PW (CC)* II 717–23]

One of Coleridge's best-known early poems, 'The Eolian Harp', distressed him later in his life because of the pantheistic merging of nature and spirit implicit in the lines 'Plastic and vast, one intellectual breeze,/ At once the Soul of each, and God of all?'

'The Eolian Harp' (1795)

My pensive Sara! thy soft cheek reclined
Thus on mine arm, most soothing sweet it is
To sit beside our Cot, our Cot o'ergrown
With white-flower'd Jasmin, and the broad-leav'd Myrtle,
(Meet emblems they of Innocence and Love!)
And watch the clouds, that late were rich with light,
Slow saddening round, and mark the star of eve
Serenely brilliant (such should Wisdom be)

Shine opposite! How exquisite the scents
Snatch'd from yon bean-field! and the world *so* hush'd!
The stilly murmur of the distant Sea
Tells us of silence.

                    And that simplest Lute,
Placed length-ways in the clasping casement, hark!
How by the desultory breeze caress'd,
Like some coy maid half yielding to her lover,
It pours such sweet upbraiding, as must needs
Tempt to repeat the wrong! And now, its strings
Boldlier swept, the long sequacious notes
Over delicious surges sink and rise,
Such a soft floating witchery of sound
As twilight Elfins make, when they at eve
Voyage on gentle gales from Fairy-Land,
Where Melodies round honey-dropping flowers,
Footless and wild, like birds of Paradise,
Nor pause, nor perch, hovering on untam'd wing!
O! the one Life within us and abroad,
Which meets all motion and becomes its soul,
A light in sound, a sound-like power in light,
Rhythm in all thought, and joyance every where –
Methinks, it should have been impossible
Not to love all things in a world so fill'd;
Where the breeze warbles, and the mute still air
Is Music slumbering on her instrument.

    And thus, my Love! as on the midway slope
Of yonder hill I stretch my limbs at noon,
Whilst through my half-clos'd eye-lids I behold
The sunbeams dance, like diamonds, on the main,
And tranquil muse upon tranquility;
Full many a thought uncall'd and undetain'd,
And many idle flitting phantasies,
Traverse my indolent and passive brain,
As wild and various as the random gales
That swell and flutter on this subject Lute!

    And what if all of animated nature
Be but organic Harps diversely fram'd,

That tremble into thought, as o'er them sweeps
Plastic and vast, one intellectual breeze,
At once the Soul of each, and God of all?

But thy more serious eye a mild reproof
Darts, O belovéd Woman! nor such thoughts
Dim and unhallow'd dost thou not reject,
And biddest me walk humbly with my God.
Meek Daughter in the family of Christ!
Well hast thou said and holily disprais'd
These shapings of the unregenerate mind;
Bubbles that glitter as they rise and break
On vain Philosophy's aye-babbling spring.
For never guiltless may I speak of him,
The Incomprehensible! save when with awe
I praise him, and with Faith that inly *feels*;
Who with his saving mercies healéd me,
A sinful and most miserable man,
Wilder'd and dark, and gave me to possess
Peace, and this Cot, and thee, heart-honour'd Maid!

CPW I 100–2 [*PW (CC)* I 231–5]

The poem 'Religious Musings', written soon after, is saturated with visions of union between nature and spirit, reinforced by language of union such as 'all in all', 'omnific' and 'omnipresent'.

Selections from 'Religious Musings' (1794–6)

... From Hope and firmer Faith to perfect Love
Attracted and absorbed: and centered there
God only to behold, and know, and feel,
Till by exclusive consciousness of God
All self-annihilated it shall make
God its Identity: God all in all!
We and our Father one!

And blest are they
Who in this fleshly World, the elect of Heaven,
Their strong eye darting through the deeds of men,
Adore with steadfast unpresuming gaze
Him, Nature's essence, mind, and energy!
And gazing, trembling, patiently ascend

Treading beneath their feet all visible things
As steps, that upward to their Father's throne
Lead gradual – else nor glorified nor loved.
They nor contempt embosom nor revenge:
For they dare know of what may seem deform
The Supreme Fair sole operant: in whose sight
All things are pure, his strong controlling love
Alike from all educing perfect good.
Their's too celestial courage, inly arm'd –
Dwarfing Earth's giant brood, what time they muse
On their great Father, great beyond compare!
And marching onwards view high o'er their heads
His waving banners of Omnipotence …

Thus from the Elect, regenerate through faith,
Pass the dark Passions and what thirsty cares
Drink up the spirit, and the dim regards
Self-centre. Lo they vanish! or acquire
New names, new features – by supernal grace
Enrobed with Light, and naturalised in Heaven.
As when a shepherd on a vernal morn
Through some thick fog creeps timorous with slow foot,
Darkling he fixes on the immediate road
His downward eye: all else of fairest kind
Hid or deformed. But lo! the bursting Sun!
Touched by the enchantment of that sudden beam
Straight the black vapour melteth, and in globes
Of dewy glitter gems each plant and tree;
On every leaf, on every blade it hangs!
Dance glad the new-born intermingling rays,
And wide around the landscape streams with glory!

There is one Mind, one omnipresent Mind,
Omnific. His most holy name is Love.
Truth of subliming import! with the which
Who feeds and saturates his constant soul,
He from his small particular orbit flies
With blest outstarting! From himself he flies,
Stands in the sun, and with no partial gaze
Views all creation; and he loves it all,
And blesses it, and calls it very good!

This is indeed to dwell with the Most High!
Cherubs and rapture-trembling Seraphim
Can press no nearer to the Almighty's throne ...

Contemplant Spirits! ye that hover o'er
With untired gaze the immeasurable fount
Ebullient with creative Deity!
And ye of plastic power, that interfused
Roll through the grosser and material mass
In organizing surge! Holies of God!
(And what if Monads of the infinite mind?)
I haply journeying my immortal course
Shall sometime join your mystic choir! Till then
I discipline my young and novice thought
In ministeries of heart-stirring song,
And aye on Meditation's heaven-ward wing
Soaring aloft I breathe the empyreal air
Of Love, omnific, omnipresent Love,
Whose day-spring rises glorious in my soul
As the great Sun, when he his influence
Sheds on the frost-bound waters – The glad stream
Flows to the ray and warbles as it flows.

CPW I 110 [*PW (CC)* I 176–91]

Notes

1 For more on Coleridge's idea of the 'book of nature' see Timothy Fulford, 'Coleridge, Boehme, and the Language of Nature', *Modern Language Quarterly: A Journal of Literary History* 52:1 (1991) and James McKusick, *Coleridge's Philosophy of Language* (New Haven: Yale University Press, 1986) 4–32.
2 *F (CC)* I 47
3 See the definitive work on the subject, Thomas McFarland, *Coleridge and the Pantheist Tradition* (Oxford: Oxford University Press, 1969).
4 Also titled Sonnet: 'As late I journey'd o'er th' extensive plain'.
5 *TL* 17 [*SWF (CC)* I 486]
6 *CPW* I 240 [*PW (CC)* I 452]
7 The full text of this poem, entitled 'Adapted from Fulke Greville's *Alaham*', can be found in *PW (CC)* I 802.

The poet's eye in his tipsy hour
Hath a magnifying power
Or rather he ~~diverts his eyes~~/ his soul emancipates his eyes
Of the accidents of size/
In unctuous cones of kindling Coal
Or smoke from his Pipe's bole
His eye can see
Phantoms of sublimity.

CN I 791 21.71

Chapter Three

Artistic Vision: 'Nature, or the divine Art'[1]

Coleridge's great creative works involved many ways of seeing nature, including the different levels from which it could be viewed. In the first chapter we saw some of the primary materials for his literary productions, consisting of the objective descriptions of nature in the notebooks. In the second chapter, we observed the finished products, in the form of highly polished lyric poems. Chapter 3 presents Coleridge's artistic theories about shaping and refining visions of nature in the practice of literature. Not only did these theories inform all of his writing, but they also significantly influenced later literary criticism.

One of the key elements of Coleridge's poetical theory is his seminal concept of symbol.[2] Rather than being 'a translation of abstract notions into a picture-language', symbolism for Coleridge is a manifestation of abstract spiritual truths in material form, 'characterized by a translucence of the special in the individual, or of the general in the special, or of the universal in the general; above all by the translucence of the eternal through and in the temporal'.[3] A symbol is not an empty or random signifier; rather it 'always partakes of the reality which it renders intelligible; and while it enunciates the whole, abides itself as a living part in that unity of which it is the representative'.[4] In other words a symbol is 'consubstantial' or sharing spiritual essence with that which it symbolizes, which suggests a profound metaphysical connection between the natural and spiritual worlds.

Coleridge's definition of the creative imagination is another concept that assumes an intimate union between the spiritual and material worlds.[5] Artistically, the imagination 'dissolves, diffuses, dissipates, in order to re-create: or where this process is rendered impossible, yet still at all events it struggles to idealize and unify. It is essentially *vital*, even as all objects (*as* objects) are essentially fixed and dead.'[6] The poet's imagination creates a miniature world in poetry, but this world is not 'fixed and dead', but an echo of the living powers working in nature itself. Even more profoundly, Coleridge posits that imagination is 'the living power and prime agent of all human perception, and as a repetition in the finite mind of the eternal act of creation in the infinite I AM',[7] This stunning connection between imagination, God's creation of the world, and the power of perception itself, reveals the centrality of vision in Coleridge's world view. Vision is a spiritual and creative power, not only artistically but metaphysically: it not only perceives reality, it also participates in creating reality.

The powers of imagination and symbol-making, because of their metaphysical implications, are not the ordinary abilities of the literary craftsman. Instead they are the domain of the poet-prophet, an individual gifted with extraordinary powers of vision. Coleridge uses the term 'genius' to denominate these powers, which include a heightened sensitivity to nature's outer forms, an ability to read nature for inward meaning, the capacity to perceive and create symbols, and of course mastery of the artistic power of imagination. Finally, for all of his confidence about the abilities of the poet-prophet, Coleridge also acknowledges that these exalted artistic powers are rarefied and difficult to sustain. The final selections in this chapter suggest the deep-seated anxiety which besets poets when their imaginative powers fail, and nature and spirit seem divided and irreconcilable.

I. Symbols 'consubstantial with the truths, of which they are the *conductors*'[8]

Symbols have the power to bridge the material and spiritual worlds in various ways; they exist not only in art, but in nature, the Bible, language and even the human thought process itself. Coleridge's seminal definition of symbol below is not just an artistic theory, but a metaphysical proposition.

From Lay Sermons, *on the power of particular passages in the Bible*

In the Scriptures they are the living *educts* of the imagination; of that reconciling and mediatory power, which incorporating the reason in images of the sense, and organizing (as it were) the flux of the senses by the permanence and self-circling energies of the reason, gives birth to a system of symbols, harmonious in themselves, and consubstantial with the truths of which they are the *conductors*. These are the *wheels* which Ezekiel beheld, when the hand of the Lord was upon him, and he saw visions of God as he sate among the captives by the river of Chebar. *Whithersoever the Spirit was to go, the* wheels *went, and thither was their spirit to go: – for the spirit of the living creature was in the wheels also.* The truths and the symbols that represent them move in conjunction and form the living chariot that bears up (for *us*) the throne of the Divine Humanity. Hence, by a derivative, indeed, but not a divided, influence, and though in a secondary yet in more than a metaphorical sense, the Sacred Book is worthily intitled the WORD OF GOD. Hence too, its contents present to us the stream of time continuous as life and a symbol of eternity, inasmuch as the past and the future are virtually contained in the present. According therefore to our relative position on the banks of this stream the Sacred History becomes prophetic, the Sacred Prophecies historical, while the power and substance of both inhere in its laws, its promises, and its comminations. In the Scriptures therefore both Facts and Persons must of necessity have a twofold significance, a past and a future, a temporary and a perpetual, a particular and a universal application. They must be at once portraits and ideals.

Eheu! paupertina philosophia in paupertinam religionem ducit: – A hunger-bitten and idea-less philosophy naturally produces a starveling and comfortless religion. It is among the miseries of the present age that it recognizes no *medium* between *literal* and *metaphorical*. Faith is either to be buried in the dead letter, or its name and honors usurped by a counterfeit product of the mechanical understanding, which in the blindness of self-complacency confounds symbols with allegories. Now an allegory is but a translation of abstract notions into a picture-language, which is itself nothing but an abstraction from objects of the senses;

the principal being more worthless even than its phantom proxy, both alike unsubstantial, and the former shapeless to boot. On the other hand a symbol ὅ ἔστιν ἀεί ταυυτηγόριχον is characterized by a translucence of the special in the individual, or of the general in the special, or of the universal in the general; above all by the translucence of the eternal through and in the temporal. It always partakes of the reality which it renders intelligible; and while it enunciates the whole, abides itself as a living part in that unity of which it is the representative. The other are but empty echoes in which the fancy arbitrarily associates with apparitions of matter, less beautiful but not less shadowy than the sloping orchard or hill-side pasture-field seen in the transparent lake below.

Shedd I 436–7 [LS (CC) 28–31]

The selections below reveal how fundamental symbol is to Coleridge's understanding of the human mind. Symbols are not just artistic signifiers, but part of the human thought process itself.

From his notebook at Malta, April 1805

Saturday Night, April 14, 1805 – In looking at the objects of Nature while I am thinking, as at yonder moon dim-glimmering thro' the dewy window-pane, I seem rather to be seeking, as it were *asking*, a symbolical language for something within me that already and forever exists, than observing anything new. Even when that latter is the case, yet still I have always an ~~obscure~~cure feeling as if that new phænomenon were the dim Awaking of a forgotten or hidden Truth of my inner Nature/ It is still interesting as a Word, a Symbol! It is Λογος, the Creator! <and the Evolver!>

CN II 2546 17.104

From his notebook, November 1804

Hard to express that sense of the analogy or likeness of a Thing which enables a Symbol to represent it, so that we think of the Thing itself – & yet knowing that the Thing is not present to us. – Surely, on this universal fact of words & images depends by more or less mediations the *imitation* instead of *copy* which is illustrated in very nature *shakespearianized/* – that Proteus Essence that could assume the very form, but yet known & felt not to be the Thing by that difference of the Substance which made every atom of the

Form another thing/ – that likeness not identity – an exact web, every line of direction miraculously the same, but the one worsted, the other silk.

CN II 2274 21.341

From Biographia Literaria

The best part of human language, properly so called, is derived from reflection on the acts of the mind itself. It is formed by a voluntary appropriation of fixed symbols to internal acts, to processes and results of imagination ...

Shedd III 405 [*BL (CC)* II 54]

From his notebook, May 1808

All minds must think by some *symbols* – the strongest minds possess the most vivid Symbols in the Imagination – yet this ingenerates a *want*, ποθον *desiderium*, for vividness of Symbol: which something that is *without*, that has the property of *Outness* (a word which Berkley preferred to 'Externality') can alone fully gratify/ even that indeed not fully – for the utmost is only an approximation to that absolute *Union*, which the soul sensible of its imperfection in itself, of its *Halfness*, yearns after, whenever it exists free from meaner passions ...

CN III 3325 21 1/2.19

Coleridge's notion of symbol has profound metaphysical implications. The selection below discusses symbols 'employed by nature to express to my own mind how I have felt in my the ground of my Being', suggesting an intimate connection between nature, humanity and the divine.

From his notebook, February–May 1807

And because, the strongest words, the words most steeped in passion, would be poor and inadequate to express, *how* I have felt. When Nature has made the Heart ache, and beat, and swell, and sink, and sicken ... when the very limbs, the feet, the arms, seemed incapable of moving unless the mind recreated a new power by some sudden *flash* of resolve to let them indeed cease to be, as a fainting and overwearied man runs with violent speed to the place in which he is to rest/ when such symbols as these have been employed by nature to express to my own mind *how* I have felt in ~~my~~ the ground of my Being, and yet still most inadequately hereby expressed it, what can modifications of air by the organs of articulation do?

CN II 3027 11.85

From Aids to Reflection

Herein the Apostle places the pre-eminence, the peculiar and distinguishing excellence, of the Christian religion. The ritual is of the same kind (ὁμοούσιον) though not of the same order, with the religion itself, – not arbitrary or conventional, as types and hieroglyphics are in relation to the things expressed by them; but inseparable, consubstantiated as it were, and partaking therefore of the same life, permanence, and intrinsic worth with its spirit and principle.

Shedd I 128 [*AR (CC)* 31]

II. Natural symbols

In addition to theorizing about symbol, Coleridge created his own natural symbols to illustrate complex abstract ideas. Some examples from his prose follow; they are notable not only for their vividness and aptness, but for the way in which they illustrate (or more correctly consubstantiate) the spiritual powers at work in nature.

From Biographia Literaria

Most of my readers will have observed a small water-insect on the surface of rivulets, which throws a cinque-spotted shadow fringed with prismatic colours on the sunny bottom of the brook; and will have noticed, how the little animal *wins* its way up against the stream, by alternate pulses of active and passive motion, now resisting the current, and now yielding to it in order to gather strength and a momentary *fulcrum* for a further propulsion. This is no unapt emblem of the mind's self-experience in the act of thinking. There are evidently two powers at work, which relatively to each other are active and passive; and this is not possible without an intermediate faculty, which is at once both active and passive. In philosophical language, we must denominate this intermediate faculty in all its degrees and determinations, the Imagination …

Shedd III 236 [*BL (CC)* I 124–5]

*The sun, with its associations of light, life, warmth, vision and omnipresence
is one of Coleridge's favourite symbols of God and his divine power.*[9]

From Lay Sermons

Religion is the sun whose warmth indeed swells, and stirs, and
actuates the life of nature, but who at the same time beholds all
the growth of life with a master-eye, makes all objects glorious on
which he looks, and by that glory visible to others.

Shedd I 449 [*LS (CC)* 48]

From his notebook, October–November 1806

A bodily Substance, an unborrow'd Self, God in God immanent,
the eternal Word, That goes forth yet remains, Crescent and Full,
and Wanes. Yet ever ~~one~~ entire and one/ – At the same time <it
dawns & sets & crowns the Height of Heaven> the dawning, setting
Son, at the same time the Tenant of each Sign Thro' all the zodiac/
~~Yet~~ While each in its own Hour Boasts & beholds ~~the~~ exclusive
Presence, ~~the~~ a Peculiar Orb. Each the great Traveller's Inn/Yet still
the unmoving Sun – Great genial Agent on all finite Souls, And by
that action ~~cloathes itself with~~ puts on finiteness absolute Infinite
whose dazzling robe Flows in rich folds & plays in shooting Hues
of infinite Finiteness.

CN II 2921 16.370–1

*In the selections below Coleridge presents the seed and the caterpillar's
chrysalis as evidence of a spiritual 'antecedent unity' that informed the
workings of nature. The seed containing the entire plant within itself, and
the caterpillar leaving room in its chrysalis for 'antennæ yet to come' are
used as complex symbols of spiritual potential.*

From Aids to Reflection

Again: in the world we see everywhere evidences of a unity, which
the component parts are so far from explaining, that they necessarily pre-suppose it as the cause and condition of their existing as
those parts; or even of their existing at all. This antecedent unity, or
cause and principle of each union, it has since the time of Bacon and
Kepler been customary to call a law. The crocus, for instance, or any
other flower, the reader may have in sight, or choose to bring before
his fancy. That the root, stem, leaves, petals, &c. cohere to one plant,

is owing to an antecedent power or principle in the seed, which existed before a single particle of the matters that constitute the size and visibility of the crocus, had been attracted from the surrounding soil, air, and moisture. Shall we turn here to the seed? Here too the same necessity meets us. An antecedent unity – I speak not of the parent plant, but of an agency antecedent in the order of operance, yet remaining present as the conservative and reproductive power – must here too be supposed. Analyze the seed with the finest tools, and let the solar microscope come in aid of your senses, – what do you find? Means and instruments, a wondrous fairy tale of nature, magazines of food, stores of various sorts, pipes, spiracles, defences – a house of many chambers, and the owner and inhabitant invisible! Reflect further on the countless millions of seeds of the same name, each more than numerically differenced from every other: and further yet, reflect on the requisite harmony of all surrounding things, each of which necessitates the same process of thought, and the coherence of all of which to a system, a world, demands its own adequate antecedent unity, which must therefore of necessity be present *to* all and *in* all, yet no wise excluding or suspending the individual law or principle of union in each.

Shedd I 150–1 [*AR (CC)* 75–6]

From Biographia Literaria

They, and only they, can acquire the philosophic imagination, the sacred power of self-intuition, who within themselves can interpret and understand the symbol, that the wings of the air-sylph are forming within the skin of the caterpillar; those only, who feel in their own spirit the same instinct, which impels the chrysalis of the horned fly to leave room in its *involucrum* for *antennæ* yet to come. They know and feel, that the *potential* works *in* them, even as the *actual* works on them! In short, all the organs of sense are framed for a corresponding world of sense; and we have it. All the organs of spirit are framed for a correspondent world of spirit; though the latter organs are not developed in all alike.

Shedd III 328 [*BL (CC)* I 241–2]

From his notebook, December 1804

I addressed a Butterfly <on a Pea-blossom> thus – Beautiful Psyche, Soul of a Blossom that art visiting & hovering o'er thy

former friends whom thou hast left –. Hadst I forgot the Caterpillar
or did I dream like a mad metaphysician the Caterpillar's hunger
for Plants was Self-love – recollection-feeling, & a lust that in its
next state refined itself into Love? – Dec. 12, 1804.

CN II 2317 21.501

Natural images that evidence organic powers of growth, change and
progress are especially attractive to Coleridge, especially given his belief
that nature and spirit are governed by the same spiritual laws and
processes.

From Lay Sermons

By the happy organization of a well-governed society the contradictory interests of ten millions of such individuals may neutralize
each other, and be reconciled in the unity of the national interest.
But whence did this happy organization first come? Was it a tree
transplanted from Paradise, with all its branches in full fruitage?
Or was it sowed in sunshine? Was it in vernal breezes and gentle
rains that it fixed its roots, and grew and strengthened? Let history
answer these questions. With blood it was planted; it was rocked in
tempests; the goat, the ass, and the stag gnawed it; the wild boar
has whetted his tusks on its bark. The deep scars are still extant
on its trunk, and the path of the lightning may be traced among
its higher branches. And even after its full growth, in the season if
its strength, *when its height reached to the heaven, and the sight thereof*
to all the earth, the whirlwind has more than once forced its stately
top to touch the ground: it has been bent like a bow, and sprang
back like a shaft.

Shedd I 432 [*LS (CC)* 21–2]

From The Friend

The progress of the species neither is nor can be like that of a
Roman road in a right line. It may be more justly compared to that
of a river, which, both in its smaller reaches and larger turnings,
is frequently forced back towards its fountains by objects which
cannot otherwise be eluded or overcome; yet with an accompanying impulse that will ensure its advancement hereafter, it is
either gaining strength every hour, or conquering in secret some
difficulty, by a labour that contributes as effectually to further it in

its course, as when it moves forward uninterrupted in a line, direct as that of the Roman road with which we began the comparison.

Shedd II 362 [*F (CC)* I 392]

From his notebook, December 1799

The Serpent by which the ancients emblem'd the Inventive faculty appears to me, in its mode of motion most exactly to emblem a writer of Genius. He varies his course yet still glides onwards – all lines of motion are his – all beautiful, & all propulsive –

> Circular base of rising folds that tower'd
> Fold above fold a surging maze, his Head
> Crested aloft, and Carbuncle his eyes,
> With burnish'd Neck of verdant Gold, erect
> Amidst the circling spires that on the Grass
> Floated Redundant –
> So varied he & of his tortuous train
> Curls many a wanton wreath;
> yet still he proceeds & is proceeding. – /

CN I 609 4.25

From his notebook, December 1804

Tuesday Morning, 18 Dec. 8 °clock. – Beautiful circumstance the improvement of the flower from the Root up to that crown of its Life & Labors, that bridal chamber of its Beauty & its twofold Love, the nuptial & the parental – the womb, the cradle, the nursery of the future Garden-insect analogies.

CN II 2349 21.533

III. Artistic vision

Coleridge believed that in creating art, the poet engages with the same creative powers that form nature itself. The following selections reveal his exalted conception of art, as 'the Mediatress, the reconciliator of Man and Nature'.[10] *Through the poet or artist's exalted powers of vision, he could harmonize the romantic triad of nature, humanity and the divine by mediating the spiritual powers that informed all three. The first selection, from the notes for Lecture 13 of the* Lectures on Literature, *is an important summary of Coleridge's artistic theory.*

From his notebook, March 1818

Thirteenth Lecture, Tuesday, 10 March, 1818.

Man communicates by articulation of Sounds, and paramountly by the memory in the Ear – Nature by the impressions of Surfaces and Bounds on the Eye, and thro' the Eye gives significance and appropriation, and thus the conditions of Memory (or the capability of being remembered) to Sounds, smells, &c. Now *Art* (I use the word collectively for Music, Painting, Statuary, and Architecture) is the Mediatress, the reconciliator of Man and Nature. –

The ~~simplest or~~ primary Art is *Writing*, primary if we regard the purpose, abstracted from the different modes of realizing it – the *steps*, of which the instances are still presented to us in the lower degrees of civilization – gesticulation and rosaries or Wampum, in the lowest – picture Language – Hieroglyphics – and finally, Alphabetic/ These all alike consist in the *translation*, as it were, of Man into Nature – the use of the visible in place of the Audible . . .

Poetry likewise is purely *human* – all its materials are *from* the mind, and all the products are *for* the mind. It is the Apotheosis of the former state – viz. Order and Passion – *N.b.* how by excitement of the Associative Power Passion itself imitates Order, and the *order* resulting produces a pleasurable *Passion* (whence Metre) and thus elevates the Mind by making its feelings the Objects of its reflection/ and how recalling the Sights and Sounds that had accompanied the occasions of the original passion it impregnates them with an interest not their own by means of the Passions, and yet tempers the passion by the calming power which all *distinct* images exert on the human soul. (This *illustrated*.)

In this way Poetry is the ~~Perp~~ Preparation for Art: inasmuch as it avails itself of the forms of Nature to recall, to express, and to modify the thoughts and feelings of the mind – still however thro' the medium of *articulate Speech*, which is so peculiarly human that in all languages it is the ordinary ~~distinction~~ phrase by which Man and Nature are contra-distinguished – it is the original force of the word *brute* – and even now mute, and dumb do not convey the absence of sound, but the absence of articulate Sounds.

As soon as the human mind is intelligibly addressed by any outward medium, exclusive of articulate Speech, ~~or as~~ so soon does *Art* commence. But please to observe, that I have layed stress on the words, *human mind* – excluding thereby all results common to Man and all sentient creatures – and consequently, confining it to the effect produced by the congruity of the animal impression with the reflective Powers of the mind – so that not the Thing presented, but that which is *re*-presented, by the Thing, is the source of the Pleasure. – In this sense Nature itself is to a religious Observer the Art of God – and for the same cause Art itself might be defined, as of a middle nature between a Thought and a Thing, or, as before, the union and reconciliation of that which is Nature with that which is exclusively Human. – Exemplify this by a good Portrait, which becomes more and more like in proportion to its excellence as a Work of Art – While a real *Copy*, a Fac Simile, ends in shocking us. –

Taking therefore *mute* as opposed not to sound but to articulate Speech, ~~the~~ the oldest definition of Painting is in fact the true and the best definition of the Fine Arts in general – *muta Poesis* – *mute* Poet~~rysy~~ – and of course, *Poesy* –/– (and as all Languages perfect themselves by a gradual process of desynonymizing words originally equivalent, as Propriety, Property – I, Me – Mister, Master – &c/ I have cherished the wish, to use the word, Poesy, as the generic or common term, ~~of~~ distinguishing that species of Poesy, which is not *muta* Poesis, by its usual name, *Poetry/*) while all the other species, which collectively form the *Fine Arts*, there would remain this as the common definition – that they all, like Poetry, are to express intellectual purposes, Thoughts, Conceptions, Sentiments that have their origin in the human Mind, but not, as Poetry, by means of articulate Speech, but as Nature, or the divine Art, does, by form, ~~proportion~~, color, magnitude, Sound, and proportion, silently or musically. –

Well – it may be said – but who has ever thought otherwise. We all know, that Art is the imitatress of Nature. – And doubtless, the Truths, I hope to convey, would be barren Truisms, if all men meant the same by the words, *imitate* and *nature*. But it would be flattering mankind at large, to presume that this is the Fact./ First, imitate – The impression on the wax is not an imitation but a *Copy* of the Seal – the Seal itself is an Imitation./ But farther – in order to form a philosophic conception, we must seek for the *kind* – as the *heat* in Ice – invisible Light – &c – but for practical purposes, we must have reference to the degree ...

So Nature – i.e. natura naturata – & hence the natural Question/ What *all* and every thing? – No, but the Beautiful. – And what is the

Beautiful? – The definition is at once undermined. – / If the Artist painfully *copies* nature, what an idle rivalry! If he proceeds from a Form, that answers to the notion of Beauty, namely, the many seen as one – what an emptiness, an unreality – as in Cypriani – The *essence* must be mastered – the natura naturans, & this presupposes *a bond* between *Nature* in this higher sense and the soul of Man ...

The wisdom in Nature distinguished from Man by the coinstantaneity of the Plan & the Execution, the Thought and the Production – In Nature there is no reflex act – but the same powers without reflection, and consequently without Morality. (Hence *Man* the *Head* of the visible Creation – *Genesis.*) Every step antecedent to full consciousness found in Nature – so to place them as for some one effect, totalized & fitted to the limits of a human Mind, as to elicit and as it were superinduce *into* the forms the reflection, to which they approximate – this is the mystery of Genius in the Fine Arts – Dare I say that the Genius must act on the feeling, that *Body* is but a striving to become Mind – that it is *mind*, in its essence –?

As in every work of *Art* the Conscious ~~appears~~ – is so impressed on the Unconscious, as to appear *in* it (ex. gr. Letters on a Tomb compared with Figures constituting a Tomb) – so is the Man of Genius the Link that combines the two – but for that reason, he must partake of both – Hence, there is in Genius itself an unconscious activity – nay, that is *the* Genius in the man of Genius. –

This is the true Exposition of the Rule, that the Artist must first *eloign* himself from Nature in order to return to her with full effect. – Why this? – Because – if he began by mere painful copying, he would produce Masks only, not forms breathing Life – he must out of his own mind create forms according to the several Laws of the Intellect, in order to produce in himself that co-ordination of Freedom & Law, that involution of the Obedience in the Prescript, and of the Prescript in the ~~tendency~~ impulse to obey, which assimilates him to Nature – enables him to understand her –. He absents himself from her only in his own Spirit, which has the same ground with Nature, to learn her unspoken language, in its main radicals, before he approaches to her endless compositions of those radicals – Not to acquire cold notions, lifeless technical Rules, but living and life-producing Ideas, which contain their own evidence/ and in that evidence the certainty that they are essentially one with the germinal causes in Nature, his Consciousness being the focus and mirror of both – for this does he for a time abandon the external *real*, in order to return to it with a full sympathy with its internal & actual –. Of all, we see, hear, or touch, the substance is and must be in ourselves – and therefore there is no alternative *in reason* between the dreary (& thank heaven! almost impossible) belief that every thing around us is but a phantom, or that the Life which is in us is in them likewise – and that to know is to *resemble* ...

Art would be or should be the Abridgment of Nature. Now the Fullness of Nature is without character as Water is purest when without taste, smell or color – but this is the Highest, the Apex, not the whole – & Art is to give *the whole* ad hominem/hence each step of Nature has its Ideal, & hence too the possibility of a climax up to the perfect Form, of harmonized Chaos –

CN III 4397 22.73

This conception of art above as 'the Abridgment of Nature' required special faculties for the poet, who must not 'acquire cold notions, lifeless technical Rules, but living and life-producing Ideas'. In order to mediate the spiritual and natural worlds, he must possess the following powers of vision:

From his notebook, 1808–11

1. Sense of Beauty – this thro' the whole poem, even to almost effeminacy of sweetness ...

2. With things remote from his own feelings – and in which the romanticity gives a vividness to the naturalness of the sentiments & feelings –

3. Love of natural Objects ...

4. Fancy, or the aggregative Power – Full gently now &c – the bringing together Images dissimilar in the main by some one point or more of Likeness ...

5. – That power of & energy of what a ~~late~~ living ~~poem~~oet has grandly & appropriately. To flash upon that inward Eye Which is the Bliss of Solitude – & to make every thing present by ~~the~~ a Series of Images – This an absolute Essential of Poetry, & of itself would form a poet, tho' not of the highest Class – It is however a most hopeful Symptom, & the V[enus] & A[donis] is one continued Specimen/

6. Imagination/ power of modifying one image or feeling by the precedent or following ones –.– So often afterwards to be illustrated that at present I shall speak only of – one of its effects – namely, that of combining many circumstances ~~by~~ into one moment of thought to produce that ultimate end of human Thought, and human Feeling, Unity and thereby the reduction of the Spirit to its Principle & Fountain, who alone is truly *one* …

7. <The describing natural objects by ~~inspiring~~ cloathing them appropriately with human passions/
Lo, here the gentle Lark/>

8. ~~Power~~ Energy, depth, and activity of Thought without which a man may be a pleasing and affecting Poet; but never a great one.

CN III 3247 25.11 1808–11

IV. Powers of the poet

The poet is elevated to a prophetic figure capable of engaging simultaneously with the spiritual and material worlds. In the passages below, the extraordinary capacities of the poet are revealed, from 'a more than ordinary Sympathy with the Objects, Emotions, or Incidents contemplated by the Poet' and 'a more than common sensibility, with a more than ordinary Activity of ~~Mind~~ the ~~Fancy~~ Mind as far as respects the Fancy & Imagination'[11] and, above all, an ability to harmonize all the faculties of vision, since 'The poet, described in ideal *perfection, brings the whole soul of man into activity, with the subordination of its faculties to each other, according to their relative worth and dignity.'[12] The poet must master all levels of vision, from the lowest levels of objective vision to the highest transcendental intuitions.*

From Biographia Literaria

What is poetry? – is so nearly the same question with, what is a poet? – that the answer to the one is involved in the solution of the other. For it is a distinction resulting from the poetic genius itself, which sustains and modifies the images, thoughts, and emotions of the poet's own mind. The poet, described in *ideal* perfection, brings the whole soul of man into activity, with the subordination of its faculties to each other according to their relative worth and dignity. He diffuses a tone, and spirit of unity, that blends, and (as it were) *fuses*, each into each, by that synthetic and magical power, to which

I would exclusively appropriate the name of Imagination. This power, first put in action by the will and understanding, and retained under their irremissive, though gentle and unnoticed, control, *laxis effertur habenis*, reveals itself in the balance or reconcilement of opposite or discordant qualities: of sameness, with difference; of the general with the concrete; the idea with the image; the individual with the representative; the sense of novelty and freshness with old and familiar objects; a more than usual state of emotion with more than usual order; judgment ever awake and steady self-possession with enthusiasm and feeling profound or vehement; and while it blends and harmonizes the natural and the artificial, still subordinates art to nature; the manner to the matter; and our admiration of the poet to our sympathy with the poetry .... Finally, Good Sense is the Body of poetic genius, Fancy its Drapery, Motion its Life, and Imagination the Soul that is every where, and in each; and forms all into one graceful and intelligent whole.

Shedd III 373–4 [*BL (CC)* II 15–18]

From Biographia Literaria

It has been before observed that images, however beautiful, though faithfully copied from nature, and as accurately represented in words, do not of themselves characterize the poet. They become proofs of original genius only as far as they are modified by a predominant passion; or by associated thoughts or images awakened by that passion; or when they have the effect of reducing multitude to unity, or succession to an instant; or lastly, when a human and intellectual life is transferred to them from the poet's own spirit,

> Which shoots its being through earth, sea, and air.

Shedd III 378 [*BL (CC)* II 23]

From Biographia Literaria

No man was ever yet a great poet, without being at the same time a profound philosopher. For poetry is the blossom and the fragrancy of all human knowledge, human thoughts, human passions, emotions, language. In Shakspeare's poems the creative power and the intellectual energy wrestle as in a war embrace. Each in its excess of strength seems to threaten the extinction of the other. At length in the drama they were reconciled, and fought each with its shield before the breast of the other. Or like two rapid streams, that, at their first meeting within narrow and rocky banks, mutually strive to repel each other, and intermix reluctantly and in tumult; but soon finding a wider channel and more yielding shores, blend, and dilate, and flow on in one current and with one voice.

Shedd III 381 [*BL (CC)* II 25–6]

From his notebook, 1811–16[13]

– In animated Prose the Beauties of Nature, the Passions & Accidents of Human Nature are often expressed in the natural Language, which the contemplation of them would suggest to a pure & benevolent mind – yet still we nor the Writers call the Work a Poem, tho' no work could deserve that name, which did not include all this together with a something else. What is this? It is theat pleasurable emotion, that peculiar state or degree of Excitement, which arises in the Poet's mind himself, in the act of composition – & in order to understand this we must combine a more than ordinary Sympathy with the Objects, Emotions, or Incidents contemplated by the Poet in consequence of a more than common sensibility, with a more than ordinary Activity of Mind the Fancy Mind as far as respects the Fancy & Imagination – Hence a more vivid reflection of the Truths of Nature & the Human Heart united with that constant exertion of Activity which modifies & corrects these truths by that sort of pleasurable Emotion, which the exertion of all our faculties give in a certain degree, but which the full play of those Powers of Mind, which are spontaneous rather than voluntary, in which the Effort required bears no proportion to the activity enjoyed – / – This is the state which permits the production of a highly pleasurable Whole, of which each part shall communicate for itself a distinct and conscious pleasure – & hence arises the definition, which now I trust is intelligible – that Poetry is a species of composition, distinguished from opposed to Science as having for its Objective intellectual pleasure for its Object and attaining its end by the Language natural to us in states of excitement; but distinguished from other species, not excluded by this criterion, by permitteding a pleasure from the Whole consistent with a p consciousness of pleasurable excitement from the component parts, & the perfection of which is to communicate from each part the greatest immediate pleasure compatible with the largest Sum of Pleasure on the whole. –

CN III 4111 M.12

From the Lectures on Literature

Contemplate the Plants & the lower species of animal Life, as Insects – then we may find at once an instance & an illustration of the poetic process. In them we find united the conquest of all the circumstances of place, soil, climate, element &c over the living power, & at the same time the victory of the living Power over these circumstances – every living object in nature exists as the reconciliation of contradictions, by the law of Balance. – The vital principle of the Plant can embody, that is, can manifest itself, make itself manifest only by embodying itself in the materials that immediately surround it, and in the very elements, into which it may be decomposed, bears witness of the its birth place & the conditions of its outward growth – On the other hand, it takes them up into itself, forces them into parts of its own Life, modifies & transmutes every power by which it is itself modified: & the result is, a living whole, in which we may in thought & by artificial Abstraction distinguish the material <Body> from the indwelling Spirit, the contingent or accidental from the universal & essential, but in reality, in the thing itself, we cannot separate them.

Lects 1809–19 (CC) I 447

V. Genius: 'genius places things *in a new light*'[14]

Rather than genius referring to a very narrow and specific area of expertise, for Coleridge genius refers to heightened perceptive powers, mastery of the mind, and an ability to create vivid and fresh impressions. The selections below demonstrate the high levels of vision achieved by the man of genius.

From his notebook

To perceive and feel the Beautiful, the Pathetic, and the Sublime in Nature, in Thought, or in Action – this combined with the power of conveying such Perceptions and Feelings to the minds and hearts of others under the most pleasurable Forms of Eye and Ear – this is poetic Genius.

IS 151

From a marginal comment on Sir Thomas Browne's Religio Medici

This is the true characteristic of Genius – our destiny & instinct is to unriddle the World, & he is the man of Genius who feels this instinct fresh and strong in his nature – who perceives the riddle & the mystery of all things even the commonest & needs no strange and out of the way Tales or Images to stimulate him into wonder & a deep Interest.

CM (CC) I 747

From Biographia Literaria

But where the ideas are vivid, and there exists an endless power of combining and modifying them, the feelings and affections blend more easily and intimately with these ideal creations than with the objects of the senses; the mind is affected by thoughts, rather than by things; and only then feels the requisite interest even for the most important events and accidents, when by means of meditation they have passed into *thoughts*. The sanity of the mind is between superstition with fanaticism on the one hand, and enthusiasm with indifference and a diseased slowness to action on the other. For the conceptions of the mind may be so vivid and adequate, as to preclude that impulse to the realizing of them, which is the strongest and most restless in those, who possess more than mere *talent* (or the faculty of appropriating and applying the knowledge of others), – yet still want something of the creative, and self-sufficing power of absolute *genius*. For this reason therefore, they are men of *commanding* genius. While the former rest content between thought and reality, as it were an *intermundium* of which their own living spirit supplies the *substance*, and their imagination the ever-varying *form*; the latter must impress their preconceptions on the world without, in order to present them back to their own view with the satisfying degree of clearness, distinctness, and individuality. These in tranquil times are formed to exhibit a perfect poem in palace, or temple, or landscape-garden; or a tale of romance in canals that join sea with sea, or in walls of rock, which, shouldering back the billows, imitate the power, and supply the benevolence of nature to sheltered navies; or in aqueducts that, arching the wide vale from mountain to mountain, give a Palmyra to the desert.

Shedd III 165 [*BL (CC)* I 31–3]

A comment on Wordsworth's genius, from Biographia Literaria

It was the union of deep feeling with profound thought; the fine balance of truth in observing with the imaginative faculty in modifying the objects observed; and above all the original gift of spreading the tone, the *atmosphere*, and with it the depth and height of the ideal world around forms, incidents, and situations, of which, for the common view, custom had bedimmed all the lustre, had dried up the sparkle and the dew drops. 'To find no contradiction in the union of old and new; to contemplate the ANCIENT of days with feelings as fresh, as if all had then sprang forth at the first creative fiat; characterizes the mind that feels the riddle of the world, and may help to unravel it. To carry on the feelings of childhood into the powers of manhood; to combine the child's sense of wonder and novelty with the appearances which every day for perhaps forty years had rendered familiar;

> With sun and moon and stars throughout the year,
> And man and woman;

this is the character and privilege of genius, and one of the marks which distinguish genius from talents. And therefore is it the prime merit of genius and its most unequivocal mode of manifestation, so to represent familiar objects as to awaken in the minds of others a kindred feeling concerning them and that freshness of sensation which is the constant accompaniment of mental, no less than of bodily, convalescence. Who has not a thousand times seen snow fall on water? Who has not watched it with a new feeling, from the time that he has read Burns' comparison of sensual pleasure

> To snow that falls upon a river
> A moment white – then gone for ever!

'In poems, equally as in philosophic disquisitions, genius produces the strongest impressions of novelty, while it rescues the most admitted truths from the impotence caused by the very circumstance of their universal admission. Truths, of all others the most awful and mysterious, yet being at the same time of universal interest, are too often considered as *so* true, that they lose all the life and efficiency of truth, and lie bed-ridden in the dormitory of the soul, side by side, with the most despised and exploded errors.' THE FRIEND ...

BL (CC) I 80–2

From Biographia Literaria

Like a green field reflected in a calm and perfectly transparent lake, the image is distinguished from the reality only by its greater softness and lustre. Like the moisture or the polish on a pebble, genius neither distorts nor false-colours its objects; but on the contrary brings out many a vein and many a tint, which escape the eye of common observation, thus raising to the rank of gems what had been often kicked away by the hurrying foot of the traveller on the dusty high-road of custom.

Shedd III 491 [*BL (CC)* II 148–9]

From his notebook, 1810

Man of genius places things *in a new light* – this trivial phrase better expresses the appropriate effects of Genius than Pope's celebrated Distich –

What oft was thought but ne'er so well exprest –

It has been *thought* DISTINCTLY, but only possessed, as it were, unpacked & unsorted – the poet not only *displays* what tho' often seen in its unfolded mass had never been opened out, but he likewise adds something, namely, Lights & Relations. Who has not seen a Rose, or a sprig of Jasmine, of Myrtle, & &c &c? – But behold these same flowers in a posy or flowerpot, painted by a man of genius – or assorted by the hand of a woman of fine Taste & instinctive sense of Beauty? –

CN III 4016 24.48

From a marginal comment on the New Testament

I have too clearly before me the idea of a poet's genius to deem myself other than a very humble poet; but in the very possession of the idea, I know myself so far a poet as to feel assured that I can understand and interpret a poem in the spirit of poetry, and with the poet's spirit. Like the ostrich, I cannot fly, yet have I wings that give me the feeling of flight; and as I sweep along the plain, can look up toward the bird of Jove, and can follow him and say: – 'Sovereign of the air, – who descendest on thy nest in the cleft of the inaccessible rock, who makest the mountain pinnacle thy perch and halting-place, and, scanning with steady eye the orb of glory right above thee, imprintest thy lordly talons in the stainless snows, that shoot back and scatter round his glittering shafts, – I pay thee homage. Thou art my king. I give honour due to the vulture, the falcon, and all thy noble baronage; and no less to the lowly bird, the sky-lark, whom thou permittest to visit thy court, and chant her matin song within its cloudy curtains; yet the linnet, the thrush, the swallow are my brethren: – but still I am a bird, though but a bird of the earth.

'Monarch of our kind, I am a bird, even as thou; and I have shed plumes, which have added beauty to the beautiful, and grace to terror, waving over the maiden's brow and on the helmed head of the war-chief, and majesty to grief, dropping o'er the car of death!'

Shedd V 120 [*CM (CC)* I 482–3]

VI. Imagination: 'that synthetic and magical power'[15]

The power of imagination, like the creation of symbols, is much more than a clever artistic capability: it is an echo of profound spiritual powers at work throughout the universe. Coleridge calls the imagination 'this greatest faculty of the human mind'[16] because it not only perceives nature, but half-creates what it sees, harmonizing with the same creative powers that are at work in nature. 'Images tho' taken immediately from Nature & most accurately represented in words, do yet not characterize the Poet. – In order to do this, they must either be blended with or merged in, other images, the offering of the Poet's Imagination.'[17] The imagination is a blending, modifying and unifying power that marks the apex of creative vision, breathing life into the static forms of art.

From Biographia Literaria

The Imagination then I consider either as primary, or secondary. The primary Imagination I hold to be the living power and prime agent of all human perception, and as a repetition in the finite mind of the eternal act of creation in the infinite I AM. The secondary Imagination I consider as an echo of the former, co-existing with the conscious will, yet still as identical with the primary in the *kind* of its agency, and differing only in *degree*, and in the *mode* of its operation. It dissolves, diffuses, dissipates, in order to re-create: or where this process is rendered impossible, yet still at all events it struggles to idealize and unify. It is essentially *vital*, even as all objects (*as* objects) are essentially fixed and dead.

Shedd III 363 [*BL (CC)* I 304]

From his notebook at sea, while studying the form of ship sails, April 1804

... the whole is made up of parts, each part referring at once to each & to the whole/ – and nothing more administers to the Picturesque than this phantom of complete visual wholeness in an object, which visually does not form a whole, by the influence ab intra of the sense of its perfect Intellectual Beauty or Wholeness. – To all these must be added the Lights & Shades, sometimes *sunshiny*, sometimes *snowy*: sometimes shade-coloured, sometimes dingy – whatever effect distance, air tints, reflected Light, and the feeling connected with *the* Object (for all Passion unifies as it were by natural Fusion) have in bringing out, and in melting down, differences & contrast, accordingly as the mind finds it necessary to the completion of the idea of Beauty, to prevent sameness or discrepancy. – Of a Fleet of Ships more may be said: & probably more will suggest itself & of less obvious kind, on after quiet Looking: now that the Intellect has done its main business & rests.

CN II 2012 9.118

From his Lectures on Literature

– Instances of the poetic Power of making every thing present to the Imagination/ both the forms, & the passions that modify these forms either actually, as in the representation of Love or Anger or other human affections; or imaginatively by the different manner, in which inanimate objects, or objects unimpassioned themselves, are seen by the mind in moments of strong excitement, and according to the kind of the excitement – whether of Jealousy, or Rage, or Love, in its only appropriate sense of the word, or of the lower Impulses of our nature, <or finally of the poetic feeling/> – It is perhaps chiefly in the power of producing or reproducing the latter, that the poet stands distinct

Lects 1808–19 (CC) I 66–7

From his notebook, March 1808

... Imagination or the power by whyich one image or feeling is made to modify many others, & by a sort of *fusion to force many into one* – ... Various are the workings of this greatest faculty of the human mind – both passionate & tranquil – in its tranquil & purely pleasurable operation it acts chiefly by producing with out of many things, as it would have appeared in the description of an ordinary mind, described slowly & in suce unimpassioned succession, a oneness/ even as Nature, the greatest of Poets, acts upon us when we open our eyes upon an extended prospect – Thus the flight of the Adonis from the enamoured Goddess in the dusk of the Evening –

> Look! how a bright star shooteth from the Sky,
> So glides he in the night from Venus' Eye–.

How many Images & feelings are here brought together without effort & without discord – the beauty of Adonis – the rapidity of his flight – the yearning yet hopelessness of the enamoured gazer – and a shadowy ideal character thrown over the whole – /or its acts by hum impressing the stamp of humanity, of human feeling, over inanimate Objects – The Pines shorn by the <Sea> wind and seen in twilight/
Then

> Lo! here the gentle Lark –

and lastly, which belongs only to a great poet, the power of so carrying on the Eye of the Reader as to make him almost lose the consciousness of words – to make him *see* every thing – & this without exciting any painful or laborious attention, without any *anatomy* of description, (a fault not uncommon in descriptive poetry) but with the sweetness & easy movement of nature –

CN III 3290 25.18

From his notebook, April 1811

The image-forming or rather re-forming power, the imagination in its passive sense, which I would rather call Fancy = Phantasy ... may not inaptly be compared to the Gorgon Head, which *looked* death into every thing – and this not by accident, but from the nature of the faculty itself, the province of which is to give consciousness to the Subject by presenting to it its conceptions *objectively* but the Soul differences itself from any other Soul for the purposes of symbolical knowledge by *form* or body only – but all form as body, i.e. as shape, & not as forma efformans, is dead – Life may be *inferred*, even as intelligence is from black marks on white paper – but the black marks themselves *are truly 'the dead* letter'. Here then is the error – not in the faculty itself, without which there would be no *fixation*, consequently, no distinct perception or conception, but in the gross idolatry of those who abuse it, & make that the goal & end which should be only a means of arriving at it. Is it any excuse to him who treats a living being as inanimate Body, that he ~~we~~ cannot arrive at the knowledge of the living Being but thro' the Body which is its Symbol & outward & visible Sign? –

CN III 4066 17.197

From his notebook, October–November 1811

I have said before that Images tho' taken immediately from Nature & most accurately represented in words, do yet not characterize the Poet. – In order to do this, they ~~ha~~ must either be blended with or merged in, other images, the offering of the Poet's Imagination, by the Passion, ~~which~~ by the specific modification of pleasurable Feelings which the contemplation of the Image had awakened in the Poet himself –

Full many a glorious morning have I seen
Flatter the Mountain Tops with Sovereign Eye –

or by blending it with some deeper emotion, arising out of and consonant with the state or circumstances of the Person describing it –

CN III 4115 M.15

VII. The crisis of imagination: 'My genial spirits fail.'[18]

Despite his optimistic statements regarding the visionary power of the imagination, Coleridge suffered crippling doubts about his own powers as a poet. Ironically, one of his greatest poems, 'Dejection: an Ode', is inspired by a crisis of inspiration: namely the devastation that he felt when his own imaginative powers failed. The final section of this chapter reveals the extreme difficulty of reaching the high levels of vision that Coleridge praised so highly. In the selections below, he seeks to awaken his imagination in moments when 'Life seems emptied of all genial Powers'.[19]

From his notebook, November 1804–5

Soother of Absence. Days & weeks & months pass on/ & now a year/ and the Sun, the Sea, the Breeze has its influences on me, and good and sensible men – and I feel a pleasure upon me, & I am to the outward view of all cheerful, & have myself no distinct consciousness of the contrary, for I use my faculties, not indeed as once, but freely – but oh [Sara]! I am never happy, never deeply gladdened – I know not, I have forgotten what the *Joy* is of ~~that~~ which the Heart is full as of a deep & quiet fountain overflowing insensibly, or the gladness of Joy, when the fountain overflows ebullient. – S.T.C.

CN II 2279 21.473

'Dejection: An Ode' (1802)

> Late, late yestreen I saw the new Moon,
> With the old Moon in her arms;
> And I fear, I fear, my Master dear!
> We shall have a deadly storm.

> *Ballad of Sir Patrick Spence*

I

> Well! If the Bard was weather-wise, who made
>   The grand old ballad of Sir Patrick Spence,
>   This night, so tranquil now, will not go hence
> Unroused by winds, that ply a busier trade
> Than those which mould yon cloud in lazy flakes,
> Or the dull sobbing draft, that moans and rakes
>   Upon the strings of this Æolian lute,
>   Which better far were mute.
> For lo! the New-moon winter-bright!
> And overspread with phantom light,
>   (With swimming phantom light o'erspread
>   But rimmed and circled by a silver thread)
> I see the old Moon in her lap, foretelling
>   The coming-on of rain and squally blast.
> And oh! that even now the gust were swelling,

And the slant night-shower driving loud and fast!
Those sounds which oft have raised me, whilst they awed,
    And sent my soul abroad,
Might now perhaps their wonted impulse give,
Might startle this dull pain, and make it move and live!

II

A grief without a pang, void, dark, and drear,
  A stifled, drowsy, unimpassioned grief,
  Which finds no natural outlet, no relief,
    In word, or sigh, or tear –
O Lady! in this wan and heartless mood,
To other thoughts by yonder throstle woo'd,
  All this long eve, so balmy and serene,
Have I been gazing on the western sky,
  And its peculiar tint of yellow green:
And still I gaze – and with how blank an eye!
And those thin clouds above, in flakes and bars,
That give away their motion to the stars;
Those stars, that glide behind them or between,
Now sparkling, now bedimmed, but always seen:
Yon crescent Moon as fixed as if it grew
In its own cloudless, starless lake of blue;
I see them all so excellently fair,
I see, not feel, how beautiful they are!

III

  My genial spirits fail;
  And what can these avail
To lift the smothering weight from off my breast?
  It were a vain endeavour,
  Though I should gaze for ever
On that green light that lingers in the west:
I may not hope from outward forms to win
The passion and the life, whose fountains are within.

IV

O Lady! we receive but what we give,
And in our life alone does Nature live:
Ours is her wedding garment, ours her shroud!

And would we aught behold, of higher worth,
Than that inanimate cold world allowed
To the poor loveless ever-anxious crowd,
  Ah! from the soul itself must issue forth,
A light, a glory, a fair luminous cloud
    Enveloping the Earth –
And from the soul itself must there be sent
  A sweet and potent voice, of its own birth,
Of all sweet sounds the life and element!

V

Oh pure of heart! thou need'st not ask of me
What this strong music in the soul may be!
What, and wherein it doth exist,
This light, this glory, this fair luminous mist,
This beautiful and beauty-making power.
  Joy, virtuous Lady! Joy that ne'er was given,
Save to the pure, and in their purest hour,
Life, and Life's effluence, cloud at once and shower,
Joy, Lady! is the spirit and the power,
Which wedding Nature to us gives in dower
  A new Earth and new Heaven,
Undreamt of by the sensual and the proud –
Joy is the sweet voice, Joy the luminous cloud –
  We in ourselves rejoice!
And thence flows all that charms or ear or sight,
  All melodies the echoes of that voice,
All colours a suffusion from that light.

VI

There was a time when, though my path was rough,
  This joy within me dallied with distress,
And all misfortunes were but as the stuff
  Whence Fancy made me dreams of happiness:
For hope grew round me, like the twining vine,
And fruits, and foliage, not my own, seemed mine.
But now afflictions bow me down to earth:
Nor care I that they rob me of my mirth;
  But oh! each visitation
Suspends what nature gave me at my birth,

My shaping spirit of Imagination.
For not to think of what I needs must feel,
But to be still and patient, all I can;
And haply by abstruse research to steal
From my own nature all the natural man –
This was my sole resource, my only plan:
Till that which suits a part infects the whole,
And now is almost grown the habit of my soul.

VII

Hence, viper thoughts, that coil around my mind,
Reality's dark dream!
I turn from you, and listen to the wind,
Which long has raved unnoticed. What a scream
Of agony by torture lengthened out
That lute sent forth! Thou Wind, that rav'st without,
Bare crag, or mountain-tairn, or blasted tree,
Or pine-grove whither woodman never clomb,
Or lonely house, long held the witches' home,
Methinks were fitter instruments for thee,
Mad Lutanist! who in this month of showers,
Of dark-brown gardens, and of peeping flowers,
Mak'st Devils' yule, with worse than wintry song,
The blossoms, buds, and timorous leaves among.
Thou Actor, perfect in all tragic sounds!
Thou mighty Poet, e'en to frenzy bold!
What tell'st thou now about?
'Tis of the rushing of a host in rout,
With groans, of trampled men, with smarting wounds –
At once they groan with pain, and shudder with the cold!
But hush! there is a pause of deepest silence!
And all that noise, as of a rushing crowd,
With groans, and tremulous shudderings – all is over –
It tells another tale, with sounds less deep and loud!
A tale of less affright,
And tempered with delight,
As Otway's self had framed the tender lay, –
'Tis of a little child
Upon a lonesome wild,
Not far from home, but she hath lost her way:

And now moans low in bitter grief and fear,
And now screams loud, and hopes to make her mother hear.

VIII

'Tis midnight, but small thoughts have I of sleep:
Full seldom may my friend such vigils keep!
Visit her, gentle Sleep! with wings of healing,
　　And may this storm be but a mountain-birth,
May all the stars hang bright above her dwelling,
　　Silent as though they watched the sleeping Earth!
　　　With light heart may she rise,
　　　Gay fancy, cheerful eyes,
　　Joy lift her spirit, joy attune her voice;
To her may all things live, from pole to pole,
Their life the eddying of her living soul!
　　O simple spirit, guided from above,
Dear Lady! friend devoutest of my choice,
Thus mayest thou ever, evermore rejoice.

CPW I 362–8 [*PW (CC)* II 697–702]

In the following poem, Coleridge responds to a crisis of imagination by escaping into an artistic world, thus rehabilitating his vision. By mid-poem he exclaims 'Thanks, gentle artist! now I can descry/ Thy fair creation with a mastering eye,/ And all awake!'

'The Garden of Boccaccio' (1828)

Of late, in one of those most weary hours,
When life seems emptied of all genial powers,
A dreary mood, which he who ne'er has known
May bless his happy lot, I sate alone;
And, from the numbing spell to win relief,
Call'd on the Past for thought of glee or grief.
In vain! bereft alike of grief and glee,
I sate and cow'r'd o'er my own vacancy!
And as I watch'd the dull continuous ache,
Which, all else slumb'ring, seem'd alone to wake;
O Friend! long wont to notice yet conceal,
And soothe by silence what words cannot heal,
I but half saw that quiet hand of thine
Place on my desk this exquisite design,

Boccaccio's Garden and its faery,
The love, the joyaunce and the gallantry!
An Idyll, with Boccaccio's spirit warm,
Framed in the silent poesy of form.

Like flocks adown a newly-bathed steep
Emerging from a mist: or like a stream
Of music soft that not dispels the sleep,
But casts in happier moulds the slumberer's dream,
Gazed by an idle eye with silent might
The picture stole upon my inward sight.
A tremulous warmth crept gradual o'er my chest,
As though an infant's finger touch'd my breast.
And one by one (I know not whence) were brought
All spirits of power that most had stirr'd my thought
In selfless boyhood, on a new world tost
Of wonder, and in its own fancies lost;
Or charm'd my youth, that, kindled from above,
Loved ere it loved, and sought a form for love;
Or lent a lustre to the earnest scan
Of manhood, musing what and whence is man!

Wild strain of Scalds, that in the sea-worn caves
Rehearsed their war-spell to the winds and waves;
Or fateful hymn of those prophetic maids,
That call'd on Hertha in deep forest glades;
Or minstrel lay, that cheer'd the baron's feast;
Or rhyme of city pomp, of monk and priest,
Judge, mayor, and many a guild in long array,
To high-church pacing on the great saint's day:
And many a verse which to myself I sang,
That woke the tear, yet stole away the pang
Of hopes, which in lamenting I renew'd:
And last, a matron now, of sober mien
Yet radiant still and with no earthly sheen,
Whom as a faery child my childhood woo'd
Even in my dawn of thought – Philosophy;
Though then unconscious of herself, pardie,
She bore no other name than Poesy;
And, like a gift from heaven, in lifeful glee,
That had but newly left a mother's knee,

Prattled and play'd with bird and flower, and stone,
As if with elfin playfellows well known,
And life reveal'd to innocence alone.

Thanks, gentle artist! now I can descry
Thy fair creation with a mastering eye,
And all awake! And now in fix'd gaze stand,
Now wander through the Eden of thy hand;
Praise the green arches, on the fountain clear
See fragment shadows of the crossing deer;
And with that serviceable nymph I stoop
The crystal, from its restless pool, to scoop.
I see no longer! I myself am there,
Sit on the ground-sward, and the banquet share.
'Tis I, that sweep that lute's love-echoing strings,
And gaze upon the maid who gazing sings:
Or pause and listen to the tinkling bells
From the high tower, and think that there she dwells.
With old Boccaccio's soul I stand possest,
And breath an air like life, that swells my chest.

The brightness of the world, O thou once free,
And always fair, rare land of courtesy!
O Florence! with the Tuscan fields and hills,
And famous Arno, fed with all their rills;
Thou brightest star of star-bright Italy!
Rich, ornate, populous, – all treasures thine,
The golden corn, the olive, and the vine.
Fair cities, gallant mansions, castles old,
And forests, where beside his leafy hold
The sullen boar hath heard the distant horn,
And whets his tusks against the gnarléd thorn;
Palladian palace with its storied halls;
Fountains, where love lies listening to their falls;
Gardens, where flings the bridge its airy span,
And Nature makes her happy home with man;
Where many a gorgeous flower is duly fed
With its own rill, in its own spangled bed,
And wreathes the marble urn, or leans its head,
A mimic mourner, that with veil withdrawn
Weeps liquid gems, the presents of the dawn; –

Thine all delights, and every muse is thine;
And more than all, the embrace and intertwine
Of all with all in gay and twinkling dance!
Mid gods of Greece and warriors of romance
See! Boccace sits, unfolding on his knees
The new-found roll of old Maeonides;
But from his mantle's fold, and near the heart,
Peers Ovid's Holy Book of Love's sweet smart!

O all-enjoying and all-blending sage,
Long be it mine to con thy mazy page,
Where, half conceal'd, the eye of fancy views
Fauns, nymphs, and wingéd saints, all gracious to thy muse!

Still in thy garden let me watch their pranks,
And see in Dian's vest between the ranks
Of the trim vines, some maid that half believes
The vestal fires, of which her lover grieves,
With that sly satyr peeping through the leaves!

CPW I 478 [*PW (CC)* II 1089–95]

This final poem, composed late in Coleridge's life, takes a much darker and more melancholy view of his loss of imaginative power:

'Work without Hope'

Lines Composed 21st February 1825

All Nature seems at work. Slugs leave their lair –
The bees are stirring – birds are on the wing –
And Winter slumbering in the open air,
Wears on his smiling face a dream of Spring!
And I the while, the sole unbusy thing,
Nor honey make, nor pair, nor build, nor sing.

Yet well I ken the banks where amaranths blow,
Have traced the fount whence streams of nectar flow.
Bloom, O ye amaranths! bloom for whom ye may,
For me ye bloom not! Glide, rich streams, away!
With lips unbrightened, wreathless brow, I stroll:
And would you learn the spells that drowse my soul?
Work without hope draws nectar in a sieve,
And hope without an object cannot live.

CPW I 447 [*PW (CC)* II 1030–3]

Notes

1 *CN* III 4397 22.73
2 For more on Coleridge's definition of symbol, see J. Robert Barth, *The Symbolic Imagination: Coleridge and the Romantic Tradition* (Princeton: Princeton University Press, 1977); Owen Barfield, *What Coleridge Thought* (London: Oxford University Press, 1972); Timothy Fulford, *Coleridge's Figurative Language* (Basingstoke: Macmillan, 1991); Stephen Prickett, *Coleridge and Wordsworth: The Poetry of Growth* (Cambridge: Cambridge University Press, 1970) and Nicholas Reid, *Coleridge, Form and Symbol: Or The Ascertaining Vision* (Aldershot: Ashgate Publishing, 2006).
3 *Shedd* I 436–7 [*LS (CC)* 29]
4 *Shedd,* I 436–7 [*LS (CC)* 29]
5 See James Engell's definitive work *The Creative Imagination: Enlightenment to Romanticism* (Cambridge, MA: Harvard University Press, 1981) and I.A. Richards, *Coleridge on Imagination* (London: K. Paul, Trench, Trubner, 1934).
6 *Shedd* III 363 [*BL (CC)* I 304]
7 *Shedd* III 363 [*BL (CC)* I 304]
8 *Shedd* I 436–7 [*LS (CC)* 29]
9 See John Beer, *Coleridge the Visionary* (London: Chatto & Windus, 1959) 92–3 for discussion of Coleridge's use of the sun as a spiritual metaphor.
10 *CN* III 4397 22.73
11 *CN* III 4111 M.12
12 *Shedd* III 373–4 [*BL (CC)* II 15]
13 This also appears in *Lects 1808–19 (CC)* I 217. This selection is crossed out with a single vertical line in the notebook, but is still clearly legible.
14 *CN* III 4016 24.48
15 *Shedd* III 373–4 [*BL (CC)* II 15]
16 *CN* III 3290 25.18
17 *CN* III 4115 M.15
18 *CPW* I 362–8 [*PW (CC)* II 697]
19 *CPW* I 478 [*PW (CC)* II 1089]

Chapter Four

Natural and Supernatural

For all of his interest in the natural world, Coleridge was also intrigued by phenomena that could not be explained by natural laws: namely, the supernatural. Here the question of nature and vision arises again: what forces modify or distort perception of the natural world? In what situations does the mind's eye dominate the physical eye? This subject was touched upon earlier in the optical illusions section of the first chapter, with Coleridge's observations concerning situations in which the perceiver modified the perceived. This chapter focuses on even more dramatic cases of altered states of perception, such as mystical visions, dreams, fevers and opium reveries, and accounts of supernatural phenomena like ghosts, which raise questions about the nature of perception itself.

Coleridge's lifelong struggles with mysticism also revolve around this intersection of nature and vision. Although he was fascinated with various mystical writings, he resisted the validity of mystical systems. His reluctance stemmed not from a disbelief that perceptions of the supernatural were possible, but rather from an instinct that vision is subject to misinterpretation, especially if it is under the sway of modifying forces such as ignorance, strong emotional predilections or fanaticism. His accounts of ghosts and apparitions also reveal suspicions about the supernatural, as when he writes, 'A lady once asked me if I believed in ghosts and apparitions. I answered with truth and simplicity: *No, madam! I have seen far too many myself.*'[1] However he does not discard these tales as fabrications; rather he values them as 'interesting as facts and data for psychology, and affording some valuable materials for a theory of perception and its dependence on the memory and imagination'.[2] Coleridge's interest in the supernatural and the nature of perception was far ahead of its time, anticipating the later development of modern psychology.

If Coleridge was sceptical about the objective reality of supernatural phenomena, he was far more comfortable with the use of the supernatural in literature.[3] Throughout his literary work, he uses supernatural elements to create strange, fresh, fantastic imagery that engages the readers' imagination and transports them to visionary worlds. The second half of the chapter illustrates this use of the supernatural in literature, including allegorical visions, poems influenced by opium use, and finally selections from the supernatural poems of *Lyrical Ballads*, all of which demonstrate the power of vision to embellish, modify and even half-create perceptions of the natural world.

In this first selection, Coleridge muses upon the relationship between mind and nature, asking which force is more powerful. He concludes that both are 'potent magicians' but it is hard to determine which power, in the end, dominates perception:

From a letter to James Gillman, 10 October 1825

In youth and early manhood the mind and nature are, as it were, two rival artists both potent magicians, and engaged, like the King's daughter and the rebel genii in the Arabian Nights' Enternts., in sharp conflict of conjuration, each having for its object to turn the other into canvas to paint on, clay to mould, or cabinet to contain. For a while the mind seems to have the better in the contest, and makes of Nature what it likes, takes her lichens and weather-stains for types and printer's ink, and prints maps and fac similes of Arabic and Sanscrit MSS. on her rocks; composes country dances on her moonshiny ripples, fandangos on her waves, and waltzes on her eddy-pools, transforms her summer gales into harps and harpers, lovers' sighs and sighing lovers, and her winter blasts into Pindaric Odes, Christabels, and Ancient Mariners set to music by Beethoven, and in the insolence of triumph conjures her clouds into whales and walruses with palanquins on their backs, and chases the dodging stars in a sky-hunt! But alas! alas! that Nature is a wary wily long-breathed old witch, tough-lived as a turtle and divisible as the polyp, repullulative in a thousand snips and cuttings, *integra et in toto*! She is sure to get the better of Lady *Mind* in the long run and to take her revenge too; transforms our to-day into a canvas dead-coloured to receive the dull, featureless portrait of yesterday: not alone turns the mimic mind, the ci-devant sculptress with all her kaleidoscopic freaks and symmetries! into clay, but *leaves* it such a *clay* to cast dumps or bullets in; and lastly (to end with that which suggested the beginning) she mocks the mind with its own metaphor.

CLE II 742 [*CL* V 496–7]

I. Mysticism

Although Coleridge disagreed with mystical writers such as Böhme and Swedenborg,[4] *he also admired their defiance of materialists who 'contemplate nothing but parts, and all parts are necessarily little. And the universe to them is but a mass of* little things.'[5] *If the mystics were wrong, at least they erred on the side of believing that spiritual forces interpenetrated the material world. Additionally, Coleridge desired to make sense of remarkable childhood experiences and intuitions that the supernatural is indeed perceivable, as demonstrated in the selections below.*

From his notebook, July–August 1804

Saw in early youth as in a Dream the Birth of the Planets; & my eyes beheld as *one* what the Understanding afterwards divided into 1. the origin of the masses, 2. the origin of their motions, and 3. the site or position of their Circles & Ellipses – all the deviations too were *seen* as in one intuition of one, the self-same, necessity – & this necessity was a Law of Spirit – & all was Spirit – and in matter each all beheld the past activity of others or their own – this Reflection, this Echo, is matter – its only essence, if essence it be – and of this too I saw the necessity and understood it – but I understood not, how infinite multitude and manifoldness could be one. Only I saw & understood, that it was yet more out of my power to comprehend how it could be otherwise – & thus in this unity I worshipped in the depth of knowledge that passes all understanding the Being of all things – and in Being their sole Goodness – and I saw that God is the one, *the* Good – possesses it not, but is it.

CN II 2151 21.452

From a letter to Thomas Poole, 16 October 1797

My father (who had so little of parental ambition in him, that he had destined his children to be blacksmiths, etc., and had accomplished his intention but for my mother's pride and spirit of aggrandizing her family) my father had, however, resolved that I should be a parson. I read every book that came in my way without distinction; and my father was fond of me, and used to take me on his knee and hold long conversations with me. I remember that at eight years old I walked with him one winter evening from a farmer's house, a mile from Ottery, and he told me the names of the stars and how Jupiter was a thousand times larger than our world, and that the other twinkling stars were suns that had worlds rolling round them; and when I came home he shewed me how they rolled round. I heard him with a profound delight and admiration: but without the least mixture of wonder or incredulity. For from my early reading of fairy tales and genii, etc., etc., my mind had been habituated *to the Vast*, and I never regarded *my* senses in any way as the criteria of my belief. I regulated all my creeds by my conceptions, not by my *sight*, even at that age. Should children be permitted to read romances, and relations of giants and magicians and genii? I know all that has been said against it; but I have formed my faith in the affirmative. I know no other way of giving the mind a love of the Great and the Whole. Those who have been led to the same truths step by step, through the constant testimony of their senses, seem to me to want a sense which I possess. They contemplate nothing but *parts*, and all *parts* are necessarily little. And the universe to them is but a mass of *little things*. It is true, that the mind *may* become credulous and prone to superstition by the former method; but are not the experimentalists credulous even to madness in believing any absurdity, rather than believe the grandest truths, if they have not the testimony of their own senses in their favour?

CLE I 16–17 [*CL* I 354]

Coleridge discusses how the systems of mystical writers are flawed, but also helped him overcome materialism in favour of more spiritual world views.

From Biographia Literaria

For the writings of these Mystics acted in no slight degree to prevent my mind from being imprisoned within the outline of any single dogmatic system. They contributed to keep alive the *heart* in the *head*; gave me an indistinct, yet stirring and working presentment, that all the products of the mere *reflective* faculty partook of Death, and were as the rattling twigs and sprays in winter, into which a sap was yet to be propelled from some root to which I had not penetrated, if they were to afford my soul either food or shelter. If they were too often a moving cloud of smoke to me by day, yet they were always a pillar of fire throughout the night, during my wanderings through the wilderness of doubt, and enabled me to skirt, without crossing, the sandy deserts of utter unbelief.

Shedd III 255 [*BL (CC)* I 152]

From Aids to Reflection

Of poor Jacob Behmen I have delivered my sentiments at large in another work. Those who have condescended to look into his writings must know that his characteristic errors are: first, the mistaking the accidents and peculiarities of his own overwrought mind for realities and modes of thinking common to all minds: and secondly, the confusion of Nature, that is, the active powers communicated to matter, with God the Creator. And if the same persons have done more than merely looked into the present Volume, they must have seen, that to eradicate, and, if possible, to preclude both the one and the other, stands prominent among its avowed objects.

Shedd I 350–1 [*AR (CC)* 384]

Mystical vision entails stepping away from mundane, everyday vision and taking a larger view of the universe; Coleridge appreciated this as a mode of refreshing perception.

From his notebook, September 1807

Our mortal existence a stoppage in the blood of Life – a brief eddy in the everflowing Ocean of pure Activity, from wind or concourse of currents – who beholds Pyramids, yea, Alps and Andes, giant Pyramids, the work of Fire, raising monuments like a generous Victor, o'er its own conquest, tombstones of a world destroyed – yet, these too float adown the Sea of Time, & melt away, Mountains of floating Ice/–

CN II 3151 12.66

From The Friend

Could we emancipate ourselves from the bedimming influences of custom, and the transforming witchcraft of early associations, we should see as numerous tribes of *fetisch*-worshippers in the streets of London and Paris, as we hear of on the coasts of Africa.

Shedd II 101–2 [*F (CC)* I 106]

From his notebook, November 1799[6]

Nov. 29. Evening – The unmoveableness of all things thro' which so many men moved – harsh contrast! – Compared too with the universal motion of things in Nature.

CN I 591 4.7

II. Dream states

Coleridge kept careful records of his dreams and waking states, hoping to use them towards a theory of perception, but because of his opium addiction he was subject to terrible nightmares. Since the effects of opium were poorly understood in the nineteenth century, he unwittingly subjected himself to endless cycles of addiction and withdrawal that drastically affected his emotional equilibrium, and probably account for some of the sensations below.[7]

From his notebook, January 1811

Jan. 25. 1811. –

Elucidation of my all-zermalming argument on the subject of ghosts & apparitions by what occurred last night in my sleep – I drew my legs up suddenly: for a great pig was leaping out direct against them. No! – a great pig appeared to leap out against me because by a fear-engendering disease of the stomach, affecting the circulation of the Blood or nervous power my Legs were suddenly twitched up.

Night-mair is, I think, always – even when it occurs in the midst of Sleep, and not as it more commonly does after a waking Interval, a state not of Sleep but of Stupor of the outward organs of Sense, not in words indeed but yet in fact distinguishable from the suspended power of the senses in true Sleep; while the volitions of *Reason* i.e. comparing &c, are awake, tho' disturbed. This stupor seems occasioned by some painful sensation, of unknown locality, most often, I believe, in the lower Gut, tho' not seldom in the Stomach, which withdrawing the attention to itself from its sense of other realities present makes us asleep to them indeed but otherwise awake – and when ever this derangement occasions an interruption in the circulation, aided perhaps by pressure, awkward position, &c, the part deadened – as the hand, or his arm, or the foot & leg, on this side, transmits ~~single~~ double Touch as ~~double~~ single Touch: to which the Imagination therefore, the true inward Creatrix, instantly out of the chaos of the elements <or shattered fragments> of Memory puts together some form to fit it – which derives an over-powering sense of Reality from the circumstance, that the power of Reason being in good measure awake, most generally presents to us all the accompanying images ~~exactly as we~~ very nearly as they existed the moment before, when we fell out of anxious wakefulness into this *Reverie* – ex. gr. the bed, the curtains, the Room, & its furniture, the knowledge of who lies in the next room &c –

Last night before awaking or rather delivery from the night-mair, in which a claw-like talon-nailed Hand grasped hold of me, interposed between the curtains, I ~~haved~~ just before with my foot felt some thing seeming to move against it (– for in my foot it commenced) – I detected it, I say, by my excessive Terror, and dreadful Trembling of my whole body, Trunk & Limbs – & by my piercing out-cries – Good Heaven! (reasoned I) were this real, I never should or could be, in such an agony of Terror –

In short, this Night-mair is not properly *a Dream*; but a species of Reverie, akin to Somnambul~~ance~~ism, during which the Understanding & Moral Sense are awake tho' more or less confused, and over the Terrors of which the Reason can exert no influence ~~that~~ because it is not true Terror: i.e. apprehension of Danger, but a sensation as much as the Tooth-ache, a Cramp – I.e. the Terror does not *arise* out of ~~the~~ a painful Sensation, but is itself a specific sensation = terror corporeus sive materialis. – To explain & classify these strange sensations, the organic material Analogons (Ideas materiales <intermedias,> as the Cartesians say) of Fear, Hope, Rage, Shame, & (strongest of all) Remorse, forms at present the most difficult & at the same time the most interesting Problem of Psychology, and intimately connected with prudential morals (= the science of morals in its relation, not the ground & Law of Duty, but to the ~~known~~ empirical hindrances & fumbulations in the realizing of the Law by the human Being) –. The solution of this Problem would, perhaps, throw great doubt on this present dogma, that the Forms & Feelings of Sleep are always the reflections & confused Echoes of our waking Thought, & Experiences. –

CN III 4046 18.274

Here Coleridge does intuit that the effects of opium – 'whenever by the operation of a cathartic pill or from the want of one[8] *– might be affecting his dreams. Since opium also impacts the digestive system, a combination of physical and narcotic effects mingle in the following dream. Coleridge also attributes the awful sensations, half-mockingly, to Swedenborg's mystical theory of demons who specialize in tormenting the gut.*

From a letter to James Gillman, 2 November 1824

Upon my seriousness, I do declare that I cannot make out certain dream-devils or damned souls that play pranks with me, whenever by the operation of a cathartic pill or from the want of one, a ci-devant dinner in its metempsychosis is struggling in the lower intestines. I cannot comprehend how any thoughts, the offspring or product of my own reflection, conscience, or fancy, could be translated into such images, and agents and actions, and am half-tempted (N.B. between sleeping and waking) to regard with some favour Swedenborg's assertion that certain foul spirits of the lowest order are attracted by the precious ex-viands, whose conversation the soul half appropriates to itself, and which they contrive to whisper into the sensorium. The Honourable Emanuel has repeatedly caught them in the fact, in that part of the spiritual world corresponding to the guts in the world of bodies, and driven them away. I do not pass this Gospel; but upon my honour it is no bad apocrypha.

CLE II 729 [*CL* V 391–2]

In the following two selections, Coleridge searches for a theory of perception by carefully examining his dreams. The complexity and malleability of vision is revealed in the strange mingling of inward and outward sensations in dream states.

From his notebook in Malta, December 1804

In dreams one is much less, in the most tranquil dreams, a spectator only – one seems always about to do, or suffering or thinking, or talking – & I do not recollect that state of feeling so common when awake of thinking on one subject, & looking at another, or at a whole prospect/ till at last perhaps, or by intervals, at least, you only look passively at the prospect.

CN II 2302 21.486

From Lay Sermons

Even *the visions of the night* speak to us of powers within us that are not dreamt of in their day-dream of philosophy. The dreams, which we most often remember, are produced by the nascent sensations and inward *motiunculæ* (the fluxions) of the waking state. Hence, too, they are more capable of being remembered, because passing more gradually into our waking thoughts they are more likely to associate with our first perceptions after sleep. Accordingly, when the nervous system is approaching to the waking state, a sort of under-consciousness blends with our dreams, that in all we imagine as seen or heard, our own self is the ventriloquist, and moves the slides in the magic-lantern. We dream *about* things.

But there are few persons of tender feelings and reflecting habits, who have not, more or less often in the course of their lives, experienced dreams of a very different kind, and during the profoundest sleep that is compatible with after-recollection, – states, of which it would scarcely be too bold to say that we *dream the things themselves*: so exact, minute, and vivid beyond all power of ordinary memory is the portraiture, so marvellously perfect is our brief metempsychosis into the very *being*, as it were, of the person who seems to address us. The dullest wight is at times a Shakspeare in his dreams. Not only may we expect that men of strong religious feelings, but little religious knowledge, will occasionally be tempted to regard such occurrences as supernatural visitations; but it ought not to surprize us, if such dreams should sometimes be confirmed by the event, as though they had actually possessed a character of divination.

Shedd I 465–6 [*LS (CC)* 80–1]

III. Ghosts and apparitions

Coleridge painstakingly collected accounts of the supernatural, claiming that 'I have long wished to devote an entire work to the subject of dreams, visions, ghosts, and witchcraft, in which I might first give, and then endeavour to explain, the most interesting and best attested fact of

each.' [9] *Searching for a psychological explanation for these phenomena,*
he examined the different modes of vision implicit in these altered states.
He wished to 'explain in a more satisfactory way the mode in which our
thoughts, in states of morbid slumber, become at times perfect dramatic'
and asked 'by what law the form of the vision appears to talk to us its
own thoughts in a voice as audible as the shape is visible'. [10] *He was*
convinced that the secrets of the supernatural are bound up in modes of
vision.

From The Friend

First, I will endeavour to make my ghost theory more clear to
those of my readers, who are fortunate enough to find it obscure
in consequence of their own good health and unshattered nerves.
The window of my library at Keswick is opposite to the fire-place,
and looks out on the very large garden that occupies the whole
slope of the hill on which the house stands. Consequently, the
rays of light transmitted *through* the glass, that is, the rays from the
garden, the opposite mountains, and the bridge, river, lake, and
vale interjacent, and the rays reflected *from* it, of the fire-place, &c.,
enter the eye at the same moment. At the coming on of evening,
it was my frequent amusement to watch the image or reflection of
the fire, that seemed burning in the bushes or between the trees in
different parts of the garden or the fields beyond it, according as
there was more or less light; and which still arranged itself among
the real objects of vision, with a distance and magnitude propor-
tioned to its greater or lesser faintness. For still as the darkness
increased, the image of the fire lessened and grew nearer and more
distinct; till the twilight had deepened into perfect night, when
all outward objects being excluded, the window became a perfect
looking-glass: save only that my books on the side shelves of the
room were lettered, as it were, on their backs with stars, more or
fewer as the sky was more or less clouded, the rays of the stars
being at that time the only ones transmitted. Now substitute the
phantom from Luther's brain for the images of *reflected* light, the
fire for instance, and the forms of his room and its furniture for the
transmitted rays, and you have a fair resemblance of an apparition,
and a just conception of the manner in which it is seen together
with real objects. I have long wished to devote an entire work to the
subject of dreams, visions, ghosts, and witchcraft, in which I might
first give, and then endeavour to explain, the most interesting and

best attested fact of each, which has come within my knowledge, either from books or from personal testimony. I might then explain in a more satisfactory way the mode in which our thoughts, in states of morbid slumber, become at times perfect *dramatic*, – for in certain sorts of dreams the dullest wight becomes a Shakespeare, and by what law the *form* of the vision appears to talk to us its own thoughts in a voice as audible as the shape is visible; and this too oftentimes in connected trains, and not seldom even with a concentration of power which may easily impose on the soundest judgments, uninstructed in the *optics* and *acoustics* of the inner sense, for revelations and gifts of prescience. In aid of the present case, I will only remark, that it would appear incredible to persons not accustomed to these subtle notices of self-observation, what small and remote resemblances, what mere hints of likeness from some real external object, especially if the shape be aided by colour, will suffice to make a vivid thought consubstantiate with the real object, and derive from it an outward perceptibility. Even when we are broad awake, if we are in anxious expectation, how often will not the most confused sounds of nature be heard by us as articulate sounds? For instance, the babbling of a brook will appear for a moment the voice of a friend, for whom we are waiting, calling out our own names. A short meditation, therefore, on the great law of the imagination, that a likeness in part tends to become a likeness of the whole, will make it not only conceivable but probable, that the inkstand itself, and the dark-coloured stone on the wall, which Luther perhaps never till then noticed, might have a considerable influence in the production of the fiend, and of the hostile act by which his obtrusive visit was repelled.

A lady once asked me if I believed in ghosts and apparitions. I answered with truth and simplicity: *No, madam! I have seen far too many myself.* I have indeed a whole memorandum-book filled with records of these *phænomena*, many of them interesting as facts and *data* for psychology, and affording some valuable materials for a theory of perception, and its dependence on the memory and imagination.

Shedd II 134–6 [*F (CC)* I 145–6]

From his Table Talk, *3 January 1823*

Define a vulgar ghost with reference to all that is called ghost-like. It is visibility without tangibility; which is also the definition of a shadow. Therefore a vulgar ghost and a shadow would be the same; because two different things can not properly have the same definition. A *visible substance* without susceptibility of impact, I maintain to be an absurdity. Unless there be an external substance, the bodily eye *can not* see it; therefore, in all such cases, that which is supposed to be seen is, in fact, *not* seen, but is an image of the brain. External objects naturally produce sensation; but here, in truth, sensation produces, as it were, the external object.

In certain states of the nerves, however, I do believe that the eye, although not consciously so directed may, by a slight convulsion, see a portion of the body, as if opposite to it. The part actually seen will by common association seem the whole; and the whole body will then constitute an external object, which explains many stories of persons seeing themselves lying dead. Bishop Berkeley once experienced this. He had the presence of mind to ring the bell, and feel his pulse; keeping his eye still fixed on his own figure right opposite to him. He was in a high fever, and the brain-image died away as the door opened. I observed something very like it once at Grasmere; and was so conscious of the cause, that I told a person what I was experiencing, while the image still remained.

Of course, if the vulgar ghost be really a shadow, there must be some substance of which it is the shadow. These visible and intangible shadows, without substances to cause them, are absurd.

Shedd VI 261

IV. The supernatural in literature

Coleridge valued the power of supernatural imagery to awaken the visionary powers of his readers with its freshness and strangeness. The supernatural engages 'the same activity of mind as in dreaming, that is – an exertion of the fancy in the combination and recombination of familiar objects so as to produce novel and wonderful imagery'. [11] *The purpose of using such imagery is 'to excite a feeling analogous to the supernatural, by awakening the mind's attention from the lethargy of custom'.* [12]

From his Lectures on Literature

(a) On the Arabian Nights

The Asiatic supernatural beings are all produced by imagining an excessive magnitude, or an excessive smallness combined with great power; and the broken associations, which must have given rise to such conceptions, are the sources of the interest which they inspire, as exhibiting, through the working of the imagination, the idea of power in the will. This is delightfully exemplified in the Arabian Nights' Entertainments, and indeed, more or less, in other works of the same kind. In all these there is the same activity of mind as in dreaming, that is – an exertion of the fancy in the combination and recombination of familiar objects so as to produce novel and wonderful imagery. To this must be added that these tales cause no deep feeling of a moral kind – whether of religion or love; but an impulse of motion is communicated to the mind without excitement, and this is the reason of their being so generally read and admired.

MC 193 [*Lects 1808–19* II 191]

From Biographia Literaria

During the first year that Mr. Wordsworth and I were neighbours, our conversations turned frequently on the two cardinal points of poetry, the power of exciting the sympathy of the reader by a faithful adherence to the truth of nature, and the power of giving the interest of novelty by the modifying colours of imagination. The sudden charm which accidents of light and shade, which moonlight or sunset diffused over a known and familiar landscape, appeared to represent the practicability of combining both. These are the poetry of nature. The thought suggested itself – (to which of us I do not recollect) – that a series of poems might be composed of two sorts. In the one, the incidents and agents were to be, in part at least, supernatural; and the excellence aimed at was to consist in the interesting of the affections by the dramatic truth of such emotions, as would naturally accompany such situations, supposing them real. And real in this sense they have been to every human being who, from whatever source of delusion, has at any time believed himself under supernatural agency. For the second class, subjects were to be chosen from ordinary life; the characters and incidents were to be such, as will be found in every village and its vicinity, where there is a meditative and feeling mind to seek after them, or to notice them, when they present themselves.

In this idea originated the plan of the LYRICAL BALLADS; in which it was agreed, that my endeavours should be directed to persons and characters supernatural, or at least romantic; yet so as to transfer from our inward nature a human interest and a semblance of truth sufficient to procure for these shadows of imagination that willing suspension of disbelief for the moment, which constitutes poetic faith. Mr. Wordsworth, on the other hand, was to propose to himself as his object, to give the charm of novelty to things of every day, and to excite a feeling analogous to the supernatural, by awakening the mind's attention from the lethargy of custom, and directing it to the loveliness and the wonders of the world before us; an inexhaustible treasure, but for which, in consequence of the film of familiarity and selfish solicitude we have eyes, yet see not, ears that hear not, and hearts that neither feel nor understand.

Shedd III 364 [*BL (CC)* II 5–7]

From his notebook

In poetry, whether metrical or unbound, the super-natural will be impressive & obtain a mastery over the imagination and feelings, will tend to infect the reader, ~~with~~ and draw him to identify himself with, or substitute himself for, the *Person* of the Drama or Tale, in proportion as it is true *to Nature* – i.e. where the Poet of his free will and judgement does what the believing Narrator of a Supernatural Incident, Apparition or Charm does from ignorance & weakness of mind, – *i.e.* mistake a *Subjective* product (A saw the Ghost of Z) for an objective fact = the Ghost of Z was there to be seen; or by the magnifying & modifying power of Fear and *dreamy* Sensations, and the additive & supplementary <Turn to page 154> interpolations ~~of and~~ of the *creative* Memory and the inferences and comments of the prejudiced Judgement slipt ~~in~~ consciously into & confounded with the *Text* of the actual experience, exaggerates an unusual Natural event or appearance into the miraculous and supernatural.

The Poet must always be in perfect sympathy with the ~~person~~ Subject of the ~~Tale and~~ Narrative – and tell his tale with 'a most believing mind' – but the Tale will be then most impressive for all, when it is so constructed and ~~so~~ particularized with such traits and circumstances, that the Psychologist and thinking Naturalist shall be furnished with the Means of explaining it as a possible fact, by distinguishing and assigning the *Subjective* portion to its true owner,/ –. The Cobold of the Mine far down/ –

CN V 6301 43.37

V. Allegorical visions

Coleridge also used the 'novel and wonderful imagery'[13] *of the super-natural to illustrate complex abstract ideas in prose. Each of these selections requires the reader to dramatically alter their perception, a goal which was aided by the unfamiliarity of the supernatural imagery. The 'allegorical visions' below take the reader on weird visionary journeys of the imagination. Their dark and unsettling imagery is not intended to delight, but rather to fascinate and terrify, and provoke drastic shifts in the reader's perspective.*

In the selection below, a fictitious 'letter from a reader' (which Coleridge wrote himself) invokes supernatural imagery in a disorienting reversal of expectations.

From Biographia Literaria

Dear C.

You ask my opinion concerning your Chapter on the Imagination, both as to the impressions it made on myself, and as to those which I think it will make on the *Public*, i.e., that part of the public, who, from the title of the work and from its forming a sort of intro-duction to a volume of poems, are likely to constitute the great majority of your readers.

As to myself, and stating in the first place the effect on my *understanding*, your opinions and method of argument were not only so *new* to me, but so directly the reverse of all I had ever been accustomed to consider as truth, that even if I had comprehended your premises sufficiently to have admitted them, and had seen the necessity of your conclusions, I should still have been in that state of mind, which in your note [in Chapter IV] you have so ingen-iously evolved, as the antithesis to that in which a man is, when he makes a bull. In your own words, I should have felt as if I had been standing on my head.

The effect on my *feelings*, on the other hand, I cannot better represent, than by supposing myself to have known only our light airy modern chapels of ease, and then for the first time to have been placed, and left alone, in one of our largest Gothic cathedrals in a gusty moonlight night of autumn. 'Now in glimmer, and now in gloom'; often in palpable darkness not without a chilly sensation of terror; then suddenly emerging into broad yet visionary lights with coloured shadows of fantastic shapes yet all decked with holy insignia and mystic symbols; and ever and anon coming out full upon pictures and stone-work images of great men, with whose *names* I was familiar, but which looked upon me with countenances and an expression, the most dissimilar to all I had been in the habit of connecting with those names. Those whom I had been taught to venerate as almost super-human in magnitude of intellect, I found perched in little fret-work niches, as grotesque dwarfs; while the grotesques, in my hitherto belief, stood guarding the high altar with all the characters of Apotheosis. In short, what I had supposed substances were thinned away into shadows, while every where shadows were deepened into substances:

> If substance may be call'd what shadow seem'd,
> For each seem'd either!
>   Milton

Yet after all, I could not but repeat the lines which you had quoted from a MS. poem of your own in the Friend, and applied to a work of Mr. Wordsworth's though with a few of the words altered:

> – An Orphic tale indeed,
> A tale *obscure* of high and passionate thoughts
> To a *strange* music chaunted!

> *Shedd* III 360–1 [*BL (CC)* I 300]

The following selection also strives to reorient the reader through a strange supernatural allegory. Coleridge cleanses the vision of his readers through cathartic, frightening means, revealing that discarding comfortable and worn beliefs is difficult and even potentially traumatic.

From Lay Sermons

AN ALLEGORIC VISION

A feeling of sadness, a peculiar melancholy, is wont to take possession of me alike in spring and in autumn. But in spring it is the melancholy of hope: in autumn it is the melancholy of resignation. As I was journeying on foot through the Apennine, I fell in with a pilgrim in whom the spring and the autumn and the melancholy of both seemed to have combined. In his discourse there were the freshness and the colors of April:

> *Qual ramicel a ramo,*
> *Tal de pensier pensiero*
> *In lui germogliava.*

But as I gazed on his whole form and figure, I bethought me of the not unlovely decays, both of age and of the late season in the stately elm; after the clusters have been plucked from its entwining vines, and the vines are as bands of dried withies around its trunk and branches. Even so there was a memory on his smooth and ample forehead, which blended with the dedication of his steady eyes, that still looked – I know not, whether upward, or far onward, or rather to the line of meeting where the sky rests upon the distance. But how may I express that dimness of abstraction which lay like the flitting tarnish from the breath of a sigh on a silver mirror, and which accorded with the lustre of the pilgrim's eyes, with their slow and reluctant movement, whenever he turned them to any object on the right hand or on the left? It seemed, methought, as if there lay upon the brightness a shadowy presence of disappointments now unfelt, but never forgotten. It was at once the melancholy of hope and of resignation.

We had not long been fellow-travellers, ere a sudden tempest of wind and rain forced us to seek protection in the vaulted doorway of a lone chapelry: and we sat face to face each on the stone bench alongside the low, weather-stained wall, and as close as possible to the massy door.

After a pause of silence: 'Even thus,' said he, 'like two strangers that have fled to the same shelter from the same storm, not seldom do despair and hope meet for the first time in the porch of death!' 'All extremes meet,' I answered; 'but yours was a strange and visionary thought.' 'The better then doth it beseem both the place and me,' he replied. 'From a VISIONARY wilt thou hear a VISION? Mark that vivid flash through this torrent of rain. Fire and water. Even here thy adage holds true, and its truth is the moral of my Vision.' I entreated him to proceed. Sloping his face toward the arch and yet averting his eye from it, he seemed to seek and prepare his words: till listening to the wind that echoed within the hollow edifice, and to the rain without,

> Which stole on his thoughts with its twofold sound,
> The clash hard by and the murmur all round,

He gradually sank away, alike from me and from his own purpose, and amid the gloom of the storm and in the duskiness of that place he sat like an emblem on a rich man's sepulchre, or like a mourner on the sodded grave of an only one, an aged mourner, who is watching the waned moon and sorroweth not. Starting at length from his brief trance of abstraction, with courtesy and an atoning smile he renewed his discourse, and commenced his parable.

During one of those short furlows from the service of the body, which the soul may sometimes obtain even in this its militant state, I found myself in a vast plain, which I immediately knew to be the Valley of Life. It possessed an astonishing diversity of soils: here was a sunny spot, and there a dark one, forming just such a mixture of sunshine and shade, as we may have observed on the mountains' side in an April day, when the thin broken clouds are scattered over heaven. Almost in the very entrance of the valley stood a large and gloomy pile, into which I seemed constrained to enter. Every part of the building was crowded with tawdry ornaments and fantastic deformity. On every window was portrayed, in glaring and inelegant colors, some horrible tale or preternatural incident, so that not a ray of light could enter, untinged by the medium through which it passed. The body of the building was full of people, some of them dancing in and out, in unintelligible figures, with strange ceremonies and antic merriment, while others seemed convulsed with horror, or pining in mad melancholy. Intermingled with these, I observed a number of men, clothed in ceremonial robes, who appeared now to marshal the various groups and to direct their movements; and now with menacing countenances, to drag some reluctant victims to a vast idol, framed of iron bars intercrossed, which formed at the same time an immense cage, and the shape of a human Colossus.

I stood for a while lost in wonder, what these things might mean; when lo! one of the directors came up to me, and with a stern and reproachful look bade me uncover my head; for that the place, in which I had entered, was the temple of the only true religion, in the holier recesses of which the great Goddess personally resided. Himself too he bade me reverence, as the consecrated minister of her rites. Awe-struck by the name of religion, I bowed before the priest, and humbly and earnestly entreated him to conduct me into her presence. He assented. Offerings he took from me, with mystic sprinklings of water and with salt he purified, and with strange sufflations he exorcised me; and then led me through many a dark and winding alley, the dew-damps of which chilled my flesh, and the hollow echoes under my feet, mingled, methought, with moanings, affrighted me. At length we entered a large hall without window, or spiracle, or lamp. The asylum and dormitory it seemed of perennial night; only that the walls were brought to the eye by a number of self-luminous inscriptions in letters of a pale sepulchral light, which held strange neutrality with the darkness, on the verge of which it kept its rayless vigil. I could read them, methought; but though each one of the words taken separately I seemed to understand, yet when I took them in sentences, they were riddles and incomprehensible. As I stood meditating on these hard sayings, my guide thus addressed me: – Read and believe: these are mysteries! At the extremity of the vast hall the Goddess was placed. Her features, blended with darkness, rose out to my view, terrible, yet vacant. I prostrated myself before her, and then retired with my guide, soul-withered, and wondering, and dissatisfied.

As I re-entered the body of the temple, I heard a deep buzz as of discontent. A few whose eyes were bright, and either piercing or steady, and whose ample foreheads, with the weighty bar, ridge-like, above the eyebrows, bespoke observation followed by meditative thought; and a much larger number who were enraged by the severity and insolence of the priests in exacting their offerings, had collected in one tumultuous group, and with a confused cry of 'This is the temple of Superstition!' after much contumely, and turmoil, and cruel maltreatment on all sides, rushed out of the pile: and I, methought, joined them.

We speeded from the temple with hasty steps, and had now nearly gone round half the valley, when we were addressed by a woman, tall beyond the stature of mortals, and with a something more than human in her countenance and mien, which yet by mortals could be only felt, not conveyed by words or intelligibly distinguished. Deep reflection, animated by ardent feelings, was displayed in them; and hope, without its uncertainty, and a something more than all these, which I understood not; but which yet seemed to blend all these into a divine unity of expression. Her garments were white and matronly, and of the simplest texture. We inquired her name. My name, she replied, is Religion.

The more numerous part of our company, affrighted by the very sound, and sore from recent impostures or sorceries, hurried onwards and examined no farther. A few of us, struck by the manifest opposition of her form and manner to those of the living idol, whom we had so recently abjured, agreed to follow her, though with cautious circumspection. She led us to an eminence in the midst of the valley, from the top of which we could command the whole plain, and observe the relation of the different parts of each to the other, and of each to the whole, and of all to each. She then gave us an optic glass which assisted without contradicting our natural vision, and enabled us to see far beyond the limits of the Valley of Life: though our eye even thus assisted permitted us only to behold a light and a glory, but what we could not descry, save only that it *was*, and that it was most glorious.

And now, with the rapid transition of a dream, I had overtaken and rejoined the more numerous party, who had abruptly left us, indignant at the very name of religion. They journeyed on, goading each other with remembrances of past oppressions, and never looking back, till in the eagerness to recede from the temple of Superstition they had rounded the whole circle of the valley. And lo! there faced us the mouth of a vast cavern, at the base of a lofty and almost perpendicular rock, the interior side of which, unknown to them, and unsuspected, formed the extreme and backward wall of the temple. An impatient crowd, we entered the vast and dusky cave, which was the only perforation of the precipice. At the mouth of the cave sate two figures; the first, by her dress and gestures, I knew to be Sensuality; the second form, from the fierceness of his demeanour and the brutal scornfulness of his looks, declared himself to be the monster Blasphemy. He uttered big words, and yet ever and anon I observed that he turned pale at his own courage. We entered. Some remained in the opening of the cave, with the one or the other of its guardians. The rest, and I among them, pressed on till we reached an ample chamber, which seemed the centre of the rock. The climate of the place was unnaturally cold.

In the furthest distance of the chamber sate an old dim-eyed man, poring with a microscope over the *torso* of a statue, which had neither base, nor feet, nor head; but on its breast was carved, NATURE! To this he continually applied his glass, and seemed enraptured with the various inequalities which it rendered visible on the seemingly polished surface of the marble. Yet evermore was this delight and triumph followed by expressions of hatred, and vehement railing against a Being, who yet, he assured us, had no existence. This mystery suddenly recalled to me what I had read in the holiest recess of the temple of Superstition. The old man spoke in divers tongues, and continued to utter other and most strange mysteries. Among the rest he talked much and vehemently concerning an infinite series of causes and effects, which he explained to be – a string of blind men, the last of whom caught hold of the skirt of the one before him, he of the next, and so on till they were all out of sight; and that they all walked infallibly straight, without making one false step, though all were alike blind. Methought I borrowed courage from surprise, and asked him – 'Who then is at the head to guide them?' He looked at me with ineffable contempt, not unmixed with an angry suspicion, and then replied – 'No one; – the string of blind men goes on forever without any beginning; for although one blind man can not move without stumbling, yet infinite blindness supplies the want of sight.' I burst into laughter, which instantly turned to terror; – for as he started forward in a rage, I caught a glance of him from behind; and lo! I beheld a monster bi-form and Janus-headed, in the hinder shape and face of which I instantly recognized the dread countenance of Superstition – and in terror I awoke.

Shedd VI 154–9 [*LS (CC)* 131–7]

In the next selection, Coleridge uses another elaborate allegory to distinguish between two types of mystics. It is interesting to note that in all three of these visions, darkness and the deceptive play of moonlight represent errors in interpretation. Moonlight, which is Coleridge's favourite symbol for the modifying power of the imagination, dramatically alters vision, both inner and outer.

From Aids to Reflection

MYSTICS AND MYSTICISM

Antinous. – 'What do you call Mysticism? And do you use the word in a good or in a bad sense?'

Nous. – 'In the latter only; as far, at least, as we are now concerned with it. When a man refers to *inward feelings* and *experiences*, of which mankind at large are not conscious, as evidence of the truth of any opinion – such a man I call a Mystic: and the grounding of any theory or belief on accidents and anomalies of individual sensations or fancies, and the use of peculiar terms invented, or perverted from their ordinary significations, for the purpose of expressing these *idiosyncracies* and pretended facts of interior consciousness, I name Mysticism. Where the error consists simply in the Mystic's attaching to these anomalies of his individual temperament the character of *Reality*, and in receiving them as permanent truths, having a subsistence in the Divine Mind, though revealed to himself alone; but entertains this persuasion without demanding or expecting the same faith in his neighbours – I should regard it as a species of ENTHUSIASM, always indeed to be deprecated, but yet capable of co-existing with many excellent qualities both of head and heart ...'

We will return to the harmless species – the enthusiastic Mystics; – a species that may again be subdivided into two ranks. And it will not be other than germane to the subject, if I endeavour to describe them in a sort of allegory, or parable. Let us imagine a poor pilgrim benighted in a wilderness or desert, and pursuing his way in the starless dark with a lantern in his hand. Chance or his happy genius leads him to an *oasis* or natural garden, such as in the creations of my youthful fancy I supposed Enos the Child of Cain to have found. And here, hungry and thirsty, the way-wearied man rests at a fountain; and the taper of his lantern throws its light on an over-shadowing tree, a boss of snow-white blossoms, through which the green and growing fruits peeped, and the ripe golden fruitage glowed. Deep, vivid, and faithful are the impressions, which the lovely imagery comprised within the scanty circle of light makes and leaves on his memory. But scarcely has he eaten on the fruits and drunk of the fountain, ere scared by the roar and howl from the desert he hurries forward: and as he passes with hasty steps through grove and glade, shadows and imperfect beholdings and vivid fragments of things distinctly seen blend with the past and present shapings of his brain. Fancy modifies sight. His dreams transfer their forms to real objects; and these lend a substance and an *outness* to his dreams. Apparitions greet him; and when at a distance from this enchanted land, and on a different track, the dawn of day discloses to him a caravan, a troop of his fellow-men, his memory, which is itself half fancy, is interpolated afresh by every attempt to recall, connect, and *piece out* his recollections. His narration is received as a madman's tale. He shrinks from the rude laugh and contemptuous sneer, and retires into himself. Yet the craving for sympathy, strong in proportion to the intensity of his convictions, impels him to unbosom himself to abstract auditors; and the poor quietist becomes a penman, and, all too poorly stocked for the writer's trade, he borrows his phrases and figures from the only writings to which he has had access, the sacred books of his religion. And thus I shadow out the enthusiastic Mystic of the first sort; at the head of which stands the illuminated Teutonic theosopher and shoemaker, honest Jacob Behmen, born near Gorlitz, in Upper Lusatia, in the 17th of our Elizabeth's reign, and who died in the 22nd of her successor's.

To delineate a Mystic of the second and higher order, we need only endow our pilgrim with equal gifts of nature, but these developed and displayed by all the aids and arts of education and favorable fortune. *He* is on his way to the Mecca of his ancestral and national faith, with a well-guarded and numerous procession of merchants and fellow-pilgrims, on the established track. At the close of day the caravan has halted: the full moon rises on the desert: and he strays forth alone, out of sight but to no unsafe distance; and chance leads *him*, too, to the same oasis or islet of verdure on the sea of sand. He wanders at leisure in its maze of beauty and sweetness, and thrids his way through the odorous and flowering thickets into open spots of greenery, and discovers statues and memorial characters, grottos, and refreshing caves. But the Moonshine, the imaginative Poesy of Nature, spreads its soft shadowy charm over all, conceals distances, and magnifies heights, and modifies relations; and fills up vacuities with its own whiteness, counterfeiting substance; and where the dense shadows lie, makes solidity imitate hollowness; and gives to all objects a tender visionary hue and softening. Interpret the moonlight and the shadows as the peculiar genius and sensibility of the individual's own spirit; and here you have the other sort; a Mystic, an enthusiast of a nobler breed – a Fenelon. But the residentiary, or the frequent visitor of the favored spot, who has scanned its beauties by steady daylight, and mastered its true proportions and lineaments, – he will discover that both pilgrims have indeed been there. *He* will know, that the delightful dream, which the latter tells, is a dream of truth; and that even in the bewildered tale of the former there is truth mingled with the dream.

Shedd I 353–6 [*AR (CC)* 388–94]

VI. Opium reveries

The narcotic effects of opium could induce seemingly supernatural perceptions, including distortions of time and space on vast scales, hallucinations of demons, ghosts and angels, acute feelings of despair and melancholy, and vivid dreams and nightmares. In the following two poems, we see two extremes of supernatural visions induced by opium, from the ecstatic to the demonic.

'Kubla Khan' is unmatched in its visionary and hallucinatory splendour. The elaborate preparatory note to the poem also yields interesting insights into the altered opium-induced state in which the poem was purportedly composed.

'Kubla Khan' (1798)

OF THE FRAGMENT OF KUBLA KHAN OR, A VISION IN A DREAM, A FRAGMENT

The following fragment is here published at the request of a poet of great and deserved celebrity [Lord Byron], and, as far as the Author's own opinions are concerned, rather as a psychological curiosity, than on the ground of any supposed *poetic* merits.

In the summer of the year 1797, the Author, then in ill health, had retired to a lonely farm-house between Porlock and Linton, on the Exmoor confines of Somerset and Devonshire. In consequence of a light indisposition, an anodyne had been prescribed, from the effects of which he fell asleep in his chair at the moment that he was reading the following sentence, or words of the same substance, in 'Purchas's Pilgrimage': 'Here the Khan Kubla commanded a palace to be built, and a stately garden thereunto. And thus ten miles of fertile ground were inclosed with a wall.' The Author continued for about three hours in a profound sleep, at least of the external senses, during which time he has the most vivid confidence, that he could not have composed less than from two to three hundred lines; if that indeed can be called composition in which all the images rose up before him as *things*, with a parallel production of the correspondent expressions, without any sensation of consciousness of effort. On awaking he appeared to himself to have a distinct recollection of the whole, and taking his pen, ink, and paper, instantly and eagerly wrote down the lines that are here preserved. At this moment he was unfortunately called out by a person on business from Porlock, and detained by him above an hour, and on his return

to his room, found, to his no small surprise and mortification, that
though he still retained some vague and dim recollection of the
general purport of the vision, yet, with the exception of some eight
or ten scattered lines and images, all the rest had passed away like
the images of the surface of a stream into which a stone has been
cast, but, alas! without the after restoration of the latter!

> Then all the charm
> Is broken – all that phantom-world so fair
> Vanishes, and a thousand circlets spread,
> And each mis-shape['s] the other. Stay awhile,
> Poor youth! who scarcely dar'st lift up thine eyes –
> The stream will soon renew its smoothness, soon
> The visions will return! And lo, he stays,
> And soon the fragments dim of lovely forms
> Come trembling back, unite, and now once more
> The pool becomes a mirror.
> [From *The Picture; or, the Lover's Resolution*, 11. 91–100.]

Yet from the still surviving recollections in his mind, the Author has
frequently purposed to finish for himself what had been originally,
as it were, given to him. Σαμερον αδιον ασω [Αὔριον ἄδιον ἄσω
1834]: but the to-morrow is yet to come.

As a contrast to this vision, I have annexed a fragment of a very
different character, describing with equal fidelity the dream of pain
and disease.

KUBLA KHAN

> In Xanadu did Kubla Khan
> A stately pleasure-dome decree:
> Where Alph, the sacred river, ran
> Through caverns measureless to man
>   Down to a sunless sea.
> So twice five miles of fertile ground
> With walls and towers were girdled round:
> And here were gardens bright with sinuous rills,
> Where blossomed many an incense-bearing tree;
> And here were forests ancient as the hills,
> Enfolding sunny spots of greenery.
>
> But oh! that deep romantic chasm which slanted
> Down the green hill athwart a cedarn cover!

A savage place! as holy and enchanted
As e'er beneath a waning moon was haunted
By woman wailing for her demon-lover!
And from this chasm, with ceaseless turmoil seething,
As if this earth in fast thick pants were breathing,
A mighty fountain momently was forced:
Amid whose swift half-intermitted burst
Huge fragments vaulted like rebounding hail,
Or chaffy grain beneath the thresher's flail:
And 'mid these dancing rocks at once and ever
It flung up momently the sacred river.
Five miles meandering with a mazy motion
Through wood and dale the sacred river ran,
Then reached the caverns measureless to man,
And sank in tumult to a lifeless ocean:
And 'mid this tumult Kubla heard from far
Ancestral voices prophesying war!

The shadow of the dome of pleasure
Floated midway on the waves;
Where was heard the mingled measure
From the fountain and the caves.
It was a miracle of rare device,
A sunny pleasure-dome with caves of ice!

A damsel with a dulcimer
In a vision once I saw:
It was an Abyssinian maid,
And on her dulcimer she played,
Singing of Mount Abora.
Could I revive within me
Her symphony and song,
To such a deep delight 'twould win me,
That with music loud and long,
I would build that dome in air,
That sunny dome! those caves of ice!
And all who heard should see them there,
And all should cry, Beware! Beware!
His flashing eyes, his floating hair!
Weave a circle round him thrice,
And close your eyes with holy dread,

For he on honey-dew hath fed,
And drunk the milk of Paradise

CPW I 295–8 [*PW* I 509–14]

*While 'Kubla Khan' presents an ecstatic vision of the natural and super-
natural worlds, the following poem delves into the darkest supernatural
visions induced by opium. In addition to nightmares brought on by his
opium use, Coleridge was plagued by wracking guilt that he could not
break his addiction.*

'The Pains of Sleep' (1803)

Ere on my bed my limbs I lay,
It hath not been my use to pray
With moving lips or bended knees;
But silently, by slow degrees,
My spirit I to Love compose,
In humble trust mine eye-lids close,
With reverential resignation,
No wish conceived, no thought exprest,
Only a sense of supplication;
A sense o'er all my soul imprest
That I am weak, yet not unblest,
Since in me, round me, every where
Eternal Strength and Wisdom are.

But yester-night I prayed aloud
In anguish and in agony,
Up-starting from the fiendish crowd
Of shapes and thoughts that tortured me:
A lurid light, a trampling throng,
Sense of intolerable wrong,
And who I scorned, those only strong!
Thirst of revenge, the powerless will
Still baffled, and yet burning still!
Desire with loathing strangely mixed
On wild or hateful objects fixed.
Fantastic passions! maddening brawl!
And shame and terror over all!
Deeds to be hid which were not hid,
Which all confused I could not know,

Whether I suffered, or I did:
For all seemed guilt, remorse or woe,
My own or others still the same
Life-stifling fear, soul-stifling shame.

So two nights passed: the night's dismay
Saddened and stunned the coming day.
Sleep, the wide blessing, seemed to me
Distemper's worst calamity.
The third night, when my own loud scream
Had waked me from the fiendish dream,
O'ercome with sufferings strange and wild,
I wept as I had been a child;
And having thus by tears subdued
My anguish to a milder mood,
Such punishments, I said, were due
To natures deepliest stained with sin, –
For aye entempesting anew
The unfathomable hell within,
The horror of their deeds to view,
To know and loathe, yet wish and do!
Such griefs with such men well agree,
But wherefore, wherefore fall on me?
To be beloved is all I need,
And whom I love, I love indeed.

CPW I 389–91 [*PW* II 753–5]

VII. *Lyrical Ballads*

The two poets' collaboration on Lyrical Ballads, *in which Wordsworth would summon 'the truth of nature' while Coleridge would write about 'persons and characters supernatural' has already been discussed.*[14] *Coleridge's supernatural poems evidence the use of the weird, the terrifying and the novel to awaken the visionary powers of the reader.*

'The Rime of the Ancient Mariner' is without doubt his greatest supernatural poem. Thomas De Quincey remarked that Coleridge was contemplating writing a poem 'on delirium, confounding its own dream-scenery with external things, and connected with the imagery of high latitudes'.[15] *In the later editions of* Lyrical Ballads *the poem was*

subtitled 'A Poet's Reverie', linking it with 'Kubla Khan' as another poem about altered states of supernatural reverie.

Selections from 'The Rime of the Ancient Mariner' (1797)

The epigraph of the poem, from Thomas Burnet's Archaeologiae Philosphicae, *further sets the stage for supernatural vision:*

> Facile credo, plures esse Naturas invisibiles quam visibiles in rerum universitate. Sed horum omnium familiam quis nobis enarrabit? et gradus et cognationes et discrimina et singulorum munera? Quid agunt? quae loca habitant? Harum rerum notitiam semper ambivit ingenium humanum, nunquam attigit. Juvat, interea, non diffiteor, quandoque in animo, tanquam in tabulâ, majoris et melioris mundi imaginem contemplari: ne mens assuefacta hodiernae vitae minutiis se contrahat nimis, et tota subsidat in pusillas cogitationes. Sed veritati interea invigilandum est, modusque servandus, ut certa ab incertis, diem a nocte, distinguamus. – T. BURNET *Archaeol. Phil.* p. 68[16]

The unnatural strangeness and grotesqueness of the imagery underscores the senseless horror of killing a friendly albatross, who came to the sailors' call 'as if it were a Christian soul'.[17]

> ... All in a hot and copper sky,
> The bloody Sun, at noon,
> Right up above the mast did stand,
> No bigger than the Moon.
>
> Day after day, day after day,
> We stuck, nor breath nor motion;
> As idle as a painted ship
> Upon a painted ocean.
>
> Water, water, every where
> And all the boards did shrink;
> Water, water, every where,
> Nor any drop to drink.
>
> The very deep did rot: O Christ!
> That ever this should be!
> Yea, slimy things did crawl with legs
> Upon the slimy sea.
>
> About, about, in reel and rout
> The death-fires danced at night;

The water, like a witch's oils,
Burnt green, and blue and white.

And some in dreams assuréd were
Of the Spirit that plagued us so;
Nine fathom deep he had followed us
From the land of mist and snow ...

The 'Night-mare Life-in-Death', who gambles for the souls of the stranded
sailors, is one of Coleridge's most haunting supernatural creations. Lurid
and unnatural colours dominate the scene:

... The western wave was all a-flame.
The day was well nigh done!
Almost upon the western wave
Rested the broad bright Sun;
When that strange shape drove suddenly
Betwixt us and the Sun.

And straight the Sun was flecked with bars,
(Heaven's Mother send us grace!)
As if through a dungeon-grate he peered
With broad and burning face.

Alas! (thought I, and my heart beat loud)
How fast she nears and nears!
Are those *her* sails that glance in the Sun,
Like restless gossameres?

Are those *her* ribs through which the Sun
Did peer, as through a grate?
And is that Woman all her crew?
Is that a Death? and are there two?
Is Death that woman's mate?

Her lips were red, *her* looks were free,
Her locks were yellow as gold:
Her skin was as white as leprosy,
The Night-mare Life-in-Death was she,
Who thicks man's blood with cold.

The naked hulk alongside came,
And the twain were casting dice;
'The game is done! I've won, I've won!'
Quoth she, and whistles thrice ...

The corpses of the dead crew, who are mysteriously reanimated to work
the ship, provide the most memorable supernatural images in the poem.

... The many men, so beautiful!
And they all dead did lie:
And a thousand thousand slimy things
Lived on; and so did I.

I looked upon the rotting sea,
And drew my eyes away;
I looked upon the rotting deck,
And there the dead men lay.

I looked to heaven, and tried to pray;
But or ever a prayer had gusht,
A wicked whisper came, and made
My heart as dry as dust.

I closed my lids, and kept them close,
And the balls like pulses beat;
For the sky and the sea, and the sea and the sky
Lay like a load on my weary eye,
And the dead were at my feet.

The cold sweat melted from their limbs,
Nor rot nor reek did they:
The look with which they looked on me
Had never passed away.

An orphan's curse would drag to hell
A spirit from on high;
But oh! more horrible than that
Is the curse in a dead man's eye!
Seven days, seven nights, I saw that curse,
And yet I could not die ...

... The moving Moon went up the sky,
And no where did abide:
Softly she was going up,
And a star or two beside –

Her beams bemocked the sultry main,
Like April hoar-frost spread;
But where the ship's huge shadow lay,

The charméd water burnt alway
A still and awful red.

Beyond the shadow of the ship,
I watched the water-snakes:
They moved in tracks of shining white,
And when they reared, the elfish light
Fell off in hoary flakes.

Within the shadow of the ship
I watched their rich attire:
Blue, glossy green, and velvet black,
They coiled and swam; and every track
Was a flash of golden fire.[18]

O happy living things! no tongue
Their beauty might declare:
A spring of love gushed from my heart,
And I blessed them unaware:
Sure my kind saint took pity on me,
And I blessed them unaware.

The self-same moment I could pray;
And from my neck so free
The Albatross fell off, and sank
Like lead into the sea ...

In the final scene, out of the shadows cast by moonlight, a 'seraph-band'
of supernatural spirits sweep through the bay. The demonic and lurid
colours are replaced by the purity of white:

... The harbour-bay was clear as glass,
So smoothly it was strewn!
And on the bay the moonlight lay,
And the shadow of the Moon.

The rock shone bright, the kirk no less,
That stands above the rock:
The moonlight steeped in silentness
The steady weathercock.

And the bay was white with silent light,
Till rising from the same,
Full many shapes, that shadows were,
In crimson colours came.

A little distance from the prow
Those crimson shadows were:
I turned my eyes upon the deck –
Oh, Christ! what saw I there!

Each corse lay flat, lifeless and flat,
And, by the holy rood!
A man all light, a seraph-man,
On every corse there stood.

This seraph-band, each waved his hand:
It was a heavenly sight!
They stood as signals to the land,
Each one a lovely light;

This seraph-band, each waved his hand,
No voice did they impart –
No voice; but oh! the silence sank
Like music on my heart ...

CPW I 187–209 [*PW* (CC) I 365–411]

When writing his next poem, Coleridge strove to represent 'witchery by daylight'[19] *by evoking a state of trance and delirium; Christabel's failure to recognize the treacherous Geraldine as a threat suggests that perception in this poem is altered and distorted by supernatural forces. As in 'The Ancient Mariner', moonlight, 'the imaginative Poesy of Nature',*[20] *casts an eerie and visionary light:*

Selections from 'Christabel'

... Is the night chilly and dark?
The night is chilly, but not dark.
The thin grey cloud is spread on high,
It covers but not hides the sky.
The moon is behind, and at the full,
And yet she looks both small and dull.
The night is chill, the cloud is gray:
'Tis a month before the month of May,
And the Spring comes slowly up this way ...

The strange woman who suddenly appears possesses a weird and unearthly beauty:

... The lady sprang up suddenly,
The lovely lady, Christabel!
It moaned as near, as near can be,
But what it is she cannot tell. –
On the other side it seems to be,
Of the huge, broad-breasted, old oak tree.

The night is chill; the forest bare;
Is it the wind that moaneth bleak?
There is not wind enough in the air
To move away the ringlet curl
From the lovely lady's cheek –
There is not wind enough to twirl
The one red leaf, the last of its clan,
That dances as often as dance it can,
Hanging so light, and hanging so high,
On the topmost twig that looks up at the sky.

Hush, beating heart of Christabel!
Jesu, Maria, shield her well!

She folded her arms beneath her cloak,
And stole to the other side of the oak.
     What sees she there?

There she sees a damsel bright,
Drest in a silken robe of white,
That shadowy in the moonlight shone:
The neck that made that white robe wan,
Her stately neck, and arms were bare;
Her blue-veined feet unsandal'd were;
And wildly glittered here and there
The gems entangled in her hair.
I guess, 'twas frightful there to see
A lady so richly clad as she –
     Beautiful exceedingly! ...

The 'glimmer' and 'gloom' of moonlight creates strange and deceptive effects:

... Sweet Christabel her feet doth bare,
And jealous of the listening air
They steal their way from stair to stair,

Now in glimmer, and now in gloom,
And now they pass the Baron's room,
As still as death, with stifled breath!
And now have reached her chamber door;
And now doth Geraldine press down
The rushes of the chamber floor.

The moon shines dim in the open air,
And not a moonbeam enters here.
But they without its light can see
The chamber carved so curiously,
Carved with figures strange and sweet,
All made out of the carver's brain,
For a lady's chamber meet:
The lamp with twofold silver chain
Is fastened to an angel's feet ...

*Under the sway of Geraldine's demonic power, Christabel is overpowered
by 'a dizzy Trance':*

... A snake's small eye blinks dull and shy;
And the lady's eyes they shrunk in her head,
Each shrunk up to a serpent's eye,
And with somewhat of malice, and more of dread,
At Christabel she look'd askance! –
One moment – and the sight was fled!
But Christabel in dizzy trance
Stumbling on the unsteady ground
Shuddered aloud, with a hissing sound;
And Geraldine again turned round,
And like a thing, that sought relief,
Full of wonder and full of grief,
She rolled her large bright eyes divine
Wildly on Sir Leoline.

The maid, alas! her thoughts are gone
She nothing sees – no sight but one!
The maid, devoid of guile and sin,
I know not how, in fearful wise,
So deeply had she drunken in
That look, those shrunken serpent eyes,
That all her features were resigned

To this sole image in her mind:
And passively did imitate
That look of dull and treacherous hate!
And thus she stood, in dizzy trance,
Still picturing that look askance
With forced unconscious sympathy
Full before her father's view –
As far as such a look could be
In eyes so innocent and blue!

And when the trance was o'er, the maid
Paused awhile, and inly prayed:
Then falling at the Baron's feet,
'By my mother's soul do I entreat
That thou this woman send away!'
She said: and more she could not say:
For what she knew she could not tell,
O'er-mastered by the mighty spell ...

CPW I 215–36 [*PW (CC)* I 483–502]

Notes

1 *Shedd* II 134–6 [*F (CC)* I 145]
2 *Shedd* II 134–6 [*F (CC)* I 145]
3 At the end of the first volume of *Biographia Literaria*, Coleridge discusses a 'critical essay on the uses of the Supernatural in poetry and the principles that regulate its introduction' which was supposed to be prefixed to 'The Rime of the Ancient Mariner'; the essay either was never written or has not survived. *BL (CC)* I 306 and 306n.
4 Jakob Böhme (1575–1624) whose name was spelled various ways by Coleridge, was an untutored cobbler who wrote a series of books on mystical theology. Emanuel Swedenborg (1688–1772) was a Swedish mystic who believed he could communicate with spirits and angels.
5 *CLE* I 16–17 [*CL* I 354]
6 In *Anima Poetæ: from the unpublished notebooks of Samuel Taylor Coleridge*, ed. E.H. Coleridge (London: Heinemann, 1895) 8 4.7 the quotation continues 'In the dim light London appeared to be a huge place of sepulchres through which hosts of spirits were gliding.' This was not included in the main selection: *Anima Poetæ* is not reliable, because of drastic and sometimes inaccurate changes E.H. Coleridge made to the text.
7 For more on Coleridge's opium addiction, see Molly Lefebure, *Samuel Taylor Coleridge: A Bondage of Opium* (New York: Stein and Day, 1974)

and Norman Fruman, *Coleridge: The Damaged Archangel* (New York: G. Braziller, 1971).

8 *CLE* II 729 [*CL* V 391–2]

9 *Shedd* II 134–6 [*F (CC)* I 145]

10 *Shedd* II 134–6 [*F (CC)* I 145]

11 *MC* 193 [*Lects 1808–19* II 191]

12 *Shedd* III 364 [*BL (CC)* II 5]

13 *MC* 193 [*Lects 1808–19* II 191]

14 *Shedd* III 364 [*BL (CC)* II 5]

15 *The Collected Writings of Thomas De Quincey*, ed. David Masson. 14 vols. (Edinburgh: 1899–90) II 145.

16 This epigraph translates 'I can easily believe, that there are more Invisible than Visible Beings in the Universe; but who will declare to us the Family of all these, and acquaint us with the Agreements, Differences, and peculiar Talents which are to be found among them? It is true, human Wit has always desired a Knowledge of these Things, though it has never yet attained it. I will own that it is very profitable, sometimes to contemplate in the Minds as in a Draught, the Image of the greater and better World; lest the Soul being accustomed to the Trifles of this present Life, should contract itself too much, and altogether rest in mean Cogitations; but, in the mean Time, we must take Care to keep to the Truth, and observe Moderation, that we may distinguish certain from uncertain Things, and Day from Night' *PW (CC)* II 371.

17 *CPW* I 189. Coleridge notes an incident on his journey to Malta in May 1804 that was probably the inspiration for the albatross's fate: 'Hawk with ruffled Feathers resting on the Bowsprit – Now shot at & yet did not move – how fatigued – a third time it made a gyre, a short circuit, & returned again/ 5 times it was thus shot at / left the Vessel/ flew to another/ & I heard firing, now here, now there/ & nobody shot it/ but probably it perished from fatigue, & the attempt to rest upon the wave! – Poor Hawk! O Strange Lust of Murder in Man! – It is not cruelty/ it is mere non-feeling from non-thinking.' *CN* II 2090 15.56

18 It is interesting to note Coleridge's notebook entry at sea in 1804, depicting water life without the 'modifying colours of the imagination': 'The path from the Shore till within a good Stone throw of the Vessel thickly swarming with insect life, all busy-swarming in the path, their swarming makes – but within the Shadow of the Ship it was – scattered at distances – scattered Os, rapidly uncoiling into Serpent spirals – O how slow a word is rapidly to express the Life & time-mocking Motion of that Change, always O's before, always Spirals, coiling, uncoiling, being' *CN* II 2070 15.37.

19 *TT (CC)* I 410

20 *Shedd* I 353–6 [*AR (CC)* 388]

Chapter Five

Philosophical Vision: Solving 'The Riddle of the World'[1]

The final two chapters of *Nature and Vision* detail Coleridge's gradual turn away from envisioning the outward forms of nature, and his search instead for an intellectual framework for nature and spirit. Many events contributed to this gradual shift from literature to metaphysics, including his opium addition, financial problems, marital difficulties and his falling out with Wordsworth.[2] Although attention to objective and artistic visions of nature decreases in his later years, Coleridge never wholly abandoned it. If anything, he became even more dedicated to discovering the relation of nature to the divine in philosophy and theology.

Coleridge's philosophical writing is fraught with contentious issues. First, there is the issue of plagiarism – and his alleged photographic memory: in works like the *Biographia Literaria* large sections of Schelling are lifted almost word for word without due credit, for example.[3] Secondly, when viewed through a strictly philosophical lens, Coleridge misinterpreted and distorted certain philosophical sources, especially Kant.[4] Finally, another intellectual proclivity complicated his philosophical writing: the insatiable desire to fuse various diverse systems of thought, such as Christian metaphysics, British mechanism, German idealism, scientific theories of *Naturphilosophie*, and Platonism.[5] Striving for a unified thread connecting these vastly different philosophical sources was admirable but also doomed to failure. However, for the purposes of this volume, Coleridge's philosophical speculations illustrate one concept very clearly: his dedication to the idea of cultivating philosophical vision.

Coleridge disliked extremes of all kinds, including philosophical extremes. In particular he refused to subscribe to a simplistic explanation of nature, either as a 'mass of *little things*'[6] in a mechanistic universe, or a natural world that disappeared entirely in pure idealism. He envisioned transcending these poles to solve 'the Riddle of the World', which he claimed could never be solved 'by drawing a circle, that can never open, around it'.[7] If creating such a system was beyond Coleridge's philosophical capacity, *imagining* and *hoping for* such a system was not.

Thus we arrive at the importance of vision. Through the cleansing of perception and cultivation of philosophical vision, Coleridge believed that the true relation of nature and spirit could be discovered. This chapter investigates various modes of philosophical vision, such as the creation of proper definitions and terminology, which lead to clearness of thought; the distinguishing between different faculties of mind to establish their capacities and limits; the cultivation of scientific theory to complement philosophy, and the training of the mind according to 'principles of method'. All of the human faculties, if properly engaged and pursued to their ends, could potentially illuminate the relationship of the spiritual and natural worlds.

I. 'Eternal universal mystery':[8] – the one and the many

A central philosophical question that Coleridge wrestled with throughout his life was the question of 'how the one can be many'.[9] *He instinctively believed in a spiritual unity of all things, yet he also wished to account for the myriad multiplicity of the natural world. The following selections reveal how compelling this conundrum of the finite and infinite was for him.*

From his notebook, October 1803

Poem on Spirit – or on Spinoza – I would make a pilgrimage to the Deserts of Arabia to find the man who could make understand how the *one can be many!* Eternal universal mystery! It seems as if it were impossible; yet it *is* – & it is every where! – It is indeed a contradiction *in Terms*: and only in Terms! – It is the co presence of Feeling & Life, limitless by their very essence, with Form, by its very essence limited – determinate – definite. –

CN I 1561 21.281

From a marginal note on Johann Christian Heinroth, Lehrbuch der Anthropologie

But in fact it is demonstrably impossible, that the Riddle of the World should be solved by a Philosophy, which commences by drawing a circle, that can never open, around it; and which therefore must for ever stagger to and fro between two intolerable Positions – first, an absolute Identity, that monopolizing all *very* Being leaves only a Universe of mere Relations without focuses, to which they refer – i.e. when the Looking-glasses are themselves only Reflections. 2. A real Nature, in which Potential Being is a the bona fide Antecedent to all actual Being, and every higher Power is the Creature and Product of the lower – all therefore of the lowest.

CM (CC) II 1018

From his notebook, March 1811

What a swarm of Thoughts & Feelings, endlessly minute fragments & as it were representations of all preceding & embryos of all future Thought lie ~~compact fused & small~~ compact in any one moment – So in a single drop of water the microscope discovers, what motions, what tumult, what wars, what pursuits, what stratagems, what a circle-dance of Death & Life, Death hunting Life & Life renewed & invigorated by Death – the whole world seems here, in a many-meaning cypher – What if our existence was but that moment! – What an unintelligible affrightful Riddle, what a chaos of ~~dark tailless~~ dark limbs & trunk, tailless, headless, nothing begun & nothing ended, would it not be! And yet scarcely more than that other moment of 50 or 60 years, were that our all! each part throughout infinite diminution adapted to some other, and yet the whole means to nothing – ends every where, and yet an end no where. –

CN III 4057 18.285

From a marginal note on Johann Jahn, Appendix Hermeneuticae Seu Exercitationes Exegeticae

Take an Acorn – and consider it in its successive growth as the Object of Watchful Attention. – It is *one* – but lo! it is becoming many – Nay, it still remains One – &c &c till at length the full Idea of the Oak is mastered – the original *Unity* becoming more & more intense, as the Distinctity becomes apparent.

CM(CC) III 102

From his notebook, October 1803

But there is no *all*, in creation – It is composed of Infinites – & the Imagination bewildered by heaping Infinites on Infinites, & wearying of demanding increase of number to a number which it conceives already infin., ~~great~~ deserted by Images, and mocked by words, whose sole Substance is the inward sense of Difficulty that accompanies all our notions of infinity applied to number, turns with delight to distinct Images, & clear Ideas – contemplates *a World*, an harmonious System where an infinity of Kinds subsist each in a multitude of Individuals apportionate to its Kind in conformity to Laws existing in the divine Nature – & therefore in the nature of Things. We cannot indeed *prove* this in any other way than by finding it as impossible to deny omniform, as eternal, agency to God – by finding it impossible to conceive that an omniscient Being should not have a distinct Idea of finite Beings, or that distinct Ideas in the mind of God should be without the perfection of real Existence – i.e. imperfecti~~on~~ <But> This ~~indeed~~ is a proof, subtle indeed, ~~but so is~~ yet not more so than the difficulty. The intellect that can stand the one can understand the other, if his vices do not prevent him. Admit for a moment, that 'to conceive' is = with creation in the divine nature, synonimous with 'to beget', (a feeling of which has given to Marriage a mysterious sanctity & sacramental significance in the mind of many great & good men). Admit this, and all difficulty ceases – all Tumult is hushed – all is clear & beautiful – / We sit in the Dark, but each by the side of his little Fire in his own group, & lo! the summit of the distant mountain is smitten with Light – all night long it has dwelt there – & we look at it, & know that the Sun is not extinguished/ yea, that he is elsewhere bright and vivifying – that he is coming to us, to make our fires needless – yet even now that our Cold & Darkness are so called only in comparison with the Heat & Light of the Coming Day/ never wholly deserted of the Rays. – Ask it as a Duty to choose Good rather than evil – even tho' there were a choice. –

CN I 1619 21.377

II. Definitions of nature and spirit

Famous for his coinages of words, Coleridge felt that the proper use of terms is essential to clear thinking: 'The office of philosophical disquisition *consists in just* distinction ... *In order to obtain adequate notions of any truth, we must intellectually separate its distinguishable parts; and this is the technical* process *of philosophy.*'[10] *Cultivating philosophic modes of vision required careful definitions and distinctions: the selections below present Coleridge's attempts to philosophically define nature and spirit.*

From Philosophical Lectures

I proceed then to the definitions.

First, that which appears by weight, or what in chemistry is called ponderable substance, is in philosophic language Body.

Second, that which appears, but not by weight, or the imponderable substance, is Matter. (Thus sunshine we should not in common language call a body, though we might not hesitate to call it a material phaenomenon; but the painter alludes to a *body* of sunshine, because he alludes to the body laid on to produce the resemblance.)

Thirdly, that which does not appear, which has no outwardness, but must be either known or inferred, but cannot be directly perceived, we call spirit or power.

Fourthly, in speaking of the world without us as distinguished from ourselves, the aggregate of phenomena ponderable and imponderable, is called nature in the passive sense, – in the language of the old schools *natura naturata* – while the sum or aggregate of the powers inferred as the sufficient causes of the former (which by Aristotle and his followers were called the substantial forms) is nature in the active sense, or *natura naturans*.

Fifthly, on the other hand, when reflecting on ourselves as intelligences and therefore individualizing spiritual powers, that which affirms its own existence and whether mediately or immediately that of other beings, we call Mind. I believe, if you ask yourselves, you will find that is the strict sense which you have been accustomed consciously or unconsciously to attach to the word.

Lastly, when we contradistinguish the Mind or the percipient power from that which it perceives, the former has been (very conveniently, I think) entitled the subject and the latter the object.

Hence the mind may be defined as a subject which has its own object. And hence those who attribute a reality to bodies and to material phenomena, independent of the mind that perceives them, and yet assert equally an independent reality of the mind itself, namely those who believe in both immaterial and corporeal substances, or in the language of the day, in soul and body both, would define the body as merely and purely objective; while an idealist would declare the material and corporeal world to be wholly subjective, that is, to exist only as far as it is perceived. In other words, he, the idealist, concedes a real existence to one of the two terms only – to the *natura naturans*, in Berkeley's language, to God, and to the finite minds on which it acts, the *natura naturata*, or the bodily world, being the result, even as the tune between the wind and the Aeolian harp. I remember when I was yet young this fancy struck me wonderfully, and here are some verses I wrote on the subject:

> 'And what if all of animated nature
> Be but organic Harps diversely framed
> That tremble into thought, as o'er them sweeps
> Plastic and vast, one intellectual Breeze
> At once Soul of each and God of all.'

PL 370–1 [Lects 1818–19 (CC) *II, 555–7]*

From Aids to Reflection

I entreat the intelligent Reader, who has taken me as his temporary guide on the straight, but yet, from the number of cross roads, difficult way of religious inquiry, to halt a moment, and consider the main points which, in this last division of my Work, have been already offered for his reflection. I have attempted, then, to fix the proper meaning of the words, Nature and Spirit, the one being the *antithesis* to the other: so that the most general and *negative* definition of nature is, whatever is not spirit; and *vice versa* of spirit, that which is not comprehended in nature: or in the language of our elder divines, that which transcends nature. But Nature is the term in which we comprehend all things that are representable in the forms of time and space, and subjected to the relations of cause and effect: and the cause of the existence of which, therefore, is to be sought for perpetually in something antecedent. The word itself expresses this in the strongest manner possible: *Natura*, that which is *about to be* born, that which is always *becoming*. It follows, therefore, that whatever originates its own acts, or in any sense contains in itself the cause of its own state, must be *spiritual*, and consequently *supernatural*: yet not on that account necessarily *miraculous.* And such must the responsible Will in us be, if it be at all.

Shedd I 262 [*AR (CC)* 250–1]

From Aids to Reflection

I have already given one definition of Nature. Another, and differing from the former in words only, is this: Whatever is representable in the form of time and space, is Nature. But whatever is comprehended in time and space, is included in the mechanism of cause and effect. And conversely, whatever, by whatever means, has its principle in itself, so far as to *originate* its actions, cannot be contemplated in any of the forms of space and time; it must, therefore, be considered as s*pirit* or s*piritual* by a mind in that stage of its development which is here supposed, and which we have agreed to understand under the name of morality or the moral state: for in this stage we are concerned only with the forming of *negative* conceptions, *negative* convictions; and by spiritual I do not pretend to determine *what* the will *is*, but what it is *not* – namely, that it is not nature. And as no man who admits a will at all (for we may safely presume that no man, not meaning to speak figuratively, would call the shifting current of a stream the will of the river), can suppose it *below* nature, we may safely add, that it is supernatural; and this without the least pretence to any positive notion or insight.

Shedd I 154 [*AR (CC)* 80]

From Aids to Reflection

The power which we call Nature, may be thus defined: a power subject to the law of continuity (*lex continui; nam in natura non datur saltus*) which law the human understanding, by a necessity arising out of its own constitution, can *conceive* only under the form of cause and effect. That this *form* or law of cause and effect is, relatively to the world *without*, or to things as they subsist independently of our perceptions, only a form or mode of *thinking*; that is a law inherent in the understanding itself just as the symmetry of the miscellaneous objects seen by the kaleidoscope inheres in, or results from, the mechanism of the kaleidoscope itself – this becomes evident as soon as we attempt to apply the pre-conception directly to any operation of nature ...

These are truths which can scarcely be too frequently impressed on the mind that is in earnest in the wish to *reflect* aright. Nature is a line in constant and continuous evolution. Its *beginning* is lost in the super-natural: and *for our understanding* therefore it must appear as a continuous line without beginning or end. But where there is no discontinuity there can be no origination, and every appearance of origination in *nature* is but a shadow of our own casting. It is a reflection from our own *will* or spirit. Herein, indeed, the will consists. This is the essential character by which Will is *opposed* to Nature, as spirit, and raised *above* nature as *self-determining* spirit – this namely, that it is a power of *originating* an act or state.

Shedd I 272n [AR (CC) 267n–278n]

From a marginal note on John Donne LXXX Sermons

The error here – and it is a grievous error – consists in the word 'Nature'. There is, there can be no Light *of* Nature. There may be a Light *in* or *upon* it; but it is the Light, that shineth down into the Darkness – i.e. in Nature; and the Darkness comprehendeth it not. All Ideas, i.e. spiritual truths, are supernatural.

S.T. Coleridge

CM (CC) II 298

III. Philosophical faculties of vision

a. Sensory and supersensory

Coleridge's claim that every person is either an Aristotelian or a Platonist suggests that each prioritizes different faculties of vision: either the faculty of understanding, derived from the senses, or the faculty of reason, derived from the mind. He favoured reason over understanding, an important distinction that is discussed further in Coleridge's Writings.[11] *The following selections further elaborate these sensory and supersensory modes of vision, and emphasize the importance of cultivating philosophical vision 'as a noble way of employing and developing, and enlarging the faculties of the soul'.*[12]

From Table Talk, *2 July 1830*

Every man is born an Aristotelian or a Platonist. I do not think it possible that any one born an Aristotelian can become a Platonist;

and I am sure no born Platonist can ever change into an Aristotelian. They are the two classes of men, beside which it is next to impossible to conceive a third. The one considers reason a quality, or attribute; the other considers it a power ... Aristotle was, and still is, the sovereign lord of the understanding; – the faculty judging by the senses. He was a conceptualist, and never could raise himself into that higher state which was natural to Plato, and has been so to others, in which the understanding is distinctly contemplated, and, as it were, looked down upon from the throne of actual ideas, or living, inborn, essential truths.

Shedd VI 336 [*TT (CC)* I 172–3]

From Biographia Literaria

There is a *philosophic* (and inasmuch as it is actualized by an effort of freedom, an *artificial*) *consciousness*, which lies beneath or (as it were) *behind* the spontaneous consciousness natural to all reflecting beings. As the elder Romans distinguished their northern provinces into Cis-Alpine and Trans-Alpine, so may we divide all the objects of human knowledge into those on this side, and those on the other side of the spontaneous consciousness; *citra et trans conscientiam communem*. The latter is exclusively the domain of pure philosophy, which is therefore properly entitled *transcendental*, in order to discriminate it at once, both from mere reflection and *re*-presentation on the one hand, and on the other from those flights of lawless speculations which, abandoned by *all* distinct consciousness, because transgressing the bounds and purposes of our intellectual faculties, are justly condemned, as *transcendent*. The first range of hills, that encircles the scanty vale of human life, is the horizon for the majority of its inhabitants. On *its* ridges the common sun is born and departs. From *them* the stars rise, and touching *them* they vanish. By the many, even this range, the natural limit and bulwark of the vale, is but imperfectly known. Its higher ascents are too often hidden by mists and clouds from uncultivated swamps, which few have courage or curiosity to penetrate. To the multitude below these vapors appear, now as the dark haunts of terrific agents, on which none may intrude with impunity; and now all *a-glow*, with colors not their own, they are gazed at, as the splendid palaces of happiness and power. But in all ages there have been a few, who measuring and sounding the rivers of the vale at the feet of their furthest inaccessible falls have learnt, that the sources must be far higher and far inward; a few, who even in the level streams have detected elements, which neither the vale itself or the surrounding mountains contained or could supply. How and whence to these thoughts, these strong probabilities, the ascertaining vision, the intuitive knowledge may finally supervene, can be learnt only by the fact. I might oppose to the question the words with which Plotinus supposes Nature to answer a similar difficulty. 'Should any one interrogate her, how she works, if graciously she vouchsafe to listen and speak, she will reply, it behoves thee not to disquiet me with interrogatories, but to understand in silence, even as I am silent, and work without words.'

Likewise in the fifth book of the fifth Ennead, speaking of the highest and intuitive knowledge as distinguished from the discursive, or in the language of Wordsworth,

'The vision and the faculty divine;'

he says: 'It is not lawful to inquire from whence it sprang, as if it were a thing subject to place and motion, for it neither approached hither, nor again departs from hence to some other place; but it either appears to us or it does not appear. So that we ought not to pursue it with a view of detecting its secret source, but to watch in quiet till it suddenly shines upon us; preparing ourselves for the blessed spectacle as the eye waits patiently for the rising sun.' They, and they only, can acquire the philosophic imagination, the sacred power of self-intuition, who within themselves can interpret and understand the symbol, that the wings of the air-sylph are forming within the skin of the caterpillar; those only, who feel in their own spirits the same instinct, which impels the chrysalis of the horned fly to leave room in its *involucrum* for *antennæ* yet to come. They know and feel, that the *potential* works *in* them, even as the *actual* works on them! In short, all the organs of sense are framed for a corresponding world of sense; and we have it. All the organs of spirit are framed for a correspondent world of spirit; though the latter organs are not developed in all alike. But they exist in all, and their first appearance discloses itself in the *moral* being.

Shedd III 325–8 [*BL (CC)* I 236–42]

From Aids to Reflection

... it has been made evident: – 1. that there is an *intuition* or *imm*ediate beholding, accompanied by a conviction of the necessity and universality of the truth so beholden not derived from the senses, which intuition, when it is construed by pure sense, gives birth to the science of mathematics, and when applied to objects supersensuous or spiritual is the organ of theology and philosophy: – and 2. that there is likewise a reflective and discursive faculty, or *mediate* apprehension which, taken by itself and uninfluenced by the former, depends on the senses for the materials on which it is exercised, and is contained within the sphere of the senses. And this faculty it is, which in generalizing the notices of the senses constitutes sensible experience, and gives rise to maxims or rules which may become more and more *general*, but can never be raised into universal verities, or beget a consciousness of absolute certainty; though they may be sufficient to extinguish all doubt.

Shedd I 252–3n [*AR (CC)* 234n–235]

From a marginal note on Richard Hooker, Works

Concerning that faith, hope and charity, without which there can be no salvation; was there ever any mention made saving only in that law which God himself hath from heaven revealed? There is not in the world a syllable muttered with certain truth concerning any of these three, more than hath been supernaturally received from the mouth of the eternal God.

That reason could have discovered these divine truths is one thing; that when discovered by revelation, it is capable of apprehending the beauty and excellence of the things revealed is another. I may believe the latter, while I utterly reject the former. That all these cognitions, together with the fealty or faithfulness in the will whereby the mind of the flesh is brought under captivity to the mind of the spirit (the sensuous understanding to the reason) are super*natural*, I not only freely grant, but fervently contend. But why the very perfection of reason, namely, those ideas or truth-powers, in which both the spiritual light and the spiritual life of the Soul are co-inherent and *one*, should be called super-*rational*, I do not see. For reason is practical as well as theoretical; or even though I should exclude the practical reason, and confine the term reason to the highest intellective power, – still I should think it more correct to describe the mysteries of faith as plusquam rationalia than *super-rational*.

Shedd V 40 [*CM (CC)* II 1151]

From his notebook, April 1811

<N.B. Nature used here as the *Mundus sensibilis*.>

Important thought that Death, judged of by *corporeal* analogies, certainly implies discerption or dissolution of Parts; but Pain and Pleasure do not – nay, they seem inconceivable except under the idea of concentration. Therefore the influence of the Body on the Soul will not prove the common destiny of Both. – I feel myself not the Slave of Nature, in the sense in which animals are. Not only my Thoughts, Affections extend to Objects transnatural, as Truth, Virtue, God; not only do my Powers extend vastly beyond all those, which I could have derived from the Instruments & Organs, with which Nature has furnished me, but I can do what Nature per se cannot – I engraft, I raise heavy bodies above the clouds, and guide my course over Ocean & thro' Air – I alone am Lord of Fire & of Light – Other creatures but their *Almsfolk* – and of all the so-called Elements, Water, Earth, Air, & all their Compounds (to speak in the ever [?enduring/endearing] Language of <the> *Senses*, to which nothing can be revealed but as compact, or fluid, or aerial, or luciform) I not merely subserved myself of them, but I employ them. – Ergo, there is in me or rather *I* am, præternatural, i.e. supersensuous – but what is not nature, why should it perish with Nature? Why lose the faculty of Vision, because my spectacles are broken? – Now to this it will be objected & very forcibly too – that this Soul or Self is acted upon by Nature thro' the body – and Water or Caloric diffused thro' or collected in the brain will derange the faculties of the Soul by deranging the organization of the Brain – the Sword can not touch the Soul but by rending the flesh will rend the feelings – Therefore, the Violence of Nature may in destroying the Body mediately destroy the Soul. – It is to this Objection that my first Sentence applies – and is an important, and (I believe) a new & the only satisfactory reply I have ever heard –

The one great & *binding* ground of the Belief of God, and Hereafter is the law of Conscience – but as the aptitudes & beauty & grandeur of the World is a sweet and beneficent *Inducement* to this Belief, a constant Fuel to our Faith – so here we seek these ~~arguments~~ not as dissatisfied with the one main ground, not as 'little faith', but because believing it to be it is natural we should expect to find *traces* of it – and as a noble way of employing & developing & enlarging the faculties of the soul – & this – not by way of motive but of assimilation, producing virtue.

2nd April, 1811.

CN III 4060 21 1/2.127

From a marginal note on Richard Field, Of the Church

In the second the light of divine reason causeth approbation of that they believe: in the third sort, the purity of divine understanding apprehendeth most certainly the things believed, and causeth a foretasting of those things that hereafter more fully shall be enjoyed.

Here too Field distinguishes the understanding from the reason, as experience following perception of sense. But as perception through the mere presence of the object perceived, whether to the outward or inner sense, is not insight which belongs to the 'light of reason', therefore Field marks it by purity, that is, *unmixed* with fleshly sensations or the idola of the bodily eye. Though Field is by no means consistent in his *epitheta* of the understanding, he seldom confounds the word itself. In theological Latin, the understanding, as influenced and combined with the affections and desires, is most frequently expressed by *cor*, the heart. Doubtless the most convenient form of appropriating the terms would be to consider the understanding as the Man's intelligential faculty, whatever be its object, the sensible or the intelligible world; while reason is the tri-unity, as it were, of the spiritual eye, light and object.

Shedd V 70 [*CM (CC)* II 679–80]

b. Ascending faculties

Coleridge created a hierarchical ladder of faculties of vision, also referred to as 'organs of sense',[13] from the lowest sensory perception to the highest levels of transcendental vision. He paid special attention to these modes of vision, particularly their capacities, limits and relations to one another, since 'I dare look forward to a continuous consciousness, to a continued progression of my powers'.[14]

From a letter to Edward Coleridge, 27 July 1826

But that another world is inshrined in the Microcosm I not only believe, but at certain depths of my Being, during the solemner Sabbaths of the Spirit, I have held commune therewith, in the power of that Faith, which is 'the substance of the things hoped for', the living stem that will itself expand into the flower, which it now foreshews. How should it not be so, even on grounds of natural reason, and the analogy of inferior life? Is not nature prophetic up the whole vast pyramid of organic being? And in which of her numberless predictions has nature been convicted of a lie? Is not every organ announced by a previous instinct or act? The Larva of the Stag-beetle lies in its Chrysalis like an infant in the coffin of an adult, having left an empty space half the length it occupies – and this space is the exact length of the horn which distinguishes the perfect animal, but which, when it constructed its temporary Sarcophagus, was not yet in existence. Do not the eyes, ears, lungs of the unborn babe, give notice and furnish proof of a transuterine, visible, audible atmospheric world? We have eyes, ears, touch, taste, smell; and have we not an answering world of shapes, colours, sounds, and sapid and odorous bodies? But likewise – alas for the man for whom the one has not the same evidence of fact as the other – the Creator has given us spiritual senses, and sense-organs – ideas I mean – the idea of the good, the idea of the beautiful, ideas of eternity, immortality, freedom, and of that which contemplated relatively to WILL is Holiness, in relation to LIFE is Bliss. And must not these too infer the existence of a world correspondent to them? There is a Light, said the Hebrew Sage, compared with which the Glory of the Sun is but a cloudy veil: and is it an ignis fatuus given to mock us and lead astray? And from a yet higher authority we know, that it is a light that lighteth every man that cometh into the world. And are there no objects to reflect it? Or must we seek its analagon in the light of the glow-worm, that simply serves to distinguish one reptile from all the rest, and lighting, inch by inch, its mazy path through weeds and grass, leaves all else before, and behind, and around it in darkness? No! Another and answerable world there is: and if any man discern it not, let him not, whether sincerely or in contemptuous irony, pretend a defect of faculty as the cause. The sense, the light, and the conformed objects are all there and for all men. The difference between man and man in relation thereto, results from no difference in their several gifts and powers of *intellect*, but in the will. As certainly as the individual is a man, so certainly *should* this other world be present to him: yea, it is his proper home. But he is an absentee and *chooses* to live abroad. His freedom and whatever else he possesses which the dog and the ape do not possess, yea, the whole revenue of his humanity is derived from this – but with the Irish Landowner in the Theatres, Gaming-houses, and Maitresseries of Paris, so with *him*. He is a voluntary ABSENTEE! I repeat it again and again – the cause is altogether in the WILL: and the defect of intellectual power, and 'the having no turn or taste for subjects of this sort', are effects and consequences of the alienation of the WILL – *i.e.* of the Man himself. There may be a defect, but there was not a deficiency, of the intellect.

CCS 212–15 [*CL* VI 595–6]

From Biographia Literaria

In an article contributed by me to Mr. Southey's Omniana, *On the soul and its organs of sense*, are the following sentences. 'These (the human faculties) I would arrange under the different senses and powers; as the eye, the ear, the touch, &c.; the imitative power, voluntary and automatic; the imagination, or shaping and modifying power; the fancy, or the aggregative and associative power; the understanding, or the regulative, substantiating and realizing power; the speculative reason, *vis theoretica et scientifica*, or the power by which we produce, or aim to produce unity, necessity, and universality in all our knowledge by means of principles *à priori*; the will, or practical reason; the faculty of choice (*Germanice*, Willkühr) and (distinct both from the moral will and the choice) the *sensation* of volition, which I have found reason to include under the head of single and double touch.'

Shedd III 354 [*BL (CC)* I 293]

From Aids to Reflection

It may be an additional aid to reflection, to distinguish the three kinds severally, according to the faculty to which each corresponds, the part of our human nature which is more particularly its organ. Thus: the prudential corresponds to the sense and the understanding; the moral to the heart and conscience; the spiritual to the will and the reason, that is, to the finite will reduced to harmony with, and in subordination to, the reason, as a ray from that true light which is both reason and will, universal reason, and will absolute.

Shedd I 134 [*AR (CC)* 42]

From the Philosophical Lectures

No, the man forfeits that high principle of nature, his free agency, which though it reveals itself principally in his moral conduct, yet is still at work in all departments of his being. It is by his bold denial of this, by an inward assertion, 'I am not the creature of nature merely, nor a subject of nature, but I detach myself from her. I oppose myself as man to nature, and my destination is to conquer and subdue her, and my destination is to be lord of light, and fire, and the elements; and what my mind can comprehend, that I will make my eye to see, and what my eye can see, my mind shall instruct me to reach through the means of my hand, so that everywhere the lower part of my nature shall be taken up into the higher. And why? Because I am a free being. I can esteem, I can revere myself, and as such a being I dare look forward to permanence. As I have never yet called this body "I", but only "mine", even as I call my clothes so, I dare look forward to a continuous consciousness, to a continued progression of my powers, for I am capable of the highest distinction, that of being the object of the approbation of the God of the Universe, which no mechanism can be. Nay further, I am the cause of the creation of the world. For what cause? To a Being whose ideas are infinitely more substantial than the things which are the results, or are created from them, what motive to create things that are not capable of right or wrong? What was there in them? Not reality. They existed with an infinitely greater reality in the mind. The Deity knew in that which was God himself, which could come from God only, the will and power of becoming worthy of a return to the Maker.' This I say is so sacred a privilege, that whatever dares to tell us that we are like the trees or like the streams, links in an inevitable chain, and that the assassin is no more worthy of abhorrence than the dagger with which he murders his benefactor, that man I say teaches treason against human nature and against the God of human nature.

PL 362 [*Lects 1818–19 (CC)* II 535]

From his notebooks, June–July 1810

One excellence of the Doctrine of Plato, or of the Plotino-platonic Philosophy, is that it never suffers, much less causes or even occasions, its Disciples to forget themselves, lost and scattered in sensible Objects disjoined or *as* disjoined from themselves. It is impossible to understand the Elements of this Philosophy without an appeal, at every step & round of the Ladder, to the fact within, to the mind's Consciousness – and in addition to this, instead of lulling the Soul into an indolence of mere attention (for a comparative *Indolence* it is, even as, relatively to mere passive amusement (a musâ) or positively passive affections of Sense & Sensation, it is likewise a comparative *Effort*) but rouses it to acts and energies of creative Thought, & Recognition – of conscious re-production of states of Being. I was not originally led to the study of this Philosophy by Taylor's Translations; but in consequence of early, half-accidental, prepossession in favor of it sent in early manhood for Taylor's Translations & Commentaries – & this, I will say, that no man worthy the name of man can read the many extracts from Proclus, Porphyry, Plotinus, &c, those I mean, <those> chiefly, that relate to the moral claims of our Nature, without an ahndung, an inward omening, of a system congruous with his nature, & thence attracting it – /

CN III 3935 18.156

c. Towards a theory of perception

The relationship of the perceiver and the perceived fascinated Coleridge, who sought for a theory of perception throughout his life. The quotations below reveal his search to understand 'the union or harmonious composition of all the Faculties'[15] at work in the process of vision.

From his notebook, February–March 1801

> – and the deep power of Joy
> We see into the *Life* of Things –

i.e. – By deep feeling we make our *Ideas dim* – & this is what we mean by our Life – ourselves. I think of the Wall – it is before me, a distinct Image – here. I necessarily think of the *Idea* & the Thinking I as two distinct & opposite Things. Now <let me> think of *myself* – of the thinking Being – the Idea becomes dim, whatever it be – so dim that I know not what it is – but the Feeling is deep & steady – and this I call *I* – ~~the~~ identifying the Percipient & the Perceived–.

CN I 921 21.121

From his notebook, February 1824

The first man of Science was he, who looked into a thing, not to
learn whether it could furnish him with food, or shelter, or weapons
or Gold or ornaments, & or play-withs – but who sought to know it
for the gratification of *knowing*: while He, that first sought to *know*
in order to *be*, was the First Philosopher. – I have read of two Rivers
passing thro' the same Lake, yet all the way preserving their streams
visibly distinct: and if I mistake not, the Rhone and the Adar thro'
the Lake of Geneva. In a far finer distinction yet a subtler Union
such for the contemplative mind, are the streams of Knowing and
of Being. The Lake formed by the two streams is Man and Nature
as it exists in and for Man; and up this Lake the Philosopher sails
on the junction line of the constituent streams, still pushing upward
and sounding as he goes, towards the common Fountain-head of
both, the Mysterious Source whoichse Being is Knowledge, whose
Knowledge is Being – the adorable I am in that I am

CN IV 5130 29.249

From a manuscript note

Then rose the question in the better natures – Surely, these are not
all of the Human Being? We have hearts as well as Heads. We can
will and act, as well as think, see, and feel. Is there no communion
between the intellectual and the moral? Are the distinctions of the
Schools separates in Nature? Is there no Heart in the Head? No
Head in the Heart? Is it not possible to find a *practical* Reason, a
Light of Life, a focal power from the union or harmonious composition of all the Faculties? Lastly, there is, it is admitted, a Reason,
to which the Understanding must convert itself in order to obtain
from within what it would in vain seek for without, the knowledge
of necessary and universal conclusion – of that which is because
it must be, and not because it had been seen. May there not be a
yet higher or deeper Presence, the source of Ideas, to which even
the Reason must convert itself? Or rather is not this more truly the
Reason, and the universal Principles but the Gleam of Light from
the distant and undistinguished community of Ideas – or the Light
in the Cloud that hides the Luminary? O! let these questions be
once fully answered, and the affirmative made sure and evident
– then we shall have Philosophy, that will unite in itself the warmth
of the mystics, the definiteness of the Dialectician, and the sunny

clearness of the Naturalist, the productivity of the Experimenter and the Evidence of the Mathematician. It was solely from the want of this foundation that Raymond of Sabunde's grand Attempt was premature, and abortive. Yet how precious the result! It reminds me of the fossile animals in the heart of the mountains according to the bold speculation of Steffens, who holds them for the *first studies* of ~~plastic~~ the organized Life of Nature, left imperfect, the divine Artist being called off abruptly to quell a new gathering of the insurgent Titans.

> Where'er I find the Good, the True, the Fair
> I ask no names. God's Spirit dwelleth there!
> The unconfounded, undivided Three.
> Each for itself, and all in each, to see
> In Man, and Nature is Philosophy ...

IS 126

From his notebook, August–September 1809

What is the common principle of the Philosophical Systems of Des Cartes, (Lock?) Berkley, Hume, and Kant? That

our Senses in no way acquaint us with Things, as they are in and of themselves: that the properties, which we attribute to Things without us, yea, that this very *Outness*, are not strictly properties of the things themselves, but either constituents or modifications of our own minds. Des Cartes seems indeed to attribute a proper perceptive faculty to the Soul; but still not the Things themselves are the Objects of this perception, but certain material Ideas, modifications of our own subjective being (= Motions in the Brain &c.) – That we know only the Impressions made on us by unknown Ουκ εφ' ημιν, or <by> unknown workings εφ' ημιν; that these Impressions which we call *Things*, are truly only Ideas, or Representations, which change with the changes of the representative Faculties in the subject: ex. gr. A which in one state of the Subject appears to him as an Image of Memory or Fancy, and as existing in himself, shall in another state (a slight inflammation of the Brain perhaps, or affection in the nerves of the Brain leading to the Eye) appear an external Reality, or Self-subsistence. That therefore all our Knowledge is confined to Appearances, our philosophy a philosophy of Phænomena. Hence the whole of Berkleianism and every other mode of Cartesianism is contained in one position, and two deductions from it. Position. A sentient Being has only its own sensations as the <immediate> objects of its knowledge/ Sentiens non nisi sensationes suas noscit.

Deduction 1. All else we must *conclude*: or all else must be deduced by reasoning, it is not given by perception.

Deduction 2. But Reason at farthest justifies us only in affirming the existence of a Cause out of ourselves adequate to the effect in ourselves: by no means, in the assumption that the Cause is a duplicate of that Effect, any more than it would justify us in attributing Suns, Planets, Moons, attraction &c &c to the Creator, or Cause of the Material World. Berkley's Idealism may be thus illustrated: Our perceptions are impressions on our own minds standing to the external cause in the relation of the picture on the Canvass to the Painter, rather than in that of the Image in the Mirror to the Object reflected.

The first step therefore by which we can pass from psychology to metaphysics, is the examination of this common principle.

Have we or have we not, a faculty of Perception? Do we perceive, or do we only deduce the existence of Things? Which is the proper expression – The perception of a Table? or the Perception, Table?

Prior however to this dispute concerning the nature of our experience, we surely ought to examine the nature of the faculties by which we acquire experience, and reason concerning it. All metaphysical philosophy indeed is at last but an examination of our powers of knowledge – and the different systems are best distinguished by their different accounts of these powers – in their obvious threefold division, our sensitive faculty, or the Sense – 2. our Understanding – 3. and our reason. – We will take the two extreme systems and state each to the best advantage. Any middle systems, if such are possible, will be easily understood by adding and subtracting – .

CN III 3605 25.88

From a letter to James Gilman, 22 November 1825

First however, I must premise that by *Sense* I here mean a man's power of thinking of himself in relation to the Things and Persons, that he has to deal with, and vice versâ, the power of apprehending and looking at Things & Persons in relation to himself. Only in this way can the Self become a Subject, or the *Circumstantia Objecta*; but both would fleet on a delirium where [the] sensations are as objective as the Perceptions, and the Perceptions as subjective as the Sensations. It is only, I say, by the habit of referring a number and variety of passing objects to the same abiding *Subject*, that the *flux* of the former can be arrested, and the latter made a nucleus for them to chrystallize round. But again it is only by the habit of referring & comparing the Subject to and with the Objects, that it can be consciously known as the *same* & *abiding* – and before it can be *compared*, it must have been distinguished, thought of separately, and singly for itself – . There must be Reflection – a turning in of the Mind on itself. In order to be a Subject, the conscious Percipient and Appropriator of outward Objects, it must have been made itself an Object for itself – for so only can it know itself to be a *Subject* relatively to all else. – Now what is that which first induces the Individual to turn inward on himself? *Generally* expressed, it is *Sensibility*. But that is far *too* general. I am persuaded, that it is some *specific* sensibility, having it's seat and source in some special energy of the organic and organific Life – & connected with, growing with, & following the same fates with, some system of organs – not perhaps the structure, but yet with the functions and functional developement.

CL V 517

IV. *Naturphilosophie*

Coleridge was interested in Naturphilosophie,[16] *a nineteenth-century intellectual movement combining a blend of theoretical and experimental science with theological and philosophical systematizing. Proponents of the discipline included Schelling, Steffens and Oken[17] as well as scientists such as Volta and who experimented with electricity. The* Naturphilosophen *believed that a unified theory between nature and spirit was imminent, once further scientific discoveries in magnetism and polarity could be harmonized with theological concepts such as non-Darwinian evolution.[18] The movement was later discredited, but Coleridge's interest in the movement evidences another hope for reconciling nature and spirit.*

From his notebook, January 1811

Now a God is to all Things, to the Universe, both the system of Matter & that of mind, (mundus intelligibilis et sensibilis) the regulative *Idea*.

CN III 4047 18.275

From a letter to James Gillman, 10 November 1816

The Alphabet of Physics no less than of Metaphysics, of Physiology
no less than of Psychology is an alphabet of *Relations*, in which N
is N only because M is M and O, O. The *reality* of all alike is the A
and Ω, far rather that Ineffable which is neither Alpha separately,
nor Omega separately, nor Alpha *and* Omega by *composition*, but
the *Identity* of both, which can become an object of *Consciousness* or
Thought, even as all the powers of the material world can become
objects of *Perception*, only as two Poles or Counterpoints of the
same Line.

CL IV 688

From a letter to C.A. Tulk, 20 January 1820

If I mistake not, one formula would comprize your philosophical
faith & mine – namely, that the sensible World is but the evolution
of the Truth, Love, and Life, or their opposites, in Man – and
that in Nature Man beholds only (to use an Algebraic but close
analogy) the integration of Products, the Differentials of which
are in, and constitute, his own mind and soul – and consequently
that all true science is contained in the Lore of Symbols and
Correspondences.

CL V 19

From a letter to C.A. Tulk, September 1817

For it is not of a dead machine that I speak; but I am endeav-
oring to trace the Genesis, the φύσις, the *Natura* rerum, the *Birth*
of Things: and this under the disadvantage of beginning (as far
as the mere *science* is concerned) with the lowest, per ascensum:
whereas the only true point of view is that of Religion, namely, per
descensum. – Observe too, that the two great poles of manifestation are Continuity (Lex Continui) and Individuation – the latter
being the final cause of nature, or her object, from the Coral which
is almost confounded with Nature to the Man of Genius and *genial*
Goodness, the maximum of Individuation in the present Life;
yet so as that the whole process is *cyclical tho' progressive, and
the Man separates from Nature only that Nature may be found
again in a higher dignity in the Man. For as the Ideal is realized in
Nature, so is the Real idealized in man.

* [Imag]ine the concentric circles, from the fall of a [pebble on] a lake, perpendicular, like a Wheel, in [motion,] in[ste]ad of horizontal: or combine the images of the water with that of the Scala or Ladder: and you will have perhaps, as tolerable an exponent as the outward Senses can supply. [Note by S.T.C.] MS. New York Public Library.

CL IV 769

From his Philosophical Lectures

... that those unknown somethings, powers or whatever you may call them, that manifest themselves in the intellect of man, or what in the language of the old philosophy would be called the intelligible world, as numbers, and the essential powers of numbers, these same manifest themselves to us and are the objects of our senses, I mean as creative and organizing powers: in short, that the very powers which in men reflect and contemplate, are in their essence the same as those powers which in nature produce the objects contemplated.

PL 114 [*Lects 1818–19* I (CC) 112]

The short work entitled 'Hints Towards the Formation of a More Comprehensive Theory of Life' is Coleridge's personal attempt at systematizing in the vein of Naturphilosophie. *The following selections sketch out some of the outlines of this theory, the completion of which depends upon higher levels of vision and further scientific discovery.*

From 'Theory of Life'

To *account* for Life is one thing; to explain Life another. In the first we are supposed to state something prior (if not in time, yet in the order of Nature) to the thing accounted for, as the ground or cause of that thing, or (which comprises the meaning and force of both words) as its *sufficient cause, quae et facit, et subest.* And to this, in the question of Life, I know no possible answer, but GOD. To account for a thing is to see into the principle of its possibility, and from that principle to evolve its being.

TL 35 [*SWF (CC)* I 503]

According to the plan I have prescribed for this inquisition, we are now to seek for the highest law, or most general form, under which this tendency acts, and then to pursue the same process with this, as we have already done with the tendency itself, namely, having stated the law in its highest abstraction, to present it in the different forms in which it appears and reappears in higher and higher dignities. I restate the question. The tendency having been ascertained, what is its most general law? I answer – *polarity*, or the essential dualism of Nature, arising out of its productive unity, and still tending to reaffirm it, either as equilibrium, indifference, or identity. In its *productive* power, of which the product is the only measure, consists its incompatibility with mathematical calculus. For the full applicability of an abstract science ceases, the moment reality begins. Life then, we consider as the copula, or the unity of thesis and antithesis, position and counterposition, – Life itself being the positive of both; as, on the other hand, the two counterpoints are the necessary conditions of the *manifestations* of Life. These, by the same necessity, unite in a synthesis; which again, by the law of dualism, essential to all actual existence, expands, or *produces* itself, from the point into the *line*, in order again to converge, as the initiation of the same productive process in some intenser form of reality. Thus, in the identity of the two counter-powers, Life *sub*sists; in their strife it *con*sists: and in their reconciliation it at once dies and is born again into a new form, either falling back into the life of the whole, or starting anew in the process of individuation.

TL 50–1 [*SWF (CC)* I 518]

But we cannot force any man into an insight or intuitive possession of the true philosophy, because we cannot give him abstraction, intellectual intuition, or constructive imagination; because we cannot organize for him an eye that can see, an ear that can listen to, or a heart that can feel, the harmonies of Nature, or recognise in her endless forms, the thousand-fold realization of those simple and majestic laws, which yet in their absoluteness can be discovered only in the recesses of his own spirit, – not by that man, therefore, whose imaginative powers have been *ossified* by the continual reaction and assimilating influences of mere *objects* on his mind, and who is a prisoner to his own eye and its reflex, the passive fancy! – not by him in whom an unbroken familiarity with the organic world, as if it were mechanical, with the sensitive, but as if it were insensate, has engendered the coarse and hard spirit of a sorcerer. The former is unable, the latter unwilling, to master the absolute prerequisites.

There is neither hope nor occasion for him 'to cudgel his brains about it, he has no feeling of the business.' If he do not see the necessity from without, if he have not learned the possibility from within, of interpenetration, of total intussusception, of the existence of all in each as the condition of Nature's unity and substantiality, and of the latency under the predominance of some one power, wherein subsists her life and its endless variety, as he must be, by habitual slavery to the eye, or its reflex, the passive fancy, under the influences of the corpuscularian philosophy, he has so paralysed his imaginative powers as to be unable – or by that hardness and heart-hardening spirit of contempt, which is sure to result from a perpetual commune with the lifeless, he has so far debased his inward being – as to be unwilling to comprehend the pre-requisite, he must be content, while standing thus at the threshold of philosophy, to receive the results, though he cannot be admitted to the deliberation – in other words, to act upon *rules* which he is incapable of understanding as LAWS, and to reap the harvest with sharpened iron for which others have delved for him in the mine.

TL 57–8 [*SWF (CC)* I 525]

But my opinions will be best explained by a rapid exemplification in the processes of Nature, from the first rudiments of individualized life in the lowest classes of its two great poles, the vegetable and animal creation, to its crown and consummation in the human body; thus illustrating at once the unceasing *polarity of life, as the form of its process, and its tendency to progressive individuation as the law of its direction.*

TL 67 [*SWF (CC)* I 533]

The facts in confirmation of both the propositions are so numerous and so obvious, the advance of Nature, under the predominance of the third synthetic power, both in the intensity of life and in the intenseness and extension of individuality, is so undeniable, that we may leap forward at once to the highest realization and reconciliation of both her tendencies, that of the most perfect detachment with the greatest possible union, to the last work, in which Nature did not assist as handmaid under the eye of her sovereign Master, who made Man in his own image, by superadding self-consciousness with self-government, and breathed into him a living soul.

TL 84–5 [*SWF (CC)* I 550]

The whole force of organic power has attained an inward and centripetal direction. He has a whole world in counterpoint to him, but he contains an entire world within himself. Now, for the first time the apex of the living pyramid, it is Man and Nature, but Man himself is a syllepsis, a compendium of Nature – the Microcosm! Naked and helpless cometh man into the world. Such has been the complaint from eldest time; but we complain of our chief privilege, our ornament, and the connate mark of our sovereignty. *Porphyrigeniti sumus!* In Man the centripetal and individualizing tendency of all Nature is itself concentered and individualized – he is a revelation of Nature! Henceforward, he is referred to himself, delivered up to this own charge; and he who stands the most on himself, and stands the firmest, is the truest, because the most individual, Man. In social and political life this acme is inter-dependence; in intellectual life it is genius. Nor does the form of polarity, which has accompanied the law of individuation up its whole ascent, desert it here. As the height, so the depth. The intensities must be at once opposite and equal. As the liberty, so must be the reverence for law. As the independence, so must be the service and the submission to the Supreme Will! As the ideal genius and the originality, in the same proportion must be the resignation to the real world, the sympathy and the inter-communion with Nature. In the conciliating mid-point, or equator, does the Man live, and only by its equal presence in both its poles can that life be manifested!

TL 85–6 [*SWF (CC)* I 550]

V. Philosophical method

In another short work, 'Essays on the Principles of Method', Coleridge elaborates a method of training philosophical vision through 'the discipline, by which the human mind is purified from its idols, and raised to the contemplation of Ideas, and thence to the secure and ever-progressive, though never-ending, investigation of truth and reality by scientific method'.[19] Through this method, the mind is trained to see the unifying threads binding together the natural and spiritual worlds, since 'All Method supposes a union of several things to a common end'.[20] Although this is a philosophical process, it shades off into religious vision: 'That we acknowledge a method, even in the latter, results from the religious

*instinct which bids us "find tongues in trees; books in the running
streams; sermons in stone" and good (that is, some useful end answering
to some good purpose) in every thing.'*

From *'Essays on the Principle of Method'* in The Friend

Method, therefore, becomes natural to the mind which has been
accustomed to contemplate not *things* only, or for their sake alone,
but likewise and chiefly the *relations* of things, either their relations
to each other, or to the observer, or to the state and apprehension
of the hearers. To enumerate and analyze these relations, with the
conditions under which alone they are discoverable, is to teach the
science of method.

Shedd II 411 [*F (CC)* I 451]

On the contrary, where the habit of method is present and effective,
things the most remote and diverse in time, place, and outward
circumstance, are brought into mental contiguity and succession,
the more striking as the less expected.

Shedd II 414 [*F (CC)* I 455]

It is Shakspeare's peculiar excellence, that throughout the
whole of his splendid picture-gallery (the reader will excuse the
acknowledged inadequacy of this metaphor), we find individuality
everywhere, mere portrait nowhere. In all his various characters,
we still feel ourselves communing with the same human nature,
which is everywhere present as the vegetable sap in the branches,
sprays, leaves, buds, blossoms, and fruits, their shapes, tastes, and
odours. Speaking of the effect, that is, his works themselves, we
may define the excellence of *their* method as consisting in that just
proportion, that union and interpenetration, of the universal and
the particular, which must ever pervade all works of decided genius
and true science. For method implies a *progressive transition*, and it
is the meaning of the word in the original language. The μέθοδος
is literally *a way* or *path of transit* ... The term, method, can not
therefore, otherwise than by abuse, be applied to a mere dead
arrangement, containing in itself no principle of progression.

Shedd II 416 [*F (CC)* I 457]

The grand problem, the solution of which forms, according to
Plato, the final object and distinctive character of philosophy, is

this: *for all that exists conditionally* (that is, the existence of which is inconceivable except under the condition of its dependency on some other as its antecedent) *to find a ground that is unconditional and absolute, and thereby to reduce the aggregate of human knowledge to a system.* For the relation common to all being known, the appropriate orbit of each becomes discoverable, together with its peculiar relations to its concentrics in the common share of subordination. Thus the centrality of the sun having been established, and the law of the distances of the planets from the sun having been determined, we possess the means of calculating the distance of each from the other. But as all objects of sense are in continual flux, and as the notices of them by the sense must, as far as they are true notices, change with them, while scientific principles or laws are no otherwise principles of science than as they are permanent and always the same, the latter were appropriated to the pure reason, either as its products or as implanted in it. And now the remarkable fact forces itself on our attention, namely, that the material world is found to obey the same laws as had been deduced independently from the reason; and that the masses act by a force, which can not be conceived to result from the component parts, known or imaginable. In magnetism, electricity, galvanism, and in chemistry generally, the mind is led instinctively, as it were, to regard the working powers as conducted, transmitted, or accumulated by the sensible bodies, and not as inherent. This fact has, at all times, been the stronghold alike of the materialists and of the spiritualists, equally solvable by the two contrary hypotheses, and fairly solved by neither.

Shedd II 420–1 [*F (CC)* I 461–2]

... what is the ground of the coincidence between reason and experience; or between the laws of matter and the ideas of the pure intellect. The only answer which Plato deemed the question capable of receiving, compels the reason to pass out of itself and seek the ground of this agreement in a supersensual essence, which being at once the *ideal* of the reason and the cause of the material world, is the pre-establisher of the harmony in and between both. Religion therefore is the ultimate aim of philosophy, in consequence of which philosophy itself becomes the supplement of the sciences, both as the convergence of all to the common end, namely, wisdom; and as supplying the copula, which, modified in each in the comprehension of its parts in one whole, is in its principles common to all, as integral parts of one system. And this is method, itself a distinct science, the immediate offspring of philosophy, and the link or *mordant* by which philosophy becomes scientific, and the sciences philosophical.

Shedd II 422 [*F (CC)* I 463]

But with the clear insight that the purpose of the writer is not so much to establish any particular truth, as to remove the obstacles, the continuance of which is preclusive of all truth, the whole scheme assumes a different aspect, and justifies itself in all its dimensions. We see, that to open anew a well of springing water, not to cleanse the stagnant tank, or fill bucket by bucket, the leaden cistern; that the education of the intellect, by awakening the principle and *method* of self-development, was his proposed object, not any specific information that can be *conveyed into it* from without; – not to assist in storing the passive mind with the various sorts of knowledge most in request, as if the human soul were a mere repository or banqueting-room, but to place it in such relations of circumstance as should gradually excite the germinal power that craves no knowledge but what it can take up into itself, what it can appropriate, and reproduce in fruits of its own.

Shedd II 429–30 [*F (CC)* I 472–3]

All method supposes a union of *several* things to a common end, either by disposition, as in the works of man; or by convergence, as in the operations and products of nature. That we acknowledge a *method*, even in the latter, results from the religious instinct which bids us 'find tongues in trees; books in the running streams; sermons in stones; and good (*that is, some useful end answering to some good purpose*) in every thing.' In a self-conscious and thence reflecting being, no instinct can exist without engendering the belief of an object corresponding to it, either present or future, real or capable of being realized; much less the instinct, in which humanity itself is grounded; – that by which, in every act of conscious perception, we at once identify our being with that of the world without us, and yet place ourselves in contra-distinction to that world. Least of all can this mysterious pre-disposition exist without evolving a belief that the productive power, which is in nature as nature, is essentially one (that is, of one kind) with the intelligence, which is in the human mind above nature: however disfigured this belief may become by accidental forms or accompaniments, and though like heat in the thawing of ice, it may appear only in its effects.

Shedd II 449–50 [*F (CC)* I 497–8]

I am aware that it is with our cognitions as with our children. There is a period in which the method of nature is working for them; a period of aimless activity and unregulated accumulation, during which it is enough if we can preserve them in health and *out of harm's way*. Again, there is a period of orderliness, of circumspection, of discipline, in which we purify, separate, define, select, arrange, and settle the nomenclature of communication. There is also a period of dawning and twilight, a period of anticipation, affording trials of strength. And all these, both in the growth of the sciences and in the mind of a rightly-educated individual, will precede the attainment of a scientific method .... Alas! how many examples are now present to my memory, of young men the most anxiously and expensively be-school-mastered, be-tutored, be-lectured, any thing but *educated*; who have received arms and ammunition, instead of skill, strength, and courage; varnished rather than polished; perilously over-civilized, and most pitiably uncultivated! And all from inattention to the method dictated by nature herself, to the simple truth, that as the forms in all organized existence, so must all true and living knowledge proceed from within; that it may be trained, supported, fed, excited, but can never be infused, or impressed.

Shedd II 451–2 [*F (CC)* I 499–500]

In the pursuits of commerce the man is called into action from without, in order to appropriate the outward world, as far as he can bring it within his reach, to the purposes of his senses and sensual nature. His ultimate end is appearance and enjoyment. Where on the other hand the nurture and evolution of humanity is the final aim, there will soon be seen a general tendency toward, an earnest seeking after, some ground common to the world and to man, therein to find the one principle of permanence and identity, the rock of strength and refuge, to which the soul may cling amid the fleeting surge-like objects of the senses. Disturbed as by the obscure quickening of an inward birth; made restless by swarming thoughts, that, like bees when they first miss the queen and mother of the hive, with vain discursion seek each in the other what is the common need of all; man sallies forth into nature – in nature, as in the shadows and reflections of a clear river, to discover the originals of the forms presented to him in his own intellect. Over these shadows, as if they were the substantial powers and presiding spirits of the stream, Narcissus-like, he hangs delighted: till finding nowhere a representative of that free agency which yet is a *fact* of immediate consciousness sanctioned and made fearfully significant by his prophetic *conscience*, he learns at last that what he *seeks* he has *left behind*, and that he but lengthens the distance as he prolongs the search … he separates the *relations* that are wholly the creatures of his own abstracting and comparing intellect, and at once discovers and recoils from the discovery, that the *reality*, the *objective* truth, of the objects he has been adoring, derives its whole and sole evidence from an obscure sensation, which he is alike unable to resist or to comprehend, which compels him to contemplate as without and independent of himself what yet he could not contemplate at all, were it not a modification of his own being.

Shedd II 459–60 [*F (CC)* I 508–9]

Long indeed will man strive to satisfy the inward querist with the phrase, laws of nature. But though the individual may rest content with the seemly metaphor, the race can not. If a law of nature be a mere generalization, it is included in the above as an act of the mind. But if it be other and more, and yet manifestable only in and to an intelligent spirit, it must in act and substance be itself spiritual: for things utterly heterogeneous can have no intercommunion. In order therefore to the recognition of himself in nature man must first learn to comprehend nature in himself, and its laws in the ground of his own existence. Then only can he reduce *phænomena* to principles; then only will he have achieved the method, the self-unravelling clue, which alone can securely guide him to the conquest of the former; – when he has discovered in the basis of their union the necessity of their differences; in the principle of their continuance the solution of their changes. It is the idea of the common centre, of the universal law, by which all power manifests itself in opposite yet interdependent forces ἡ γὰρ ΔΥΑΣ ἀεὶ παρὰ Μονάδι κάθηται, καὶ νοεραῖς ἀστράπτει τομαῖς) – which enlightening inquiry, multiplying experiment, and at once inspiring humility and perseverance will lead him to comprehend gradually and progressively the relation of each to the other, and of all to each.

Shedd II 461–2 [*F (CC)* I 511]

For be it not forgotten, that this discourse is confined to the evolutions and ordonnance of knowledge, as prescribed by the constitution of the human intellect. Whether there be a correspondent reality, whether the Knowing of the Mind has its correlative in the Being of Nature, doubts may be felt. Never to have felt them, would indeed betray an unconscious unbelief, which traced to its extreme roots will be seen grounded in a latent disbelief. How should it be so? if to conquer these doubts, and out of the confused multiplicity of seeing with which 'the films of corruption' bewilder us, and out of the unsubstantial shows of existence, which, like the shadow of an eclipse, or the chasms in the sun's atmosphere, are but *negations* of sight, to attain that *singleness of eye*, with which '*the whole body shall be full of light*' be the purpose, the means, and the end of our probation, the method which is 'profitable to all things, and hath the promise in this life and in the life to come!' Imagine the unlettered African, or rude yet musing Indian, poring over an illumined manuscript of the inspired volume, with the vague yet deep impression that his fates and fortunes are in some unknown manner connected with its contents. Every tint, every group of characters has its several dream. Say that after long and dissatisfying toils, he begins to sort, first the paragraphs that appear to resemble each other, then the lines, the words – nay, that he has at length discovered that the whole is formed by the recurrence and interchanges of a limited number of cyphers, letters, marks, and points …. The poor Indian too truly represents the state of learned and systematic ignorance – arrangement guided by the light of no leading idea, mere orderliness without method!

But see! the friendly missionary arrives. He explains to him the nature of written words, translates them for him into his native sounds, and thence into the thoughts of his heart – how many of these thoughts then first evolved into consciousness, which yet the awakening disciple receives, and not as aliens! Henceforward, the book is unsealed for him; the depth is opened out; he communes with the spirit of the volume as a living oracle. The words become transparent, and he sees them as though he saw them not.

F (CC) I 512–13[21]

Look round you, and you behold everywhere an adaptation of means to ends. Meditate on the nature of a being whose ideas are creative, and consequently more real, more substantial than the things that, at the height of their *creaturely* state, are but their dim reflexes; and the intuitive conviction will arise that in such a being there could exist no motive to the creation of a machine for its own sake; that, therefore, the material world must have been made for the sake of man, at once the high-priest and representative of the Creator, as far as he partakes of that reason in which the essences of all things co-exist in all their distinctions yet as one and indivisible. But I speak of man in his idea, and as subsumed in the divine humanity, in whom alone God loved the world.

Shedd II 466–7 [*F (CC)* I 516]

If then in all inferior things from the grass on the house top to the giant tree of the forest, to the eagle which builds in its summit, and the elephant which browses on its branches, we behold – first, a subjection to universal law by which each thing belongs to the Whole, as interpenetrated by the powers of the Whole; and, secondly, the intervention of particular laws by which the universal laws are suspended or tempered for the weal and sustenance of each particular class, and by which each species, and each individual of each species, becomes a system in and for itself, a world of its own – if we behold this economy everywhere in the irrational creation, shall we not hold it probable that a similar temperament of universal and general laws by an adequate intervention of appropriate agency, will have been effected for the permanent interest of the creature destined to move progressively towards that divine idea which we have learnt to contemplate as the final cause of all creation, and the centre in which all its lines converge?

F (CC) I 517[22]

If it be objected, that in nature, as distinguished from man, this intervention of particular laws is, or with the increase of science will be, resolvable into the universal laws which they had appeared to counterbalance, we will reply: Even so it may be in the case of miracles; but wisdom forbids her children to antedate their knowledge, or to act and feel otherwise or further than they know. But should that time arrive, the sole difference, that could result from such an enlargement of our view, would be this; – that what we now consider as miracles in opposition to ordinary experience, we should then reverence with a yet higher devotion as harmonious parts of one great complex miracle, when the antithesis between experience and belief would itself be taken up into unity of intuitive reason.

And what purpose of *philosophy* can this acquiescence answer? A gracious purpose, a most valuable end; if it prevent the energies of philosophy from being idly wasted, by removing the contrariety without confounding the distinction between philosophy and faith. The philosopher will remain a man in sympathy with his fellow-men. The head will not be disjoined from the heart, nor will speculative truth be alienated from practical wisdom. And vainly without the union of both shall we expect an opening of the inward eye to the glorious vision of that existence which admits of no question out of itself, acknowledges no predicate but the I AM IN THAT I AM! ... As every faculty, with every the minutest organ of our nature, owes its whole reality and comprehensibility to an existence incomprehensible and groundless, because the ground of all comprehension; not without the union of all that is essential in all the functions of our spirit, not without an emotion tranquil from its very intensity, shall we worthily contemplate in the magnitude and integrity of the world that life-ebullient stream which breaks through every momentary embankment, again, indeed, and evermore to embank itself, but within no banks to stagnate or be imprisoned.

But here it behoves us to bear in mind, that all true reality has both its ground and its evidence in the *will*, without which as its complement science itself is but an elaborate game of shadows, begins in abstractions and ends in perplexity. For considered merely intellectually, individuality, as individuality, is only conceivable as with and in the universal and infinite, neither before nor after it. No transition is possible from one to the other, as from the architect to the house, or the watch to its maker. The finite form can neither be laid hold of, nor can it appear to the mere speculative intellect as any thing of itself real, but merely as an apprehension, a frame-work which the human imagination forms by its own limits, as the foot measures itself on the snow; and the sole truth of which we must again refer to the divine imagination, in virtue of its omniformity. For even as thou art capable of beholding the transparent air as little during the absence as during the presence of light, so canst thou behold the finite things as actually existing neither with nor without the substance. Not without, – for then the forms cease to be, and are lost in night: not with it, – for it is the light, the substance shining through it, which thou canst alone really see.

The ground-work, therefore, of all pure speculation is the full apprehension of the difference between the contemplation of reason, namely, that intuition of things which arises when we possess ourselves, as one with the whole, which is substantial knowledge, and that which presents itself when transferring reality to the negations of reality, to the ever-varying frame-work of the uniform life, we think of ourselves as separated beings, and place nature in antithesis to the mind, as object to subject, thing to thought, death to life. This is abstract knowledge, or the science of the mere understanding. By the former, we know that existence is its own predicate, self-affirmation, the only attribute in which all others are contained, not as parts, but as manifestations. It is an eternal and infinite self-rejoicing, self-loving, with a joy unfathomable, with a love all-comprehensive. It is absolute; and the absolute is neither singly that which affirms, nor that which is affirmed; but the identity and living *copula* of both.

Shedd II 468–70 [*F (CC)* I 518–21]

Thus I prefaced my inquiry into the s*cience* of method with a principle deeper than science, more certain than demonstration. For that the *very* ground, saith Aristotle, is groundless or self-grounded, is an identical proposition. From the indemonstrable flows the sap that circulates through every branch and spray of the demonstration. To this principle I referred the choice of the final object, the control over time, or, to comprise all in one, the method of the will. From this I started, or rather seemed to start; for it still moved before me, as an invisible guardian and guide, and it is this the re-appearance of which announces the conclusion of the circuit, and welcomes me at the goal. Yea (saith an enlightened physician), there is but one principle, which alone reconciles the man with himself, with others, and with the world; which regulates all relations, tempers all passions, gives power to overcome or support all suffering, and which is not to be shaken by aught earthly, for it belongs not to the earth; namely, the principle of religion, the living and substantial faith *which passeth all understanding*, as the cloud-piercing rock, which overhangs the stronghold of which it had been the quarry and remains the foundation. This elevation of the spirit above the semblances of custom and the senses to a world of spirit, this life in the idea, even in the supreme and godlike, which alone merits the name of life, and without which our organic life is but a state of somnambulism; this it is which affords the sole sure anchorage in the storm, and at the same time the substantiating principle of all true wisdom, the satisfactory solution of all the contradictions of human nature, of the whole riddle of the world. This alone belongs to and speaks intelligibly to all alike, the learned and the ignorant, if but the *heart* listens. For alike present in all, it may be awakened, but it cannot be given. But let it not be supposed, that it is a sort of *knowledge*: no! it is a form of being, or indeed it is the only knowledge that truly *is*, and all other science is real only as far as it is symbolical of this. The material universe, saith a Greek philosopher, is but one vast complex Mythos, that is, symbolical representation, and mythology the *apex* and complement of all genuine physiology. But as this principle cannot be implanted by the discipline of logic, so neither can it be excited or evolved by the arts of rhetoric. For it is an immutable truth, that what comes from the heart, that alone goes to the heart; what proceeds from a divine impulse, that the godlike alone can awaken.

Shedd II 471–2 [*F (CC)*] I 523–4]

Notes

1 *CM (CC)* II 1018
2 See Richard Holmes' biography *Coleridge: Darker Reflections: 1804–1834* (New York: Pantheon Books, 1998).
3 For differing views of Coleridge's plagiarism, see James Engell, *BL (CC)* 'Editor's Introduction'; Richard Holmes, *Coleridge: Darker Reflections*, 281; Thomas McFarland, *Coleridge and the Pantheist Tradition*, Chapter One; and Norman Fruman, *Coleridge: The Damaged Archangel* (New York: G. Braziller, 1971).
4 For more on Coleridge's reading of Kant see Giuseppe Micheli, *The Early Reception of Kant's Thought in England: 1785–1805* (London: Routledge/Thoemmes Press, 1993) and Rene Wellek, *Immanuel Kant in England: 1793–1838* (London: Routledge/Thoemmes Press, 1993).
5 For more on the philosophical sources of Coleridge's thought, see Douglas Hedley, *Coleridge, Philosophy, and Religion: Aids to Reflection and the Mirror of the Spirit* (Cambridge: Cambridge University Press, 2000); David Newsome, *Two Classes of Men: Platonism and English Romantic Thought* (London: Butler and Tanner, 1974); Gerald McNiece, *The Knowledge that Endures: Coleridge, German Philosophy, and the Logic*

of Romantic Thought (New York: St. Martin's Press, 1992) and Seamus Perry, *Coleridge and the Uses of Division* (Oxford: Clarendon Press, 1999).

6 *CLE* I 16–17 [*CL* I 354]

7 *CM (CC)* II 1018

8 *CN* I 1561 21.281

9 *CN* I 1561 21.281

10 *BL (CC)* II 11

11 See Chapter 4 of David Vallins' volume *Coleridge's Writings: On the Sublime* for more on the important reason/understanding distinction.

12 *Shedd* V 551 [*CN* III 4060 21 1/2.127]

13 *Shedd* III 325–8 [*BL (CC)* I 236]

14 *PL* 362 [*Lects 1818–19* (CC) II 535]

15 *IS* 126

16 For more on Coleridge's interest in *Naturphilosophie*, see Raimonda Modiano, *Coleridge and the Concept of Nature* (Tallahassee: Florida State University Press, 1985); Trevor Levere, *Poetry Realized in Nature: Samuel Taylor Coleridge and Early Nineteenth-century Science* (Cambridge: Cambridge University Press, 1981); and Chapter 5 of David Vallins, *Coleridge and the Psychology of Romanticism: Feeling and Thought* (New York: St. Martin's Press, 2000). Modiano provides an excellent summary of the over-arching aims of the *Naturphilosophen*, who 'generally conceived the universe as a complicated web of polar forces, operating in distinct though related modes, in both inorganic and organic nature, matter and spirit. They commonly rejected the Newtonian atomistic conception of nature, proposing instead a dynamic theory which explained the manifestations of given phenomena on the basis of original forces opposed to one another' (Modiano, 141).

17 Friedrich Schelling (1775–1854) was a German Idealist philosopher who was very influential for Coleridge; Henrik Steffens (1773–1845) was a Norwegian-born academic; Lorenz Oken (1779–1851) was a German pupil of Schelling. All three attempted to reconcile science, philosophy and religion in a manner characteristic of *Naturphilosophie*.

18 See David Vallins' volume *Coleridge's Writings: On the Sublime* for more on this theological notion of evolution, in which natural forms ascend towards higher levels of spirituality.

19 *F (CC)* I 492

20 *Shedd* II 422 [*F (CC)* I 463]

21 This passage does not appear in *Shedd*, so the *F (CC)* text is presented here instead.

22 This passage appears in *Shedd*, but in a greatly modified form, so the *F (CC)* text is presented here instead.

... the whole march of nature and history, from the first impregnation of Chaos by the Spirit converges toward this kingdom as the final cause of the world. Life begins in detachment from Nature, and ends in union with God.

Shedd V 513 [*CM (CC)* III 417]

Chapter Six

Religious Vision: 'an inward eye, which is both eye and light'[1]

Underlying and informing all of Coleridge's literary work is a reverence for religion and a yearning for the divine. Towards the end of his life, he became increasingly preoccupied with finding an acceptable theological framework for his wide-ranging ideas.[2] This coincided with a turn away from the observations of the physical eye, to focus instead on cultivating spiritual vision: 'In order therefore for a man to understand, or even to know of, God, he must have a god-like spirit communicated to him, wherewith, as with an inward eye, which is both eye and light, he sees the spiritual truths.'[3] While vision becomes increasingly spiritual and abstract in these religious musings, nature has not been abandoned, since observing the natural world has 'solemnized the long marriage of our souls by its outward Sign and natural Symbol. It is now registered in both worlds, the world of Spirit and the world of the Senses.'[4] Here we see the ultimate goal of Coleridge's lifelong commitment to vision: apprehending a transparent unity between nature, God and the human mind.

Religious vision crowns the ascending series of faculties discussed in *Nature and Vision*. Because of the transcendent nature of religious truth, Coleridge conceives of faith as a high level of seeing, that continues on where other powers of perception have reached their limits. However, faith alone was not enough to satisfy Coleridge's penchant for system. He was attracted to the theological doctrine of

Trinitarianism because it offered a potential solution to nature and spirit, in a tri-partite God who manifested himself in both material and spiritual ways. He struggled with these religious formulations until his final days.

If religious vision is the perfection of vision, it is also the hardest to achieve. It is important to note the hypothetical language Coleridge uses in discussing the highest levels of vision. The conditional language that dominates many of these passages suggests that he *hoped for* and *believed in* the possibility of transparency between nature and spirit, but did not underestimate the difficulty – if not impossibility – of such vision, due to humanity's perceptive flaws. Because of this, Coleridge outlines the necessity of 'the art of reflection' in order to cultivate religious vision, which is the subject of the first set of quotations.

I. The art of reflection

Coleridge's influential book Aids to Reflection *was intended as a spiritual manual to develop the inward powers of reflection. His aim is nothing less than to 'form the human mind anew after the Divine Image'*[5] *by cleansing and awakening higher powers of perception. Reflection becomes a kind of rejuvenating and redemptive process, intended 'to rouse and emancipate the soul'.*[6]

From a marginal note on Manuel Lacunza y Diaz, The Coming of Messiah

O Almighty God, Absolute God! Eternal I am! Ground of my Being, Author of my existence, & its ultimate End! Mercifully cleanse my Heart enlighten my Understanding & strengthen my Will, that if it be needful or furtherant to the preparation of my soul & of thy Church for the Advent of thy Kingdom, that I should be led into the right belief respecting the Second Coming of the son of Man into the World, the Eye of my mind may be quickened into quietness & singleness of Sight.

CM(CC) III 437

From Aids to Reflection

Reader! You have been bred in a land abounding with men, able in arts, learning, and knowledges manifold, this man in one, this in another, few in many, none in all. But there is one art, of which every man should be master, the art of reflection. If you are not a thinking man, to what purpose are you a man at all?

Shedd I 116 [*AR (CC)* 9]

As a fruit tree is more valuable than any one of its fruits singly, or even than all it fruits of a single season, so the noblest object of reflection is the mind itself, by which we reflect: And as the blossoms, the green and the ripe fruit, of an orange-tree are more beautiful to behold when on the tree and seen as one with it, than the same growth detached and seen successively, after their importation into another country and different clime; so is it with the manifold objects of reflection, when they are considered principally in reference to the reflective power, and as part and parcel of the same. No object, of whatever value our passions may represent it, but becomes foreign to us as soon as it is altogether unconnected with our intellectual, moral, and spiritual life.

Shedd I 118 [*AR (CC)* 13]

Among the various undertakings of men, can there be mentioned one more important, can there be conceived one more sublime, than an intention to form the human mind anew after the Divine Image? The very intention, if it be sincere, is a ray of its dawning.

Shedd I 125 [*AR (CC)* 25]

Awakened by the cock-crow – (a sermon, a calamity, a sick-bed, or a providential escape) – the Christian pilgrim sets out in the morning twilight, while yet the truth (νόμος τέλειος ὁ τῆς ἐλευθερίας) is below the horizon. Certain necessary consequences of his past life and his present undertaking will be seen by the refraction of its light: more will be apprehended and conjectured. The phantasms, that had predominated during the hours of darkness, are still busy. Though they no longer present themselves as distinct forms, they yet remain as formative motions in the pilgrim's soul, unconscious of its own activity and over-mastered by its own workmanship. Things take the signature of thought. The shapes of the recent dream become a mould for the objects in the distance, and these again give an outwardness to and a sensation of reality of the shapings of the dream. The bodings inspired by the long habit of selfishness, and self-seeking cunning, though they are now commencing the process of their purification into that fear which is the beginning of wisdom, and which, as such, is ordained to be our guide and safeguard, till the sun of love, the perfect law of liberty, is fully arisen – these bodings will set the fancy at work, and haply, for a time, transform the mists of dim and imperfect knowledge into determinate superstitions.

Shedd I 130–1 [*AR (CC)* 35–6]

The more consciousness in our thoughts and words, and the less in our impulses and general actions, the better and more healthful the state both of head and heart. As the flowers from an orange-tree in its time of blossoming, that burgeon forth, expand, fall, and are momently replaced, such is the sequence of hourly and momently charities in a pure and gracious soul.

Shedd I 166 [*AR (CC)* 96]

Now I do not hesitate to assert, that it was one of the great purposes of Christianity, and included in the process of our redemption, to rouse and emancipate the soul from this debasing slavery to the outward senses, to awaken the mind to the true *criteria* of reality, namely, permanence, power, will manifested in act, and truth operating as life. *My words,* said Christ, *are spirit*: and they (that is, the spiritual powers expressed by them) *are truth*; that is, very being. For this end our Lord, who came from heaven to *take captivity captive,* chose the words and names, that designate the familiar yet most important objects of sense, the nearest and most concerning things and incidents of corporeal nature; water, flesh, blood, birth, bread. But he used them in senses, that could not without absurdity be supposed to respect the mere *phænomena,* water, flesh, and the like; in senses that by no possibility could apply to the colour, figure, specific mode of touch or taste produced on ourselves, and by which we are made aware of the presence of the things and *understand* them – *res, quae sub apparitionibus istis statuendae sunt.* And this awful recalling of the drowsed soul from the dreams and phantom world of sensuality to *actual* reality, – how it has been evaded! These words, that were spirit, – these mysteries, which even the Apostles must wait for the Paraclete, in order to comprehend – these spiritual things which can only be *spiritually* discerned, – were mere metaphors, figures of speech, oriental hyperboles! 'All this means only morality!' Ah! how far nearer to the truth would these men have been, had they said that morality means all this!

Shedd I 363–4 [*AR (CC)* 406–7]

From his notebook, February 1805

Of the incalculable advantage of chiefly dwelling on the virtues of the Heart, of Habits of Feeling, & harmonious action, the music of the adjusted String at the impulse of the Breeze ... – No actions should be distinctly described but ~~should~~ such as manifestly tend to awaken the Heart to ~~such~~ efficient Feelings, whether of Fear or of Love, ~~as tend to fill~~ actions that falling back on the Fountain, <keep it full,> or clear out the mud from its pipes, ~~to~~ & make it play in its abundance, & shining in that purity, in which at once the Purity & the Light ~~or Defecation~~ is each the cause of the ~~Light~~ other, the Light purifying, and the purified receiving and reflecting the Light, sending it off to others, not like the polish'd mirror by rejection from itself, but by transmission thro' itself. S.T.C.

CN II 2435 17.9

Although religious vision is necessarily abstract, nature has not been abandoned: 'Holy Writ' and 'insight into the nature of Life'[7] are corresponding studies that offer insight into the divine:

From his notebook, May 1827

5 May 1827. – To the right understanding of the most awefully concerning declarations of Holy Writ there has been no greater obstacle, than the want of insight into the nature of *Life* – what it is and what it is not. But in order to this the mind must have been raised to the contemplation of the IDEA, the Life celestial to wit – or the distinctive essence and character of the Holy Spirit./ – Here Life is *Love*, communicative out-pouring Love. Ergo, the terrestrial or the Life of Nature (ever the shadow and opposite of the Divine) is appropriative, absorbing, *appetence*. But the great mistake is, that the Soul cannot continue to be without *Life* – ~~and~~ for if so, with what propriety can the portion of the reprobate Soul be called Death? What if the natural Life have two possible terminations – true Being, & the falling back into the dark Will? –

CN V 5505 23.30

In this beautiful letter to a young boy, Coleridge exhorts his charge to consider 'his true self to be the butterfly' so that 'he will not on that account neglect the caterpillar'. Rather than idling away in childish pleasures, he should acknowledge 'the eyes of this true self are to be formed, its wing to grow, and its powers and instincts to be gradually matured and disciplined'. Religious vision should be cultivated at the youngest age, to allow time for these faculties to develop into their full potential.

From a letter to James Gillman, Jr., August 1823?

My Dear James, – What is true of all human beings in respect to another world may be said of lads of your age in respect to the present life.

They are caterpillars, with the future butterfly not only enclosed, but already forming and unfolding within them. Great is the distance, on the scale of creation, between the poor reptile and a youth like you. The ladder, resembling that which Jacob saw in a dream (Genesis, chapter 28, verse 12) is of vast height: and the reptile is almost on the lowest round, and the youth but a few rounds from the top, of that portion of the ladder, I mean, which is within our view.

But yet, my dear James, the most important, nay, the only *essential* and *permanent* difference between you and your green-frocked sister on the cabbage-leaf, is this: that by the gift of reason and reflection, God has put it in *your* power, and has left it to your own choice, *which* of the two you consider to be your true and proper self, the caterpillar, (that is, your present boy nature) or the butterfly (that is, the man which is growing within you) behind the mask (larva) of the former.

If a lad of 15 years of age is unhappy enough to regard the mere *larva* as his true and only self, if he thinks, feels, and acts as if he was nothing else but the caterpillar, and therefore with the caterpillar only, and with nothing else would concern himself; if he resolves neither to know or care about any self but his present and immediate havings, likings, and cravings, the consequence will, nay, *must* be, that he will not retain his caterpillar life and state of being an hour the longer on this account, but will pass into a poor lame starveling lop-sided butterfly, dragging and trailing his soiled and tatterdemallion wings along the ground, which instead of being the means and organs of elevation and liberty – the means of at once *rising* in the world, and of becoming his own master – are an additional burthen, and an object of mingled scorn and commiseration.

If, on the other hand, he considers his true self to be the butterfly, he will not on that account neglect the caterpillar – on the contrary, he will carefully attend to it, only not (at all events, not *principally*) for *its own* sake, but as the thing, out of which his true and precious self is to burst into open view, as the school within which the eyes of this true self are to be formed, its wings to grow, and its powers and instincts to be gradually matured and disciplined.

It is true, this process cannot be carried on well or effectually without sometimes crossing and contradicting the caterpillar – that is his present boyish wants and wishes, likes and dislikes. But what then? I am no better (you should say to yourself) than the real garden caterpillar, I am *indeed* a caterpillar if I cannot or will not make the crawler go *my* way and not his. In short and to vary the simile, I would have you, my dear young friend, consider the outside and visible James of the present and the two or three following years, as the *mule*, on which the inward and *man* James is riding on a life and death journey. If he flings and kicks and runs restive, you must spur and lash and *force* him on, or else the mule will have disappeared, and have left an *Ass* in its place.

CH 130–2 [*CL* V 296–7]

II. Spiritual vision

a. Yearning for oneness

Coleridge's religious writings are marked by a persistent longing for oneness with God. This union requires 'that most glorious birth of the God-like within us'[8] *– or in other words, a high level of religious vision. The following selections further explore 'the act and habits of reverencing the invisible, as the highest both in ourselves and in nature'.*[9]

From Lay Sermons

O what a mine of undiscovered treasures, what a new world of power and truth would the Bible promise to our future meditation, if in some gracious moment one solitary text of all its inspired contents should but dawn upon us in the pure untroubled brightness of an IDEA, that most glorious birth of the God-like within us, which even as the Light, its material symbol, reflects itself from a thousand surfaces, and flies homeward to its Parent Mind enriched with a thousand forms, itself above form and still remaining in its own simplicity and identity! O for a flash of that same Light ...

Shedd I 450 [*LS (CC)* 50]

From The Friend

No object, not even the light of a solitary taper in the far distance, tempts the benighted mind from before; but its own restlessness dogs it from behind, as with the iron goad of destiny. What then is or can be the preventive, the remedy, the counteraction, but the habituation of the intellect to clear, distinct, and adequate conceptions concerning all things that are the possible object of clear conception, and thus to reserve the deep feelings which belong, as by a natural right, to those obscure ideas that are necessary to the moral perfection of the human being, notwithstanding, yea, even in consequence, of their obscurity – to reserve these feelings, I repeat, for objects, which their very sublimity renders indefinite, no less than their indefiniteness renders them sublime, – namely, to the ideas of being, form, life, the reason, the law of conscience, freedom, immortality, God!

Shedd II 101 [*F (CC)* I 106]

Religion, in its widest sense, signifies the act and habits of reverencing the invisible, as the highest both in ourselves and in nature. To this the senses and their immediate objects are to be made subservient, the one as its organs, the other as its exponents; and as such, therefore, having on their own account no true value, because no inherent *worth*. They are, in short, a *language*; and taken independently of their representative function, from words they become mere empty sounds, and differ from noise only by exciting expectations which they cannot gratify – fit ingredients of the idolatrous charm, the potent *abracadabra*, of a sophisticated race, who had sacrificed the religion of faith to the superstition of the senses, a race of animals, in whom the presence of reason is manifested solely by the absence of instinct.

Shedd II 402 [*F (CC)* I 440]

b. Inward vision

Spiritual vision, as the highest human mode of perception, is abstract, intuitive, and in places mystical in its evocation of that which lies beyond the material senses. In these passages, the power of vision is directed inward, becoming an intuitive 'inward Light'.[10]

From his notebooks, May–June 1805

~~With~~ all the merely bodily Feelings subservient to our Reason, coming only at its call, and obeying its Behests with a gladness not without awe, like servants who work under the Eye of their Lord, we have solemnized the long marriage of our Souls by its outward Sign & natural Symbol. It is now registered in both worlds, the world of Spirit and the world of the Senses. We therefore record our deep Thankfulness to Him, from whose absolute Unity all Union derives its possibility, existence, and meaning, subscribing our names with the blended Blood of this great Sacrament.

CN II 2600 17.211

From his notebooks, November 1803

In Plotinus the system of the Quakers is most beautifully expressed, in the 5th Book of the fifth Ennead: speaking of 'the inward Light.' It is not lawful to enquire from whence it originated, for it neither approached hither, nor again departs from hence to some other place, but it either appears to us, or it does not appear. So that we ought not to pursue it, as if with a view of discovering its latent ~~abode~~ Original, but to abide in Quiet, till it suddenly shines upon us; preparing ourselves for the blessed Spectacle, like the eye waiting patiently for the rising Sun.

CN I 1678 21.406

From Lay Sermons

Only by the intuition and immediate spiritual consciousness of the idea of God, as the One and Absolute, at once the ground and the cause, who alone containeth in himself the ground of his own nature, and therein of *all* natures, do we arrive at the third, which alone is a real *objective* necessity. Here the immediate consciousness decides: the idea is its own evidence, and is insusceptible of all other. It is necessarily groundless and indemonstrable; because it is itself the ground of all possible demonstration. The reason hath faith in itself, in its own revelations. ΛΌΓΟΣ ῈΦΗ. *Ipse dixit.* So it is: for it is so! All the necessity of causal relations (which the mere understanding reduces, and must reduce to co-existence and regular succession in the objects of which they are predicated, and to habit and association in the mind predicating) depends on, or rather inheres in, the ideas of the omnipresent and absolute; for this it is, in which the possible is one and the same with the real and the necessary.

Shedd I 439 [*LS (CC)* 32]

From The Friend

I have asked then for its birth-place in all that constitutes our relative individuality, in all that each man calls exclusively himself. It is an alien of which they know not: and for them the question itself is purposeless, and the very words that convey it are as sounds in an unknown language, or as the vision of heaven and earth expanded by the rising sun, which falls but as warmth on the eyelids of the blind. To no class of *phænomena* or particulars can it be referred, itself being none; therefore, to no faculty by which these alone are apprehended. As little dare we refer it to any form of abstraction or generalization; for it has neither co-ordinate or *analogon*; it is absolutely one; and that it is, and affirms itself TO BE, is its only predicate. And yet this power, nevertheless, is; – in supremacy of being it IS: – and he for whom it manifests itself in its adequate idea, dare as little arrogate it to himself as his own, can as little appropriate it either totally or by partition, as he can claim ownership in the breathing air, or make an inclosure in the cope of heaven. He bears witness of it to his own mind, even as he describes life and light: and, with the silence of light, it describes itself and dwells in *us* only as far as we dwell in *it*. The truths which it manifests are such as it alone can manifest, and in all truth it manifests itself. By what name then canst thou call a truth so manifested? Is it not revelation? Ask thyself whether thou canst attach to that latter word any consistent meaning not included in the idea of the former. And the manifesting power, the source and the correlative of the idea thus manifested – is it not God?

Shedd II 464–5 [*F (CC)* I 515–16]

c. Ascending faculties

The long selections from Lay Sermons *that follow discuss the different faculties involved in spiritual vision. In Coleridge's view 'every new knowledge' is 'but a new organ of sense and insight into this one all-inclusive verity, which, still filling the vessel of the understanding, still dilates it to a capacity of yet other and yet greater truths'.*[11] *Religious vision is the consummation of all the perceptive powers that exist below it, and nature aids in the cultivation of vision at every stage, since it is 'the great book of his servant Nature' wherein are found 'correspondencies and symbols of the spiritual world'.*[12]

From Lay Sermons

St. Paul indeed thought otherwise. For though he too teaches us, that in the religion of Christ there is *milk for babes*: yet he informs us at the same time, that there is *meat for strong men*: and to the like purpose one of the Fathers has observed that in the New Testament there are shallows where the lamb may ford, and depths where the elephant must swim. The Apostle exhorts the followers of Christ to the continual study of the new religion, on the ground that in the mystery of Christ, which in other ages was not made known to the sons of men, and in the riches of Christ which no research could exhaust, there were contained all the treasures of knowledge and wisdom. Accordingly in that earnestness of spirit, which his own personal experience of the truth inspired, he prays with a solemn and a ceremonious fervor, that being *strengthened with might in the inner man, they might be able to comprehend with all saints what is the breadth and length and depth and height*, of that living principle, at once the giver and the gift of that anointing faith, which in endless evolution *teaches us of all things, and is truth!* For all things are but parts and forms of its progressive manifestation, and every new knowledge but a new organ of sense and insight into this one all-inclusive verity, which, still filling the vessel of the understanding, still dilates it to a capacity of yet other and yet greater truths, and thus makes the soul feel its poverty by the very amplitude of its present, and the immensity of its reversionary wealth. All truth is indeed simple, and needs no extrinsic ornament. And the more profound the truth is, the more simple: for the whole labour and building up of knowledge is but one continued process of simplification.

Shedd VI 188–9 [*LS (CC)* 179]

The completing power which unites clearness with depth, the plentitude of the sense with the comprehensibility of the understanding, is the imagination, impregnated with which the understanding itself becomes intuitive, and a living power. The reason, (not the abstract reason, not the reason as the mere *organ* of science, or as the faculty of scientific principles and schemes *à priori*; but reason), as the integral *spirit* of the regenerated man, reason substantiated and vital, *one only*, yet *manifold, overseeing all, and going through all* understanding; *the breath of the power of God, and a pure influence from the glory of the Almighty*; which *remaining in itself* regenerateth all other powers, *and in all ages entering into holy souls maketh them friends of God and prophets*; (Wisdom of Solomon, c. vii.), this reason without being either the sense, the understanding, or the imagination, contains all three within itself, even as the mind contains its thoughts, and is present in and through them all; or as the expression pervades the different features of an intelligent countenance ...

The object of the preceding discourse was to recommend the Bible, as the end and centre of our reading and meditation. I can truly affirm of myself, that my studies have been profitable and availing to me only so far, as I have endeavoured to use all my other knowledge as a glass enabling me to receive more light in a wider field of vision from the word of God. If you have accompanied me thus far, thoughtful reader, let it not weary you if I digress for a few moments to another book, likewise a revelation of God – the great book of his servant Nature. That in its obvious sense and literal interpretation it declares the being and attributes of the Almighty Father, none but the *fool in heart* has ever dared gainsay. But it has been the music of gentle and pious minds in all ages, it is the *poetry* of all human nature, to read it likewise in a figurative sense, and to find therein correspondencies and symbols of the spiritual world.

I have at this moment before me, in the flowery meadow, on which my eye is now reposing, one of its most soothing chapters, in which there is no lamenting word, no one character of guilt or anguish. For never can I look and meditate on the vegetable creation without a feeling similar to that with which we gaze at a beautiful infant that has fed itself asleep at its mother's bosom, and smiles in its strange dream of obscure yet happy sensations. The same tender and genial pleasure takes possession of me, and this pleasure is checked and drawn inward by the like aching melancholy, by the same whispered remonstrance, and made restless by a similar impulse of aspiration. It seems as if the soul said to herself: from this state hast *thou* fallen! Such shouldst thou still become, thyself all permeable to a holier power! thyself at once hidden and glorified by its own transparency, as the accidental and dividuous in this quiet and harmonious object is subjected to the life and light of nature; to that life and light of nature, I say, which shines in every plant and flower, even as the transmitted power, love and wisdom of God over all fills, and shines through, nature! But what the plant *is* by an act not its own and unconsciously – *that* must *thou* make thyself to *become* – must by prayer and by a watchful and unresisting spirit, join at least with the preventive and assisting grace to *make* thyself, in that light of conscience which inflameth not, and with that knowledge which puffeth not up!

But further, and with particular reference to that undivided reason, neither merely speculative or merely practical, but both in one, which I have in this annotation endeavoured to contra-distinguish from the understanding, I seem to myself to behold in the quiet objects, on which I am gazing, more than an arbitrary illus-tration, more than a mere *simile*, the work of my own fancy! I feel an awe, as if there were before my eyes the same power as that of the reason – the same power in a lower dignity, and therefore a symbol established in the truth of things. I feel it alike, whether I contem-plate a single tree or flower, or meditate on vegetation throughout the world, as one of the great organs of the life of nature. Lo! – with the rising sun it commences its outward life and enters into open communion with all the elements, at once assimilating them to itself and to each other. At the same moment it strikes its roots and unfolds its leaves, absorbs and respires, steams forth its cooling vapour and finer fragrance, and breathes a repairing spirit, at once the food and tone of the atmosphere, into the atmosphere that feeds *it*. Lo! – at the touch of light how it returns an air akin to light, and yet with the same pulse effectuates its own secret growth, still contracting to fix what expanding it had refined. Lo! – how upholding the ceaseless plastic motion of the parts in the profoundest rest of the whole it becomes the visible *organismus* of the entire *silent* or *elementary* life of nature and, therefore, in incorporating the one extreme becomes the symbol of the other; the natural symbol of that higher life of reason, in which the whole series (known to us in our present state of being) is perfected, in which, therefore, all the subordinate gradations recur, and are re-ordained *in more abundant honor*. We had seen each in its own cast, and we now recognize them all as co-existing in the unity of a higher form, the crown and completion of the earthly, and the mediator of a new and heavenly series. Thus finally, the vegetable creation, in the simplicity and uniformity of its *internal* structure symbolizing the unity of nature, while it represents the omniformity of her delegated functions in its *external* variety and manifoldness, becomes the record and chronicle of her ministerial acts, and enchases that vast unfolded volume of the earth with the hieroglyphics of her history.

O! – if as the plant to the orient beam, we would but open out our minds to that holier light, which *'being compared with light is found before it, more beautiful than the sun, and above all the order of stars,'* (Wisdom of Solomon, vii. 29.) ungenial, alien, and adverse to our very nature would appear the boastful wisdom which, beginning in France, gradually tampered with the taste and literature of all the most civilized nations of christendom ...

Shedd I 461 [*LS (CC)* 69–74]

Man of understanding, canst thou command the stone to lie, canst thou bid the flower to bloom, where thou hast placed it in thy classification? – Canst thou persuade the living or the inanimate to stand separate even as thou hast separated them? – And do not far rather all things spread out before thee in glad confusion and heedless intermixture, even as a lightsome chaos on which the Spirit of God is moving? – Do not all press and swell under one attraction, and live together in promiscuous harmony, each joyous in its own kind, and in the immediate neighbourhood of myriad others that in the system of thy understanding are distant as the poles? – If to mint and to remember names delight thee, still arrange and classify and pore and pull to pieces, and peep into death to look for life, as monkeys put their hands behind a looking-glass! Yet consider in the first sabbath which thou imposest on the busy discursion of thought, that all this is at *best* little more than a technical memory: that like can only be known by like: that as truth is the correlative of Being, so is the act of Being the great organ of truth, that in natural no less than in moral science, *quantum sumus, scimus.*

That which we find in ourselves is (*gradu mutato*) the substance and the life of *all* our knowledge. Without this latent presence of the

'I am,' all modes of existence in the external world would flit before us as colored shadows, with no greater depth, root, or fixture, than the image of a rock hath in a gliding stream or the rainbow on a fast-sailing rain-storm. The human mind is the compass, in which the laws and actuations of all outward essences are revealed as the dips and declinations. (The application of geometry to the forces and movements of the material world is both proof and instance.) The fact, therefore, that the mind of man in its own primary and constituent forms represents the laws of nature, is a mystery which of itself should suffice to make us religious: for it is a problem of which God is the only solution, God, the one before all, and of all, and through all! – True natural philosophy is comprised in the study of the science and language of *symbols*. The power delegated to nature is all in every part: and by a symbol I mean, not a metaphor or allegory or any other figure of speech or form of fancy, but an actual and essential part of that, the whole of which it represents. Thus our Lord speaks symbolically when he says that *the eye is the light of the body*. The genuine naturalist is a dramatic poet in his own line: and such as our myriad-minded Shakspeare is, compared with the Racines and Metastasios, such and by a similar process of self-transformation would the man be, compared with the doctors of the mechanic school, who should construct his physiology on the heaven-descended, Know Thyself.

Shedd I 464 [*LS (CC)* 77–9]

d. Limits and horizons

The difficulty of high levels of religious seeing stretches the limits of human knowing, at 'the horizon of consciousness'.[13]

From Aids to Reflection

If any reflecting mind be surprised that the aids of the Divine Spirit should be deeper than our consciousness can reach, it must arise from the not having attended sufficiently to the nature and necessary limits of human consciousness. For the same impossibility exists as to the first acts and movements of our own will; – the farthest distance our recollection can follow back the traces never leads us to the first foot-mark; the lowest depth that the light of our consciousness can visit even with a doubtful glimmering, is still at an unknown distance from the ground: and so, indeed, must it be with all truths, and all modes of Being, that can neither be counted, colored, or delineated. Before and after, when applied to such subjects, are but allegories, which the sense or imagination supplies to the understanding. The position of the Aristoteleans, *nihil in intellctu quod non prius in sensu*, on which Mr. Locke's Essay is grounded, is irrefragable: Locke erred only in taking half the truth for a whole truth. Conception is consequent on perception. What we can not *imagine*, we can not, in the proper sense of the word, conceive.

Shedd I 153–4 [*AR (CC)* 79]

Most readily therefore do I admit, that there can be no contrariety between revelation and the understanding; unless you call the fact, that the skin, though sensible of the warmth of the sun, can convey no notion of its figure or its joyous light, or of the colours which it impresses on the clouds, a contrariety between the skin and the eye; or infer that the cutaneous and the optic nerves *contradict* each other.

But we have grounds to believe, that there are yet other rays of effluences from the sun, which neither feeling nor sight can apprehend, but which are to be inferred from the effects. And were it even so with regard to the Spiritual Sun, how would this contradict the understanding or the reason? It is a sufficient proof of the contrary, that the mysteries in question are not in the direction of the understanding of the speculative reason. They do not move on the same line or plane with them, and therefore cannot contradict them. But besides this, in the Mystery that most immediately concerns the Believer, that of the birth into a new and spiritual life, the common sense and experience of mankind come in aid of their faith.

Shedd I 234 [*AR (CC)* 204]

From his notebook, January–September 1821

Did you *deduce* your own being? Even that is less absurd than the conceit of *deducing* the Divine Being? Never would you have had the notion had you not had the Idea – rather, had not the Idea worked in you, like the Memory of a Name which I we cannot recollect and yet feel that we have, and which reveals its existence in the mind only by a restless anticipation & proves its prior actuality by the most explosive instantaneity with which it is welcomed & recognized on its re-emersion out of the Cloud, or its re-ascent above the horizon of Consciousness.

CN IV 4816 29.80

III. Faith

Coleridge recognized that 'Some truths, from their nature, surpass the scope of man's limited powers, and stand as the criteria of faith'.[14] *Thus faith extends human vision to its utmost boundaries, by becoming a form of intuition: 'faith must be a light, a form of knowing, a beholding of truth'.*[15] *The following selections elaborate the nuanced and complex notion of faith as a mode of vision.*

From his notebook, May–July 1811

We are born in the mountains, in the Alps – and when we hire ourselves out to the Princes of the Lower Lands, sooner or later we feel an incurable Home-sickness – & every Tune that recalls our native Heights, brings on a relapse of the Sickness. – I seem to myself like a Butterfly who having foolishly torn or bedaubed his wings, is obliged to crawl like a Caterpillar with all the restless Instincts of the Butterfly.

Our Eye rests in an horizon – still moving indeed as we move – yet still there is an Horizon & there the Eye rests – but our Hands can only pluck the Fruit a yard from us – there is no Horizon for the *Hand* – and the Hand is the symbol of earthly realities, the Eye of our Hope & Faith. And what is Faith? – it is to the Spirit of Man the same Instinct, which impels the chrysalis of the horned fly to build its involucrum as long again as itself to make room for the Antennæ, which are to come, tho' they never yet have been – O the *Potential* works *in* us even as the Present mood works *on* us! –

Love with Virtue have almost an actual Present – tho' for moments and tho' for few – but in general, we have no present unless we are brutalized – the Present belongs to the two extremes, Beast & Angel – We in youth have Hope, the Rainbow of the Morning in the West – in age, we have recollections of Hope, the Evening Rainbow in the East! – In short, all the organs of Sense are framed for a correspondingWorld of Sense: and we have it. All the organs of Spirit are framed for a correspondent World of Spirit: & we cannot but believe it.

CN III 4088 18.304

From his marginalia on Marcus Aurelius Antoninus, His Conversation with Himself

I have compared a human Soul to a Glow-worm creeping on in the night; a little, pleasing inch of Light before and behind and on either side, and a World of Darkness all around. Yea, even the vast Soununs & Systems of Heavenly Truth partake, to us, or our own littleness, & are but Glow-worms, & Sparkles, in the black Ether – Reason enlarges them indeed by her Telescope; but their true dimensions are deduced by Faith availing herself of the Instruments of Reason.

CM (CC) I 169–70

From his marginalia on Joseph Blanco White, Letters from Spain

The great Object of Christianity is FAITH – fëalty to the SPIRITUAL in our Humanity, <to> that which indeed contra-distinguishes us as *human* – to that Power, in which the Will, the Reason and the Conscience are three in One, & by which alone spiritual Truths, i.e. the only living and substantial Truths, can be discerned. To this power, under the name of Faith, every thought of the Understanding, of the 'mind of the Flesh['], must be brought into subjection – and Beliefs of particular Dogmata, i.e. the perception of the preponderance of the arguments *for* over those against their verity, is then only essential, when such Belief is implied in the state of FAITH … Belief, therefore, cannot be the proper and essential Ground of Salvation in the Soul – But Faith *is* – and by Christ himself solemnly declared to be so. Therefore, Belief cannot be the same as Faith – tho' the Belief of the truths essential to the Faith in Christ is the necessary accompaniment and consequent of the Faith.

CM (CC) I 503

From Biographia Literaria

This has been my object, and this alone can be my defence – and O! that with this my personal as well as my LITERARY LIFE might conclude! – the unquenched desire I mean, not without the consciousness of having earnestly endeavoured to kindle young minds, and to guard them against the temptations of scorners, by showing that the scheme of Christianity, as taught in the liturgy and homilies of our Church, though not discoverable by human reason, is yet in accordance with it; that link follows link by necessary consequence; that Religion passes out of the ken of Reason only where the eye of Reason has reached its own horizon; and that Faith is then but its continuation: even as the day softens away into the sweet twilight, and twilight, hushed and breathless, steals into the darkness. It is night, sacred night! the upraised eye views only the starry heaven which manifests itself alone: and the outward beholding is fixed on the sparks twinkling in the awful depth, though suns of other worlds, only to preserve the Soul steady and collected in its pure *act* of inward adoration to the great I AM, and to the filial Word that re-affirmeth it from eternity to eternity, whose choral echo is the universe.

Shedd III 594 [*BL (CC)* II 247–8]

From his 'Essay on Faith'

Faith subsists in the *synthesis* of the reason and the individual will. By virtue of the latter therefore it must be an energy, and inasmuch as it relates to the whole moral man, it must be exerted in each and all of his constituents or incidents, faculties and tendencies; – it must be a total, not a partial; a continuous, not a desultory or occasional energy. And by virtue of the former, that is, reason, faith must be a light, a form of knowing, a beholding of truth. In the incomparable words of the Evangelist, therefore – *faith must be a light originating in the Logos, or the substantial reason, which is co-eternal and one with the Holy Will, and which light is at the same time the life of men.* Now as life is here the sum or collective of all moral and spiritual acts, in suffering, doing, and being, so is faith the source and the sum, the energy and the principle of the fidelity of man to God, by the subordination of his human will, in all provinces of his nature to his reason, as the sum of spiritual truth, representing and manifesting the will Divine.

Shedd V 565 [*SWF (CC)* II 844]

From A Lay Sermon

Not, my Christian friends! by all the lamps of worldly wisdom clustered in one blaze can we guide our paths so securely as by fixing our ways on this inevitable cloud, through which all must pass, which at every step becomes darker and more threatening to the children of this world, but to the children of faith and obedience still thins away as they approach, to melt at length and dissolve into that glorious light, from which as so many gleams and reflections of the same falling on us during our mortal pilgrimage, we derive all principles of true and lively knowledge, alike in science and in morals, alike in communities and in individuals.

Shedd VI 153 [*LS (CC)* 131]

From a marginal note on The Book of Common Prayer

A Man may pray night and day, and yet deceive himself; but no man can be assured of his sincerity, who does not pray. Prayer is faith passing into act; a union of the will and the intellect realizing in an intellectual act. It is the whole man that prays. Less than this is wishing, or lip-work; a charm or a mummery. *Pray always*, says the Apostle; – that is, have the habit of prayer, turning your thoughts into acts by connecting them with the idea of the redeeming God, and even so reconverting your actions into thoughts.

Shedd V 21 [*CM (CC)* I 702]

From a marginal note on John Donne, LXXX Sermons

A question is here affirmatively stated of highest importance and of deepest interest, that is faith, so distinguished from reason, *credat* from *sciat*, that the former is an infused grace not in our power; the latter an inherent quality or faculty, on which we are able to calculate as man with man. I know not what to say to this. Faith seems to me the co-adunation of the individual will with the reason, enforcing adherence alike of thought, act, and affection to the Universal Will, revealed whether in the conscience, or by the light of reason, however the same may contravene, or apparently contradict, the will and mind of the flesh, the presumed experience of the senses and of the understanding, as the faculty, or intelligential yet animal instinct, by which we generalize the notices of the senses, and substantiate the *spectra* or *phænomena*.

Shedd V 106 [*CM (CC)* II 331–2]

From a letter to Joseph Cottle, April 1814

The supreme Governor of the world, and the Father of our spirits, has seen fit to disclose to us, much of his will, and the whole of his natural and moral perfections. In some instances he has given his *word* only, and demanded our *faith*; while, on other momentous subjects, instead of bestowing a full revelation, like the *Via Lactea*, he has furnished a glimpse only, through either the medium of inspiration, or by the exercise of those rational faculties with which he has endowed us. I consider the Trinity as substantially resting on the first proposition, yet deriving support from the last.

I recollect when I stood on the summit of Etna, and darted my gaze down the crater; the immediate vicinity was discernible, till, lower down, obscurity gradually terminated in total darkness. Such figures exemplify many truths revealed in the Bible. We pursue them, until, from the imperfection of our faculties, we are lost in impenetrable night. All truths, however, that are essential to faith, *honestly* interpreted; all that are important to human conduct, under every diversity of circumstance, are manifest as a blazing star. The promises also of felicity to the righteous, in the future world, though the precise nature of that felicity may not be defined, are illustrated by every image that can swell the imagination: while the mystery of the *lost*, in its unutterable intensity, though the language that describes it is all necessarily figurative, is there exhibited as resulting chiefly, if not wholly, from the withdrawment of the *light of God's countenance*, and a banishment from his *presence*! – best comprehended in this world, by reflecting on the desolations which would instantly follow the loss of the sun's vivifying and universally diffused *warmth*.

You, or rather *all*, should remember, that some truths, from their nature, surpass the scope of man's limited powers, and stand as the criteria of *faith*, determining, by their rejection, or admission, who among the sons of men can confide in the veracity of heaven. Those more ethereal truths, of which the Trinity is conspicuously the chief, without being circumstantially explained, may be faintly illustrated by material objects. – The eye of man cannot discern the satellites of Jupiter, nor become sensible of the multitudinous stars, whose rays have never reached our planet, and, consequently, garnish not the canopy of night; yet, are they the less *real*, because their existence lies beyond man's unassisted gaze? The tube of the philosopher, and the *celestial telescope*, – the unclouded visions of heaven will confirm the one class of truths, and irradiate the other.

The *Trinity* is a subject of which analogical reasoning may advantageously be admitted, as furnishing, at least, a glimpse of light, and with this, for the present, we must be satisfied. Infinite Wisdom deemed clearer manifestations inexpedient; and is man to dictate to his Maker? I may further remark, that where we cannot behold a desirable object distinctly, we must take the best view we can; and I think you, and every candid and enquiring mind, may derive assistance from such reflections as the following.

Notwithstanding the arguments of Spinoza, and Descartes, and other advocates of the *Material system*, (or, in more appropriate language, the *Atheistical system*!) it is admitted by all men, not prejudiced; not biased by sceptical prepossessions, that *mind* is distinct from *matter*. The mind of man, however, is involved in inscrutable darkness, (as the profoundest metaphysicians well know) and is to be estimated, (if at all) alone, by an inductive process; that is, by its *effects*. Without entering on the question, whether an extremely circumscribed portion of the mental process, surpassing instinct, may, or may not, be extended to quadrupeds, it is universally acknowledged, that the mind of man, alone, regulates all the voluntary actions of his corporeal frame. Mind, therefore, may be regarded as a distinct genus, in the scale ascending above brutes, and including the whole of intellectual existences; advancing from *thought*, (that mysterious thing!) in its lowest form, through all the gradations of sentient and rational beings, till it arrives at a Bacon, a Newton, and then, when unincumbered by matter, extending its illimitable sway through Seraph and Archangel, till we are lost in the GREAT INFINITE!

ER 89–92 [*CL* III 482–3]

IV. Trinitarianism

The religious doctrine of Trinitarianism, which presented a tri-partite God as the Father, the Son and the Holy Ghost, is a unifying link between Coleridge's theological and philosophical thought. He envisioned Trinitarianism as an all-encompassing theory accounting for 'the history of life which begins in its detachment from nature, and is to end in its union with God'. Logos, or the Word of God,[16] *incorporated humanity and nature as outflowings of divine spirit, in which 'the book of nature and the book of revelation, with the whole history of man as the intermediate link, must be the integral and coherent parts of one great work'.*[17] *More specifically, Trinitarianism conceived of an all-powerful God who could multiply himself in his creation, without compromising his unity, creativity or connection to the human or natural worlds. In his final days, Coleridge was obsessed with refining these concepts, and he recited a Trinitarian formula in his last moments of life. Although some of his coined terminology can be obfuscatory, his enduring commitment to harmonizing nature and spirit is evident.*

From his notebook, September–October 1810

A thing cannot be one and three – *at the same time.* True! – but Time does not apply to God – he is neither one in time nor three in time, for he existences not in time at all – the Eternal! .... O! the truly religious man when he is not conveying his feelings & beliefs to other men, and does not need the medium of words, O! how little does he find in his religious *sense* either of *form* or of number – it is the *Infinite!* – Alas! why do we all seek by instinct for a God – a supersensual – but because we feel the insufficiency, the unsubstantiality, of all *forms*, and formal Being of itself –/

CN III 3973 14.55

From a marginal note on Henry More, Theological Works

Yet if Christianity is to be the religion of the world, if Christ be that Logos or Word that *was in the beginning*, by whom all things *became*; if it was the same Christ who said, *Let there be light*; who in and by the creation commenced that great redemptive process, the history of life which begins in its detachment from nature, and is to end in its union with God; – if this be true, so true must it be that the book of nature and the book of revelation, with the whole history of man as the intermediate link, must be the integral and coherent parts of one great work: and the conclusion is, that a scheme of the Christian faith which does not arise out of, and shoot its beams downward into, the scheme of nature, but stands aloof as an insulated afterthought, must be false or distorted in all its particulars.

Shedd V 113 [*CM (CC)* III 919]

From his notebook

Life knows only its product, and beholds itself only as far as it is visible in its offspring. Yea, the Ground and Cause of All comprehends itself only because the Logos in its co-eternal offspring, its Product, is at the same time its adequate Idea. No Word, no God.

IS 390

From his notebook, 1825–6

The Trinity is indeed the primary Idea, out of which all other Ideas are evolved – or as the Apostle says, it is the Mystery (which is but another word for Idea) in which are hidden all the Treasures of Knowledge – But for this very case it is the example & representative of all Ideas – the it is the common Attribute of all, that the Absolute exists entire in all the plenitude of its eternal Forms, entire in each and indivisibly one in all. As a Mother listens with tender smiles at the Child that striving to repeat makes nonsense of her words, so does the Philosopher regard the attempts of the Understanding to express the Ideas of the Reason, were which it reflects and refracts in two contradictory positions – nay, demands this as a negative test of the eternal truth intended.

CN IV 5294 Fo. 47

From a marginal note on Edward Irving, Sermons, Lectures and ... Discourses

After this Ascent hath been attained, it will no longer be Sound without meaning for my Friend, when he hears it said – That the Absolute Subject in the eternal Act of Self-affirmation begetting the Son <or (which means the same)> uttering the only-begotten WORD is at once the I AM, and the Father. The <Air of the intellectual World cleansed from the> glittering Dust-atoms and Moats of the fancy; the busy discursion of the Understanding <suspended,> and the stubborn intrusions of Time and Space, repelled – let him but once have raised his Spirit to the contemplation of Deity under the form of Identity, as the Absolute Will essentially Causative of *all* Reality and therefore of his own (Causa Sui) he will welcome the appropriateness not shrink from the scholastic strangeness, of the Tri-une terms Ipseity, Alterity and Community, as Exponents of the eternal Distinctities, in which

God is the Father, the Son, and the Spirit – the Subjective, = the I Am, the Objective = the Jehovah; the subjectively Objective = the Holy Ghost, or eternal Procession of Life and Love, Communicant and Communicated. One practical conclusion He will not fail to deduce from the above, namely, never in any act to introduce any one of the Divine Tri-unity without a clear intuition of the Co-presence of all – Will, Light, Life! Good, Truth, Wisdom. For lest it never be absent from the mind, that if the Distinctityies of the Deity be incomparably more real, essential, and incomprendible, than the corresponding Names, viz. the I, the Reason, and the Personal Life or Spirit in a regenerate Man, the Unity likewise is in the same transcendency more perfect – in as much as it alone is perfect, in short absolute. As therefore in every ~~Act~~ manifestation it is *the Man* that acts, and not ~~either the power some~~ any one ~~of~~ Power singly, tho' it may very well ~~happieren~~, that this Power may give the distinct form, name and character to the Act: so it is God, the one incomprehensible God, that is manifested in very work of God: and still less, than in the case of a human Individual, dare we think ꝋ that the Son is acting without the Holy Ghost, while the Father looks on as from a distance; or that the Father can act without ~~his~~ the Son, and the Holy Ghost, who are *his* Word and *his* Breath.

CM (CC) III 12–13

From a marginal note on Jacob Böhme, Works

In the Logos, or adequate idea of the divine Beings, all Ideas possible according to Wisdom, and Goodness (which is truly all that can be meant by the words 'in the nature of Things'; for nature is the creature of God, and to be the One, the Good, the Wise, is God's nature) in the Son, I say, are contained all possible Ideas *eminenter*. But in him all are as one/ yet even as the divine act of Self-consciousness gave substantial Essence to his greater idea, even so all the included Ideas produced existing Images of themselves in the power and thro' the free goodness of Deity/ for it was better that they should be, than not be. But yet by *existence*, i.e *stare extra*, they of necessity became *finite*, & therefore inadequate, Images of their Prototypes in the divine mind; and as finite derived their distinguishing <& separate> ~~Beings~~ Natures from *not-Being*: as Plato has set forward almost inspiredly. Hence the Chasm infinitely infinite between Deity and the Creatur[e.] I merely give the order of Thought, like the anarthrous Words at the head of a Chapter. – 1. The existence of the Universe not necessary, all and the all consciousness of being comprize[d] in the Tri-une God. 2. Thro' Grace it was created, according to the divine Ideas. 3. Bu[t] the Images of those Ideas being finite and contingent had their Beings defined by negations – infinitely less than the vere entia, they were Worl[d] <was> better than vere ens non ens, tho' non vere ens. 4. From negation arose free Will and Desire. 5. From thence the possibility of Evil. – 6. From Grace a new Creation, the 5th Article having brought in the necessity of Revelation – and thence the whole Economy of Redemption, or the reduction of Soul to Spirit, of the Image to its Idea, which could only be effected by producing in them the condition of their Ideas, namely, the being all, as one, in one/ and thereby putting off the evils of separation and finiteness.

CM (CC) I 573–4

From a marginal note on Jacob Böhme, Works

As the Sun is (here conceived to be) the manifested Convergence of all the Astral Powers, subsisting from them, yet re-acting as that which is the Condition of *all* being a Whole: so the Son is the omnipresent Center of that infinite Circle, whose only Circumference is in his its own Self-comprehension, the eternal Act of which for ever constitutes that Center. The immanent Energy of the divine Consciousness is, and is the cause of, the co-eternal Filiation of the Logos, the essential Symbol of the Deity, the substantial, infinite, sole adequate, Idea, in God, of God; in and by whom the Father, thus *necessarily* self-manifested, doth *freely* in the ineffable overflowing of Goodness create, and, in proportion to the containing power, manifest himself to, all Creatures. But the contrary second Energy – in *order* (for time attributed to the Infinite Eternal is a contradiction in thought) of the Father in and through the Son, and of the Son in and from the Father, is, and is the co-eternal Procession and Procedence of, the Holy Spirit – one God, blessed over all! Unity whatich *cannot* be *divided!* Tri-unity, which cannot *but* be *distinguished.*

The main cause of our human aversion to conceive or admit the personality, or i.e. the essential Distinctness, of the Word and the

Spirit, lies in our not devoutly attending to the infinite disparateness of an eternal and creative Mind, whose ideas are anterior to their objects, from Minds whose Images and Thoughts are posterior to the Things, and produced or conditioned by their Objects! The latter – Effects, Shadows of Shadows, pene Hihilum a non vere Ente! The former super-essential Causes ὧν ἐν τῷ περισσῷ (let the imperfection of language, let the strivings of human weakness be forgiven, the growing pains of inadequate Intellect and their accompanying Distortions) ὧν ἐν τῷ περισσῷ in whose excess and overflow of *Actuality* all created Things have their Reality.

CM (CC) I 564–5

From a letter to William Rowan Hamilton, 6 April 1832

God's will be done! He knows that my first prayer is not to fall from Him, and the faith that He is God, the I AM, the God that heareth prayer – the Finite in the form of the Infinite = the Absolute Will, the Good; the Self-affirmant, the Father, the I AM, the Personeity; – the Supreme Mind, Reason, Being, the *Pleroma*, the Infinite in the form of the Finite, the Unity in the form of the Distinctity; or lastly, in the synthesis of these, in the *Life*, the *Love*, the Community, the Perichoresis, or Inter[cir]culation – and that there is *one* only God! And I believe in an apostasis, absolutely necessary, as a *possible* event, from the absolute perfection of Love and Goodness, and because WILL is the only ground and antecedent of all Being. And I believe in the descension and condescension of the Divine Spirit, Word, Father, and Incomprehensible Ground of all – and that he is a God who *seeketh* that which was lost, and that the whole world of Phænomena is a revelation of the Redemptive Process, of the Deus *Patiens*, or Deitas *Objectiva* beginning in the separation of Life from Hades, which under the control of the Law = Logos = Unity – becomes *Nature*, i.e., that which never *is* but *natura* est, is to be, from the brute Multeity, and Indistinction, and is to end with the union with God in the Pleroma.

LH 546 [*CL* VI 897]

From his notebook, April 1811

As the most far-sighted Eye even aided by the most powerful Telescope will not make a fixed Star appear larger than it does to an ordinary & unaided Sight, even so there are heights of Knowledge,

& Truths sublime, which all men ~~with~~ in possession of the ordinary human understanding may comprehend as much and as well as the profoundest Philosopher & the most learned Theologian. Such are the Truths relating to the Logos, and its Oneness with the Self-existent Deity, and of the Humanity of Christ, & its union with the Logos – . It is idle therefore to refrain from preaching on these Subjects, provided only such preparation have been made, as no man can be a Christian without. The misfortune is, that the majority are Christians in name & by birth only – let them but once according to St James have looked down steadfastly into *the Law* of Liberty or Freedom in their own Souls (the Will & the Conscience) & they are capable of whatever God has chosen to reveal.

CN III 4065 17.196

From his notebook, November 1810

Confessio Fidei
of
S.T. Coleridge
written Nov. 3. 1810.

1. I believe, that I am a Free Agent, inasmuch as, and as far as, I have a will which renders me justly responsible for my actions, omissive as well as commissive. Likewise that I possess Reason, or a Law of Right and Wrong, which uniting with my sense of moral responsibility constitutes the voice of Conscience.

2. Hence it becomes my absolute Duty to believe, and I do believe, that there is a God, that is, a Being in whom Supreme Reason and a most holy Will are one with an infinite Power ... that all holy Will is coincident with the Will of God, and therefore secure in its ultimate Consequences by his Omnipotence – having, if such similitude be not unlawful, a similar relation to the goodness of the Almighty, as a perfect Time-piece would have to the Sun.

Corollary.

The wonderful Works of God in the sensible World are a perpetual Discourse, reminding me of his Existence, and Shadowing out to me his perfections. But as all Language presupposes in the intelligent Hearer or Reader those primary notions, which it symbolizes, as well as the power of making those combinations of these primary notions, which it represents & excites us to combine

– even so I believe, that the notion of God is essential to the human Mind, that it is called forth into distinct consciousness principally by the Conscience, and auxiliarly by the manifest adaptation of means to ends in the outward Creation. It is therefore evident to my Reason, that this existence of God is absolutely & necessarily insusceptible of a scientific Demonstration – and that Scripture has so represented it. For it *commands* us to believe in one God – I am the Lord thy God: thou shalt have no other God but Me. Now all Commandment necessarily relates to the *Will*; Whereas all scientific demonstration is independent of the will, & is apodictic (or demonstrative) only as far as it is compulsory on the mind, volentem, nolentem.

3. My Conscience forbids me to propose to myself the Pains and Pleasures of this Life, as the primary motive or ultimate end of my actions – on the contrary, makes me perceive an utter disproportion-ateness and heterogeneity between the acts of the Spirit, or Virtue & Vice, and the things of the Sense, such as all earthly Rewards & Punishments must be –. Its Hopes & Fears therefore refer me to a different, and Spiritual state of Being: and I beliefve in the Life to come, not thro' arguments acquired by my Understanding or discursive Faculty, but chiefly & effectively because so to believe is my Duty, and in obedience to the Command of my Conscience.

Here ends the first Table of my Creed, which would have been my Creed, had I been born with Adam; and which therefore consti-tutes what may in this sense be called Natural Religion, i.e. the Religion of all finite rational Beings. The second Tables contains the Creed of Revealed Religion, my Belief as a Christian.

II

4. I believe, and hold it as the fundamental article of Christianity, that I am a fallen creature; that I am of myself capable of moral evil, but not of myself capable of moral good, and that Guilt is justly imputable to be me prior to any given act, or assignable moment of time, in my Consciousness. I am born a child of Wrath. This fearful Mystery I pretend not to understand – I cannot even conceive the possibility of it – but I know, that it is so! My Conscience, the sole fountain of certainty, commands me to believe it, and would itself be a contradiction, were it not so – and what is real, must be possible.

5. I receive with full and grateful Faith the assurance of Revelation, that the Word which is from all eternity with God and

is God, assumed our human nature in order to redeem me and all mankind from this our connate Corruption. My reason convinces me, that no other mode of redemption is conceivable, and, as did Socrates, would have yearned after the Redeemer, tho' it would not dare expect so wonderful an Act of Divine Love, except only as an effort of my mind to conceive the utmost of the infinite greatness of that Love!

6. I believe that this assumption of Humanity by the ~~Godhead~~ Son of God was revealed & realized to us by the Word made flesh, and manifested to us, in Christ Jesus; and that his miraculous Birth, his agony, his Crucifixion, Death, Resurrection, and Ascension, were all both Symbols of our Redemption (φαινομενα των Νουμενων) and necessary parts of the aweful process.

7. I believe in the descent and sending of the Holy Spirit, by whose free grace alone obtained for me by the merits of my Redeemer I can alone be sanctified, and restored from my natural Inheritance of Sin & Condemnation be a Child of God, and an Inheritor of the Kingdom of God.

Corollary.

The Trinity of Persons in the unity of the God would have been a necessary *Idea* of my speculative Reason, deduced from the necessary Postulate of an intelligent Creator, whose ideas being anterior to the Things must be more *actual* than those things, even as those Things are more actual than our Images derived from them; and as intelligent, must have had co-eternally an adequate Idea of Himself, in and thro' which he created all things both in Heaven & on Earth. – But this would only have been a speculative Idea, like those of Circles & other mathematical figures, to which we are not authorized by the practical Reason to attribute *Reality*. Solely in consequence of our Redemption does the Trinity become a Doctrine, the *Belief* of which as real is commanded by our Conscience. But to Christians it is commanded – and it is false candour in a Christian believing in Original Sin & Redemption therefrom, to admit that any man denying the Divinity of Christ can be a Christian ....

CN III 4005 M.7

From a marginal note on John Donne, LXXX Sermons

If this mystery be considered, as words or rather *sounds* vibrating on some certain ears, to which their Belief assigned a supernatural cause – well and good! Wh[at] else can be said! Such were the sounds – Wha[t] their meaning is, we know not/ but such sounds not being in the ordinary cour[se] of nature, we of course attribute them to something extra-natural. Bu[t] if God made man in hi[s] own Image therein, as in a mirr[or] misty, no doubt[,] at best, & now *cracked* by peculiar & inherited defects, yet still our only mirror, & therein to recontemplate all we can of God, – this word 'proceeding' may admit of an easy sense. For if man first used it to express as well as he could a notion found in himself, as Man in genere, we have to look into ourselves – & there we may find, that two events of vital Intelligence may be conceived – the first, a necessary and eternal outgoing of *Intelligence* ... from *Being* ... *with the will as an accompaniment, but* not *from* it, as a cause, in *order*, tho' not necessarily in *time*, precedent – / this is true *Filiation*; the second [an] act of *[th]e Will and Reason*, [in] their purity strict [Id]entities/ & and therefore [n]ot *begotten* or [fi]liated, but [P]ROCEEDING from [in]telligent essence [a]nd essential [i]ntelligence [c]ombining in [a]ct/ necessarily [i]n deed, & [c]o-eternally/ [f]or the co-existence [o]f absolute Spontaneity with [a]bsolute necessity is involved in the very idea of *God*, one of whose intellectual Definitions is, the Synthesis, generative a[d] extra, and annihilative tho' inconclusive quod se, of all conceivable Antitheses: even as the best moral Definition – (and O how much more godlike to *us*, in this state of antithetic Intellect is the moral beyond the intellectual!) – the best moral Definition is, God *is* LOVE! – and this is (to *us*) the high prerogative of *the moral*, that all its dictates immediately reveal [truths] of intelligence, whereas the strictly Intellectual only by more <distant and cold> deductions carries us towards the Moral. – For what is Love? Union with the desire of union – / God therefore is the Cohesion & the Oneness of all Things – & dark & dim is that system of Ethics, which does [not] take '*Oneness*' as the *root* of all Virtue!

Being, Mind, Love in action = holy Spirit, are ideas – distin-guishable, tho' not divisible, but *Will* is ~~both~~ equally incapable of distinction & or division – it is equally implied in 1. vital Being, [2]. in [e]ssential [I]ntelligence/ [an]d 3. in [re/co]-effluent Love or [h]oly Action/ Now Will [i]s the true [p]rinciple & meaning of *Identity*, of *Selfness*: even in our common Language. – The Will therefore being indistinguishably [o]ne, but the possessive Powers [t]riply distinguishable do perforce involve the notion expressed by three *Persons* and one *God*. There are three 'Personæ *Per quas sonat*' three forms of manifestation co-eternally co-existing, in which the one will is totally, all in each/ the truth of which we may *know* in our own minds, & can understand by no analogy – for the mind ministrant to diverse at the same moment, in order then either to aid the fancy, borrows <or rather steals> from the mind the idea of [the] total in omni parte, which alone furnishes the Analogy – but that both it & a myriad of other material Images do inwrap themselves in these veste non sua, & would be even no objects of conception, if they did not – yea, that even the very words, 'conception,' 'comprehension,' and all in all languages that answer to them – suppose this transinfusion from the Mind (even as if the Sun be imagined visual, it must first irradiate from itself in order for itself to perceive) is an argument better than all analogy

CM (CC) II 249–50

From 'The Trinity'

IDENTITY

The *absolute* Subjectivity, whose only attribute is the GOOD; whose only definition is, that which is essentially causative of *all* possible true Being – Ground and Cause. = The Absolute WILL: the adorable πρόπρωτον; i.e. that which, whatever is assumed as the First, must be *pre*sumed as its Antecedent. Θεὸς, without the article; & yet not as an adjective – ...

IPSËITY

The eternally self-affirmant, self-affirmed: the 'I AM, in that I AM' – (in the Hebrew literally, 'I shall be that I will to be.[']) The FATHER: the *relatively* Subjective: whose attribute is, the HOLY ONE, whose definition is, the essential Finific in the form of the Infinite. Dat sibi fines. But the Absolute WILL, the Absolute Good, in the eternal act of Self-affirmation, the Good as the Holy, co-eternally begets the divine

ALTERITY

The supreme Being; Ὁ ὄντωςῶν;The Supreme Reason – the Jehovah. The Son. The Word. whose *attribute* is the TRUE (The TRUTH, the LIGHT, the Fiat); and whose Definition, is the PLEROMA of Being, whose essential poles are Unity and Distinctity; or the *essential* Infinite in the *form* of the Finite: lastly, the relatively OBJECTIVE = Deitas objectiva in relation to the I AM or the Deitas SUBJECTIVA.

The *Objectivity*

The Distinctities in the pleroma are the Eternal IDEAS – the Subsistential Truths, <each> considered in itself an Infinite in the form of the Finite; but all considered as one with the Unity, the Eternal Son, they are the energies of the Finific. John, Chap: I – But with the relatively Subjective, and the relatively Objective, the great Idea needs only for its completion a co-eternal which is both, i.e. relatively Objective to the Subjective, relatively Subjective to the Objective. Hence the

COMMUNITY

The eternal LIFE, which is LOVE – the Spirit, relatively to the Father, the *Spirit* of Holiness, the Holy *Spirit*: relatively to the Son, the Spirit of Truth whose attribute is Wisdom. Sancta Sophia. The Good in the ~~form~~ reality of the True, in the form of actual Life = Wisdom.

SWF (CC) II 1510–12

V. Transparency of nature and spirit

Vision, carried to its highest and most transcendent levels, could apprehend a transparency between nature and spirit. Nature and the Scriptures direct the human mind to its spiritual origins; perfecting vision reveals a unity between the romantic triad of nature, humanity and the divine. In Coleridge's grand scheme, 'Life begins in detachment from Nature, and ends in union with God.'[18]

Letter to Hyman Hurwitz, 4 January 1820

Especially, if you would take the opportunity of impressing on your own Brethren the *duty* of availing themselves of that increased Light, the means, and of course therefore the moral necessity, of which God hath so greatly augmented in the present day. They should be reminded, that the glory and the contra-distinguishing character of the Old Testament collectively, contrasted with all the Books pretending to be revealed & not acknowledging the divine authority of your sacred Scriptures, is especially manifested in it's strong injunctions to seek after *Truth*. Not Veracity *only*, but likewise after *intellectual* Truth and *Knowledge*! Knowledge is not only extolled as the crown and honor of a man, but earnestly to endeavor after it's attainment is again and again enforced as one of our most sacred duties. Above all, to study the Scriptures themselves, with all the aids which ancient and modern Learning have prepared; and to regard all the great Book of natural science but as a Glass enabling them to take a deeper and more exact view of the Law which (as your Sages have profoundly said) was, before the World itself was.

CL V 5

From a marginal note of 1827 on Manuel Lacunza y Diaz, The Coming of Messiah

Again, I protest against all identification of the coming with the Apocalyptic Millennium, which in my belief began under Constantine. II. In what sense? In this and no other, that the objects of the Christian Redemption will be perfected on this earth; – that the kingdom of God and his Word, the latter as the Son of Man, in which the divine will shall *be done on earth as it is in heaven*, will *come*; and that the whole march of nature and history, from the first impregnation of Chaos by the Spirit, converges toward this kingdom as the final cause of the world. Life begins in detachment from Nature, and ends in union with God.

CM (CC) III 417

Notes

1 *Shedd* V 389
2 For more on Coleridge's theological thought, see Anthony John Harding, *Coleridge and the Inspired Word* (Kingston: McGill-Queen's University Press, 1985) as well as his volume of *Coleridge's Responses: Coleridge on the Bible,* and J. Robert Barth, *Coleridge and Christian Doctrine* (Cambridge: Harvard University Press, 1969).
3 *Shedd* V 389
4 *CN* I 2600 17.211
5 *Shedd* I 125 [*AR (CC)* 25]

6   *Shedd* I 363–4 [*AR (CC)* 406]
7   *CN* V 5505 23.30
8   *Shedd* I 450 [*LS (CC)* 50]
9   *Shedd* II 402 [*F (CC)* 440]
10 *CN* I 1678 21.406
11 *Shedd* VI 188–9 [*LS (CC)* 179]
12 *Shedd* I 461 [*LS (CC)* 69]
13 *CN* IV 4816 29.80
14 *ER* 89–92 [*CL* III 482–3]
15 *Shedd* V 565 [*SWF (CC)* II 844]
16 For an in-depth examination of Coleridge's lifelong interest in 'logos' as a philosophical and religious concept, see Mary Anne Perkins, *Coleridge's Philosophy: The Logos as Unifying Principle* (Oxford: Clarendon Press, 1994).
17 *Shedd* V 113 [*CM (CC)* III 919]
18 *Shedd* V 513 [CM (CC) III 417]

Bibliography

Abrams, M.H. *Natural Supernaturalism: Tradition and Revolution in Romantic Literature.* London: Oxford University Press, 1971.

Barfield, Owen. *What Coleridge Thought.* London: Oxford University Press, 1972.

Barth, J. Robert. *Coleridge and Christian Doctrine.* Cambridge, MA: Harvard University Press, 1969.

——. *The Symbolic Imagination: Coleridge and the Romantic Tradition.* Princeton: Princeton University Press, 1977.

Beer, John. *Coleridge's Poetic Intelligence.* London: Macmillan, 1977.

——. *Coleridge the Visionary.* London: Chatto, 1959.

Coleridge, S.T. *Aids to Reflection.* Ed. John Beer. *Collected Works of Samuel Taylor Coleridge.* Vol. 9. Princeton: Princeton University Press, 1993.

——. *Anima Poetæ: from the unpublished notebooks of Samuel Taylor Coleridge.* Ed. E.H. Coleridge. London: William Heinemann, 1895.

——. *Biographia Literaria.* Ed. James Engell and W. Jackson Bate, 2 vols. *Collected Works of Samuel Taylor Coleridge.* Vol. 7. Princeton: Princeton UP, 1983.

——. *Coleridge's Miscellaneous Criticism.* Ed. T.M. Raysor. Cambridge: Harvard University Press, 1936.

——. *Collected Letters of Samuel Taylor Coleridge.* Ed. E.L. Griggs. 6 vols. Oxford: Clarendon Press, 1956–71.

——. *Collected Works of Samuel Taylor Coleridge.* General ed. Kathleen Coburn. Associate ed. Bart Winer. Princeton: Princeton University Press, 1969–.

——. *The Complete Poetical Works of Samuel Taylor Coleridge.* Ed. E.H. Coleridge. 2 vols. Oxford: Clarendon Press, 1912.

——. *The Complete Works of Samuel Taylor Coleridge.* Ed. W.G.T. Shedd. 7 vols. New York: Harper, 1884.

——. *On the Constitution of Church and State, according to the idea of each: with aids towards a right judgment on the late Catholic Bill.* London: Hurst, Chance, 1830.

—. *The Friend.* Ed. Barbara Rooke. 2 vols. *Collected Works of Samuel Taylor Coleridge.* Vol. 4. Princeton: Princeton University Press, 1969.

—. *Hints Towards the Formation of a More Comprehensive Theory of Life.* Ed. Seth B. Watson. London: John Churchill, 1848.

—. *Inquiring Spirit: A New Presentation of Coleridge from his Published and Unpublished Prose Writings.* Ed. Kathleen Coburn. London: Routledge and Kegan Paul, 1950.

—. *Lay Sermons.* Ed. R.J. White. *Collected Works of Samuel Taylor Coleridge.* Vol. 6. Princeton: Princeton University Press, 1972.

—. *Lectures 1808-19 On Literature.* Ed. R.A. Foakes. 2 vols. *Collected Works of Samuel Taylor Coleridge.* Vol. 5. Princeton: Princeton U.P., 1987.

—. *Lectures 1818-19 On the History of Philosophy.* Ed. R.J. de J. Jackson. 2 vols. *Collected Works of Samuel Taylor Coleridge.* Vol. 8. Princeton: Princeton U.P., 2000.

—. *Lectures and Notes on Shakespere and Other English Poets.* Ed. T. Ashe. London: George Bell, 1884.

—. *Letters of Samuel Taylor Coleridge.* Ed. E.H. Coleridge. 2 vols. London: Heinemann, 1895.

—. *Marginalia.* Ed. George Whalley *et al.* 6 vols. *Collected Works of Samuel Taylor Coleridge.* Vol. 12. Princeton: Princeton University Press, 1980–2001.

—. *The Notebooks of Samuel Taylor Coleridge.* Ed. Kathleen Coburn *et al.* 5 vols. London: Routledge and Kegan Paul, 1957–.

—. *The Philosophical Lectures of Samuel Taylor Coleridge.* Ed. Kathleen Coburn. London: Routledge and Kegan Paul, 1950.

—. *Poetical Works.* Ed. J.C.C. Mays. 3 pts in 6 vols. *Collected Works of Samuel Taylor Coleridge.* Vol. 16. Princeton: Princeton University Press, 2001.

—. *Shorter Works and Fragments.* Ed. H.J. Jackson and R.J. de J. Jackson. 2 vols. *Collected Works of Samuel Taylor Coleridge.* Vol. 11. Princeton: Princeton University Press, 1995.

—. *Specimens of the Table Talk of Samuel Taylor Coleridge.* London: John Murray, 1836.

—. *Table Talk.* Ed. Carl Woodring. 2 vols. *Collected Works of Samuel Taylor Coleridge.* Vol. 14. Princeton: Princeton University Press, 1990.

—. *Unpublished Letters of Samuel Taylor Coleridge.* Ed. E.L. Griggs. 2 vols. London: Constable, 1932.

Cottle, Joseph. *Early Recollections; chiefly relating to the late Samuel Taylor Coleridge, during his long residence in Bristol.* 2 vols. London: Longman, Rees & Co. and Hamilton, Adams & Co., 1837.

De Quincey, Thomas. *The Collected Writings of Thomas De Quincey.* Ed. David Masson. 14 vols. Edinburgh: Black, 1889–90.

Engell, James. *The Creative Imagination: Enlightenment to Romanticism.* Cambridge, MA: Harvard University Press, 1981.

Fruman, Norman. *Coleridge: The Damaged Archangel.* New York: G. Braziller, 1971.

Fulford, Timothy. 'Coleridge, Böhme, and the Language of Nature'. *Modern Language Quarterly: A Journal of Literary History* 52:1 (1991): 37–52.

—. *Coleridge's Figurative Language.* Basingstoke: Macmillan, 1991.

Graves, Robert Perceval. *Life of Sir Rowan Hamilton, including selections from his poems, correspondence, and miscellaneous writings.* Dublin: Hodges, Figgis, & Co., 1882–9.

Gravil, Richard and Lefebure, Molly (eds). *The Coleridge Connection: Essays for Thomas McFarland.* London: Macmillan, 1990.

Harding, Anthony. *Coleridge's Responses: Coleridge on the Bible.*

Harding, Anthony John. *Coleridge and the Inspired Word.* Kingston: McGill-Queen's University Press, 1985.

Hedley, Douglas. *Coleridge, Philosophy, and Religion: Aids to Reflection and the Mirror of the Spirit.* Cambridge: Cambridge University Press, 2000.

Holmes, Richard. *Coleridge: Early Visions: 1772–1804.* London: Hodder and Stoughton, 1989.

—. *Coleridge: Darker Reflections: 1804–1834.* New York: Pantheon Books, 1998.

Inge, William Ralph. *The Platonic Tradition in English Religious Thought.* London: Longman, 1926.

Jasper, David. *Coleridge as Poet and Religious Thinker: Inspiration and Revelation.* London: Macmillan, 1985.

Lefebure, Molly. *Samuel Taylor Coleridge: A Bondage of Opium.* New York: Stein and Day, 1974.

Levere, Trevor. *Poetry Realized in Nature: Samuel Taylor Coleridge and Early Nineteenth-century Science.* Cambridge: Cambridge University Press, 1981.

McFarland, Thomas. *Coleridge and the Pantheist Tradition.* Oxford: Oxford University Press, 1969.

McKusick, James. *Coleridge's Philosophy of Language*. New Haven: Yale University Press, 1986.

McNiece, Gerald. *The Knowledge that Endures: Coleridge, German Philosophy, and the Logic of Romantic Thought*. New York: St. Martin's Press, 1992.

Micheli, Giuseppe. *The Early Reception of Kant's Thought in England: 1785–1805*. London: Routledge/Thoemmes Press, 1993.

Modiano, Raimonda. *Coleridge and the Concept of Nature*. Tallahassee: Florida State University Press, 1985.

Muirhead, J.H. *Coleridge as Philosopher*. London: Allen & Unwin, 1931.

Newsome, David. *Two Classes of Men: Platonism and English Romantic Thought*. London: Butler and Tanner, 1974.

Orsini, G.N.G. *Coleridge and German Idealism: A Study in the History of Philosophy with Unpublished Materials from Coleridge's Manuscripts*. Carbondale: Southern Illinois University Press, 1969.

Perkins, Mary Anne. *Coleridge's Philosophy: The Logos as Unifying Principle*. Oxford: Clarendon Press, 1994.

Perry, Seamus. *Coleridge and the Uses of Division*. Oxford: Clarendon Press, 1999.

—— *Coleridge's Responses: Coleridge on Writers and Writing*.

Prickett, Stephen. *Coleridge and Wordsworth: The Poetry of Growth*. Cambridge: Cambridge University Press, 1970.

Reid, Nicholas. *Coleridge, Form and Symbol: Or The Ascertaining Vision*. Aldershot: Ashgate Publishing, 2006.

Richards, I.A. *Coleridge on Imagination*. London: Kegan Paul, Trench, Trubner, 1934.

Vallins, David. *Coleridge and the Psychology of Romanticism: Feeling and Thought*. New York: St. Martin's Press, 2000.

Watson, Lucy E. *Coleridge at Highgate*. London: Longmans, Green and Co., 1925.

Wellek, Rene. *Immanuel Kant in England: 1793–1838*. London: Routledge/Thoemmes Press, 1993.

Wheeler, Kathleen. *Sources, Processes and Methods in Coleridge's Biographia Literaria*. Cambridge: Cambridge University Press, 1980.

Index

electricity 165, 172
emotion, feeling 23, 36, 88–90, 96, 98, 120, 122, 128, 186, 190
and thought, 93, 147, 161
Engell, James 107n, 180n.
Enos 129
enthusiasm 92, 129
Eolian harp 69–79, 99, 102, 150, 186; *see also* lute
Eolus 35
eternal, eternity 67, 158, 204, 207
evolve, evolution 152, 165–7, 174, 176, 192
'extremes meet' 124
eye 3, 7, 23, 44, 51, 54, 56–7, 64, 71, 74, 84, 97–8, 100, 108, 127, 157, 159–60, 163, 168–9, 183, 190, 194, 196, 198, 202, 208
'bodily eye' 119, 157
'inward Eye' 87, 104, 178, 182
'master-eye' 80, 105
of the Lord 3, 190
of 'this true self' 187–8
Ezekiel 76

faith 2, 4, 19, 71, 76, 155–7, 182, 191, 197–204, 208, 210
and philosophy 166, 178
and reason 201
family 49–50, 60, 62–3, 66, 110–11, 205
fanaticism 92
fancy 5, 11, 77, 87, 89, 97, 101, 115, 129, 163, 168–9, 185, 194, 205, 213 and imagination 89–90, 159
Fenelon, François de Salignac de la Mothe- 130
fever 12, 108, 119
Field, Richard 157
fiends, fiendish 134–5; *see also* devil, demon
finite and infinite 80, 178, 206–8, 213–14
flowers 83, 94, 106, 158, 195; *see also* blossoms
form 30, 66–7, 87, 92, 98, 118, 146, 150–1, 189, 204–5

fountain 88, 99–100, 133, 162, 186, 210
free, freedom 86, 158, 160, 189, 209; *see also* liberty
Freud, Sigmund 13
friend, friendship 48, 49–50, 62–3, 103
Fruman, Norman 143n., 180n.
Fulford, Timothy 73n., 107n.

galvanism 172
genial powers 100, 103
genius 2, 3, 11, 75, 83, 86, 89, 91–5, 166, 170–1
versus talent 92–3
ghosts, and apparitions 13, 108, 113, 116–19, 121, 129
Gillman, James 109, 164, 166
Gillman, James Jr. 187–8
glow-worm 158, 199
God 2, 18, 19, 30, 58, 65–6, 68–9, 71–3, 76, 80, 112, 148, 156, 160, 163, 165, 167, 177, 182–3, 187–91, 193–6, 200, 202–15; *see also* Jehovah
Goddess 125–6
grace 194, 201, 207, 211
Greece, Greek 106, 180
grief 100, 103

Hades 208
Hamilton, William Rowan 208
Harding, Anthony 215n.
Hartley, David 5, 21n.
heart 90, 157, 159, 168, 180, 183, 186
and head 111, 129, 162, 178, 185
heaven 23, 51, 63, 67–9, 71–2, 134, 202–3
and earth 101, 191, 211, 215
Hedley, Douglas 180n.
Heinroth, Johann Christian 146–7
Hertha 104
hieroglyphics 30, 38, 79, 84, 195; *see also* cyphers, picture-language
Holmes, Richard 180n.
Hooker, Richard 155
hope 64, 71, 106, 124, 198, 210
Hume, David 163
Hurwitz, Hyman 214–15